The politics of Jean Genet's late theatre

Manchester University Press

theory · practice
· performance ·

series editors
MARIA M. DELGADO
PETER LICHTENFELS

advisory board
MICHAEL BILLINGTON
SANDRA HEBRON
MARK RAVENHILL
JANELLE REINELT
PETER SELLARS

This series will offer a space for those people who practise theatre to have a dialogue with those who think and write about it.

The series has a flexible format that refocuses the analysis and documentation of performance. It provides, presents and represents material which is written by those who make or create performance history, and offers access to theatre documents, different methodologies and approaches to the art of making theatre.

The books in the series are aimed at students, scholars, practitioners and theatre-visiting readers. They encourage reassessments of periods, companies and figures in twentieth-century and twenty-first-century theatre history, and provoke and take up discussions of cultural strategies and legacies that recognise the heterogeneity of performance studies.

The series editors, with the advisory board, aim to publish innovative challenging and exploratory texts from practitioners, theorists and critics.

The politics of Jean Genet's late theatre: Spaces of revolution

CARL LAVERY

Manchester University Press
Manchester and New York

distributed in the United States exclusively by Palgrave Macmillan

Copyright © Carl Lavery 2010

The right of Carl Lavery to be identified as the author of this work has been asserted by him in accordance with the Copyright, Designs and Patents Act 1988.

Published by Manchester University Press
Oxford Road, Manchester M13 9NR, UK
and Room 400, 175 Fifth Avenue, New York, NY 10010, USA
www.manchesteruniversitypress.co.uk

Distributed in the United States exclusively by
Palgrave Macmillan, 175 Fifth Avenue,
New York, NY 10010, USA

Distributed in Canada exclusively by
UBC Press, University of British Columbia, 2029 West Mall,
Vancouver, BC, Canada V6T 1Z2

British Library Cataloguing-in-Publication Data is available

Library of Congress Cataloging-in-Publication Data is available

ISBN 978 0 7190 9015 8 paperback

First published by Manchester University Press in hardback 2010

This paperback edition first published 2013

The publisher has no responsibility for the persistence or accuracy of URLs for any external or third-party internet websites referred to in this book, and does not guarantee that any content on such websites is, or will remain, accurate or appropriate.

Printed by Lightning Source

To Melanie

CONTENTS

List of figures   *page* ix
Acknowledgements   x

PART I Politics and aesthetics

Introduction   1
1 Genet and commitment: politics and aesthetics   21
2 Tracing the shift: the event of the wound   49
3 Aesthetic politics: staging the wound   78

PART II Spatial politics in the late plays

4 Exploding the bordello in *The Balcony*: spectacle, allegory and the wound of theatre   105
5 *Détournement*, abjection and disidentification in *The Blacks*   136
6 Bringing it all back home: the battle of *The Screens*   168
7 Conclusion: Genet our contemporary   195

PART III Interviews

8	Interview with Lluís Pasqual	201
9	Interview with JoAnne Akalaitis	208
10	Interview with Ultz	215
11	Interview with Excalibah	221
	Appendix: 'Preface to *The Blacks*', translated by Clare Finburgh	227
	References	235
	Index	249

FIGURES

1 *The Screens*, Tyrone Guthrie Theatre, Minneapolis, Minnesota, 1989–90. Directed by JoAnne Akalaitis. Photo: Michal Daniel   213

2 *The Screens*, Tyrone Guthrie Theatre, Minneapolis, Minnesota, 1989–90. Directed by JoAnne Akalaitis. Photo: Michal Daniel   214

3 *The Blacks (Remixed)*, Theatre Royal Stratford East, London, 2007. Directed by Ultz and Excalibah. Photo: Jake Green   225

4 *The Blacks (Remixed)*, Theatre Royal Stratford East, London, 2007. Directed by Ultz and Excalibah. Photo: Jake Green   226

ACKNOWLEDGEMENTS

First, I would like to thank Lancaster University for granting me a period of study leave, and the Arts and Humanities Research Council (AHRC) for a Research Leave Award in 2007–08.

In an editorial sense, I am particularly indebted to Maria Delgado and Peter Lichtenfels for encouraging and supporting the project.

Thanks also to Joanna Marston at Rosica Colin Ltd for granting me permission to publish the first English-language translation of the 'Preface to *The Blacks*', which was done, with customary brilliance, by Clare Finburgh.

Many people have helped with the writing and thinking of this book. I would like to thank Elaine Aston, David Bradby, Clare Finburgh, Gerry Harris, Adrian Kear, Joe Kelleher, Andrew 'Oscar' Quick, Alan Read, Graham Saunders, Linda Taylor, David Williams and Ralph Yarrow.

Thanks are equally due to Lluís Pasqual, JoAnne Akalaitis, Excalibah, Ultz and to the photographers Jake Green and Michal Daniel for granting me the rights to reproduce images. I am also grateful, in this capacity, to William Grier (at the Tyrone Guthrie Theatre, Minneapolis).

Finally, I want to extend my gratitude to Melanie, Immanuel, Inez and Saul without whom this book *really* would not have been completed.

PART I: Politics and aesthetics

Introduction

EDWARD DE GRAZIA: I found that the possibility – or threat – of revolution, permeates your plays more than your novels; there's a possibility, or threat of revolution or insurrection in *The Maids*, for example; there's a revolution going on in *The Balcony*, and *The Blacks* contains a threat of revolution. Does this mean that you are in favour of great changes in the relationships between classes and between people?

JEAN GENET: No! It just means that you fear revolution (because you said you'd felt it as a threat), whereas I see it as a hope! (de Grazia, 1993: 315)

A revolutionary playwright

Jean Genet has long been regarded as one of the most influential artists of the twentieth century. Since the publication of Jean-Paul Sartre's existential biography *Saint Genet: Actor and Martyr* in 1952, his writing has attracted the attention of leading French thinkers and philosophers, and, in the UK and US, his work has played a major role in the development of queer and feminist studies, where his representation of sexuality and gender continues to provoke controversy.[1]

This study aims to argue for Genet's influence once again, but it does so by focusing uniquely on the politics of his late theatre. Unlike those anthologists who continue to define him, erroneously, as an absurdist theatre maker, I intend to argue for Genet as a revolutionary playwright by engaging with, and building on, the uncompromising political readings that have started to emerge in Genet scholarship in France, the UK and the USA in the past decade.[2]

Writing at the dawn of the new millennium, the French novelist and critic Marie Redonnet has no doubts about the burning relevance of Genet's political vision. For her, 'Genet is the only writer who saw with lucidity what the new face of the enemy would look like' (2000: 156; my translation). Although Redonnet strangely neglects to describe what that face is or to whom it might belong, it is safe to assume from a detailed reading of her book *Jean Genet: le poète travesti* that the 'enemy' has much in common with what the Retort collective has named the 'military-industrial–entertainment complex' of advanced capital (2006: 37).[3] Redonnet's views on Genet's political significance are endorsed by the Indian critic Rustom Bharucha. Reflecting on his own production of *The Maids* in Manila in 2002, Bharucha proposed that Genet's rejection of western political values, although not easy to assimilate on account of its 'anarchist affinities' and sympathy for 'terrorism', 'challenges us to spell out our politics in relation to where he stands'. For Bharucha, this stance is situated, necessarily, in what he calls 'the global terror of our times' (2003: 24).

The recent claims made by Redonnet and Bharucha supplement a formidable body of scholarship that has, for some time now, been concerned to unpack the political significance of Genet's writing. From the late 1960s onward, Genet has been famously championed for deconstructing

---

1 See p. 3 for specific details on the French philosophers and feminist and queer thinkers who have engaged with Genet's work.
2 I am thinking here of Jill Forbes and Michael Kelly (eds), *French Cultural Studies: An Introduction* (Oxford: Oxford University Press, 1995), pp. 157–8; and Kenneth Pickering, *Keys Concepts in Drama and Performance* (London: Palgrave Macmillan, 2005), pp. 109–10. In his 1961 collection *The Theatre of the Absurd*, Martin Esslin categorised Genet as an absurdist, as a result of which his theatre was – and often still is – discussed in anglophone scholarship in terms of metaphysics, identity and myth as opposed to politics, sociology and history (2nd enlarged edn, London: Penguin, 1968), pp. 195–228. Esslin's concept of the absurd is problematic for another reason, too: as a dramatic typology, it overlooks the key dramaturgical and scenic differences inherent in the work of the playwrights he defines as 'absurdist'.
3 The Retort collective is a group of activists and artists based in San Francisco. Four of its members, Iain Boal, T. J. Clark, Joseph Matthews and Michael Watts, are the authors of *Afflicted Powers: Capital and Spectacle in an Age of War* (London: Verso, 2006).

normative notions of gender and sexuality (Cixous, 1975; Lloyd, 1987; Millet, 1991; Bersani, 1995; Dollimore, 1995; Case, 1997; Hanrahan, 1997; Eribon, 2001; Gaitet, 2003; Eldridge, 2005; Hargreaves, 2006; Stephens, 2006); debunking racist stereotypes and critiquing western imperialism (Said, 1995; Chalaye, 1998; Hughes, 2001; Khélil, 2001; Boisseron and Ekotto, 2004); playfully subverting the epistemic violence of logocentricism (Oswald, 1989; Derrida, 1990, 2004; Bougon, 1993, 1997, 1998; Bougon and Rabaté, 1995; Finburgh, 2004); and practising a nomadic process of deterritorialisation (Guattari, 1989; Durham, 1995, 1997, 1998; Hardt, 1997; Gourgouris, 1998; Hardt and Negri, 2001; Clark, 2008).

While the readings referred to above have certainly done much to highlight the sophistication of Genet's political vision, a shift in emphasis is required if we are to engage, profitability, with the new line of enquiry advanced, wholeheartedly, by Redonnet and, more tentatively, by Bharucha. Where Genet's texts have long been regarded as favoured sites for a politics based on theoretical notions of difference and *différance*, Bharucha and Redonnet, on the other hand, encourage us to locate his politics in history, and to consider their radical opposition to today's neo-imperialist consensus that everywhere seems so depressingly routine and banally colossal.[4] This book attempts to respond to that challenge by concentrating on an aspect of Genet's political and aesthetic thought which, in my view, calls out for further clarification: his commitment to a utopian view of revolution, characterised by anti-Statism, aesthetics and radical equality.

Unlike other critics such as Jérôme Neutre (2002), Eric Marty (2003) and Bharucha who, with very different agendas in mind, have stressed how Genet politics are conditioned by a hatred of the West, I want to emphasise, instead, his commitment to inclusivity. For me, Genet's rejection of the West has less do with an attraction to the idea of the global South, as Neutre implies, than it does with discovering a utopic space, in which subjectivity might be reimagined and reconfigured in new, more egalitarian ways.[5] As Simon Critchley observes,

---

4   For an excellent argument in favour of reading Genet theoretically, see Mairéad Hanrahan (ed.), *Genet*, special edition of *Paragraph* (2004). This is not the first study to read Genet historically. Maria Shevtsova locates Genet's politics within history and sociology, but, as opposed to my approach, she considers them in relation to the Third Republic. See 'Social Actors/Stage Actors: Jean Genet and the Sociology of the Theatre', in S. Knight and S. N. Mukherjee (eds), *Words and Worlds: Studies in the Social Role of Verbal Culture* (Sydney: Sydney Studies in Society and Culture 1983), pp. 163–87.
5   To be fair to Jérôme Neutre and his superb study, *Genet: sur les routes du sud* (Paris: Fayard, 2002), he concludes his book by suggesting that Genet managed from 1967 onwards to find a space beyond the North–South binary. According to Neutre, 'Japan [for Genet] was the image of an Elsewhere that broke with the division of the world into a bipolar entity' (p. 312; my translation).

Genet was only '*at home* in Palestine' because it was 'a country that didn't exist' (1999: 39; original italics). To trace the utopian impulse in Genet's thinking, I make a distinction between the political significance of his early and late work. Whereas the politics of the former articulate the resistant desires of a radical individual interested in negating what the queer theorist Leo Bersani defines as 'structures of oppression' (1995: 174), in the latter, his coruscating attack on identity is firmly attached to pressing historical and sociological problems in France at the time, while also exploring the possibilities of collective revolt. As I argue in Chapter 2, this evolution in Genet's writing can be traced to a shattering encounter experienced aboard a train in the early to mid-1950s while in the presence of an abject travelling companion. This disturbing episode, the truth of which is impossible to determine with any certainty, haunted Genet for a decade or so, and resulted in the disclosure of what he refers to, metaphorically, as '*la blessure*', or wound, a painful epiphany, in which he discovered that his being was all void. The importance I attach to the wound in this study distinguishes my analysis of Genet's utopian politics from the one advanced by Deleuzian-inspired scholars such as Michael Hardt and Scott Durham. Where they explore the utopian potential of 'virtuality' in Genet's texts, I put the onus on the abyssal emptiness that disrupts all images and compels us to recognise the axiomatic presence of justice.

Although I have written elsewhere of the wound in terms of an ethics of alterity (Lavery, 2003), I am increasingly minded to see it as the catalyst for a politics of radical equality, based on the maxim that 'every man *is worth as much* as every other' (Genet, 2003: 91; original italics). The Genetian wound, to paraphrase the literary scholar Andrew Gibson, does more than merely reveal difference; it is 'difference that makes a difference' (2005: 62). If we take Genet's own aesthetic and political acts after 1955 as a kind of litmus test for the wound, we can see that it obliges the subject to act upon the 'truth' of her experience and to assent to a revolutionary politics grounded in what he refers to as 'a sort of universal identity' (Genet, 2003: 92). That certain critics might baulk here at Genet's language and regard it, perhaps, as indicative of a dangerously totalitarian or heteronormative move on his part is ultimately uncalled for. Genet's revolutionary universality is the very source of any politics of difference, for what it reveals is the equality of all human beings, regardless of their gender, sexuality or ethnicity. Or as Genet puts it: 'I quickly came to believe that it was this [wound] that allowed every man to be loved, *neither more nor less* than any other, and that allowed even the most revolting appearance to be loved, that is to say, taken charge of and recognized, cherished' (*ibid.*: 94; original italics). The above reflection confirms that Genet's thinking has nothing in common with the dubious universalism of liberal humanist philosophers such as John Stuart Mill or Thomas Paine.[6] Unlike them, Genet does not believe that identity is an essence or substance. No one, for instance, can possess or attain it. On the contrary, we discover the universal, Genet claims, when we become the Other in a strange and unsettling experience which takes place at the very limits of being, and which 'calls into question the plenum of the world' (*ibid.*: 98). Genet's wounded subject is decentred and homeless. She no longer belongs to any nation or State. The corollary to this 'wounded geography' is a world without nations and nationality, a world where, to use Alain Badiou's language, 'everyone who is here is from here' (2008: 57; my translation). As Genet reasons in the 1977 essay 'Chartres Cathedral: A "Bird's-Eye" View': '[i]f every man has a value equal to every other man, every corner of the earth, even the most barren, is worth every other – hence I hope I'll be forgiven, my total detachment with regard to any particular region' (2003: 155).

Returning to the arguments of Bharucha and Redonnet, and keeping their advice firmly in mind, I intend, in this study, to show how the wound emerged in Genet's theatre at the very moment when France was being decolonised and modernised. Contextualising the wound historically allows us to see how it challenged the spectacular notion of 'Frenchness' that was manufactured in the 1950s and 1960s. As with all consensual identities, this was inherently defensive and paranoid, predicated, as it was, upon the exclusion of immigrant workers from public space and the repression of the traumatic reality of the Algerian War. Where France was concerned to reinvent itself as a racially segregated nation-State, Genet's late theatre was tenaciously committed to puncturing that mythology and to keeping the promise of a different, more egalitarian future alive.

This brings me, more or less, to the five central ideas upon which the argument of this book is founded. These are: that Genet's notion of revolution is shot through with utopian assumptions; that the supposed gulf separating his late theatre from his post-1968 commitment needs to be revised and reassessed in terms of an expanded definition of the aesthetic; that his politics and aesthetics underwent a radical change of direction in the 1950s in the aftermath of his experience of the wound; that he possessed his own oblique model of committed theatre, based on the notion of wounding; and that his late theatre is a deliberate

---

6 For a good discussion of how Genet's texts deconstruct the foundations of liberal humanism, see David Lloyd, 'Genet's Genealogy: European Minorities and the Ends of the Canon', *Cultural Critique*, 6 (1987), 161–85.

attempt to undermine the consensus on decolonisation which emerged in France in the mid-1950s.

By weaving these ideas together, my aim, in this book, is to propose a different Genet, a Genet engaged in pursuing an impossible notion of revolution based on the unspeakable equality disclosed through a process of aesthetic disorientation or wounding. For some, this utopian Genet might be perilously optimistic, in the extent to which it remains silent about the ambivalence that he cultivated so carefully, and which therefore makes it relatively easy to challenge my argument with a series of counter-claims from his texts. However, my motivation for writing this book was never to offer a balanced view of Genet's politics. Rather, I wanted to highlight what a more measured approach to Genet's work, for all its exactitude and good political intentions, must invariably downplay or mistrust: namely, its hopefulness, or what I call its *promesse du bonheur*. By focusing uniquely on the utopian impulses of Genet's aesthetics and politics, I intend to make a *plaidoyer* for them. In an age which is so resolutely concerned to shore up all possible escape routes from neo-liberal consensus, I intend to wager for Genet as a playwright of the impossible, and no longer (or not simply) as a playwright of equivocation. This is a time for new exorbitant readings of Genet, readings which take his ambivalence as a given, and which strive to rescue neglected aspects of his politics rather than to reproduce well-rehearsed anxieties. It feels important to say that this utopian Genet is not, in any way, intended to replace the numerous 'political Genets' that are currently in circulation.[7] Rather, it is a Genet refracted through my own notion of what constitutes revolutionary politics. As with every reading of his work, this book is as much about me as it is Genet.

Late theatre

This monograph differs from most studies of Genet's work by concentrating on the three plays, which compose what I call his late theatre: *The Balcony, The Blacks* and *The Screens*.[8] The rationale behind this is to

---

[7] As I mentioned on p. 3, Genet's politics have been important for thinkers working in the fields of sexuality, gender and 'race'.
[8] Although *The Balcony, The Blacks* and *The Screens* have much in common with what Edward Said calls 'late style', when I use the term late theatre it is with a more basic chronological meaning in mind. See *On Late Style* (London: Bloomsbury, 2006).

come to terms with the important aesthetic and political transformation that took place in Genet's theatre from *The Balcony* onwards, and which, to my mind, has received little by way of detailed exegesis.[9] Although it would be grossly inaccurate to say that Genet broke completely with the sexual and existential themes of his novels, films and early plays, there is, in his late theatre, a new concern with global politics and overthrowing the State. These concerns are absent from his work prior to 1955.

Crucially, this thematic shift is doubled by a major alteration in dramaturgical structure. Regardless of what Jean-Paul Sartre termed the 'whirligig' in *The Maids*, the early plays, despite their unsettling theatricality, conform to the usual conventions of play-watching (1988: 611). In them, the spectator is asked to forget the material reality of theatre and encouraged to judge the actions of dramatic characters. In the late plays, by contrast, the audience is decentred and displaced, catapulted into what Una Chaudhuri has termed a 'a no-man's stage' (1986), as a result of the blurring caused by the shifting of spatial and aesthetic barriers.[10] By tracing the cause of this deconstruction of the theatrical frame back to Genet's disorientating incident aboard the train, I aim to show how the spatial politics of his late theatre are predicated upon a self-conscious attempt to *blesser*, or wound the audience. Like Antonin Artaud's notion of cruelty, wounding in Genet's late theatre is not to be confused with a physical act; it is a mode of aesthetic experience which shatters spectators ontologically in order to disclose the void of being.

This study deviates from existing scholarship on Genet for an additional reason. In contrast to many critics who downplay the relationship between the politics of Genet's theatre and his revolutionary militancy, I explain how they form part of a single project of emancipation.[11] By

---

9 Many critics reference the shift in Genet's theatre but few of them have tried to explore its cause. Exceptions are Jean-Bernard Moraly, *Jean Genet: la vie écrite* (Bordeaux: Editions de la Différence,1988); Edmund White, *Genet* (London: Chatto & Windus, 1993); Cynthia Running-Johnson, 'Reading Life Signs in Jean Genet's L'Atelier d'Alberto Giacometti and Ce qui est resté d'un Rembrandt', P. Bougon (ed), *L'Esprit Créateur*, 35: 1 (1995), 20–9; Marie-Claude Hubert, *L'Esthétique de Jean Genet* (Paris: Sedes, 1996); Simon Critchley, 'Writing the Revolution: The Politics of Truth in Genet's *Prisoner of Love*', in *Ethics, Politics and Subjectivity: Essays on Derrida, Levinas and Contemporary French Thought* (London: Verso, 1999), pp. 30–50; and Carl Lavery, 'The Politics of the Wound: Jean Genet's Ethical Commitment', *Journal of European Studies*, 33:2 (2003), 161–76.
10 This is taken from the title of Chaudhuri's outstanding semiotic analysis of Genet's theatre, *No Man's Stage: A Semiotic Study of Jean Genet's Major Plays* (Ann Arbor: UMI Research Press, 1986).
11 This position is adopted by the majority of Genet scholars, including some of his best and most brilliant commentators and biographers. See for instance: Jean-Bernard Moraly, *Les nègres au Port de la Lune: Genet et les différences* (Bordeaux: Editions de la Différence,1988); Gene A. Plunka, *The Rites of Passage of Jean Genet* (New Jersey:

doing so, I take issue with the common view that sees Genet's theatre as politicised without, necessarily, being committed. There are two problems with this point of view. First, it implies that Genet's political engagement is coterminous with his abandonment of theatre. And second, it assumes that Genet had no intention of transforming spectators politically, as if, that is, he was merely content to raise dilemmas.[12] On the contrary, I want to advocate that Genet's concept of revolution is saturated with utopian drives that are inherent to, and anticipated by, the thematic and formal politics of his late plays. In mapping this continuity, I hope to do more than trace a formal practice rooted in what Clare Finburgh has called an interplay between 'stage-craft' and 'statecraft' (2002b: 495). Rather, I am concerned with how, in Genet's theatre *and* politics, there is an onus placed on producing a sense of shock that might allow French subjects to gamble on a revolutionary future. So although I do not dispute that political activism replaced playwriting in Genet's life in the late 1960s, there is much to be gained, or so it seems to me, by approaching this break in terms of evolution rather

---

Fairleigh Dickinson Press, 1992); Nathalie Fredette, 'Genet politique: l'ultime engagement', *Etudes Françaises*, 29:2 (1993), 83–102; Albert Dichy, 'Jean Genet: Portrait of the Artist as Warrior', in B. Read and I. Birchall (eds), *Flowers and Revolution: A Collection of Writings on Jean Genet* (London: Middlesex University Press, 1997), pp. 21–5; Michel Corvin in M. Corvin and A. Dichy (eds), *Jean Genet: théâtre complet* (Paris: Gallimard, 2002) pp. xi-lxxxvii. Each of them, in their different ways, highlights the silence that followed *The Screens*, and then uses this to distinguish between the politics of his theatre and his revolutionary politics. What they are concerned to do is to show that Genet's dramatic work was political without being committed. In this narrative, Genet's role as a committed writer is reserved for his late prose work. My point is somewhat different: I want to suggest that Genet's alternative notion of engagement dates from his late theatre rather than from the essay 'Four Hours in Shatila' or the posthumously published novel *Prisoner of Love*. Genet hints at this himself in an interview in 1969 with Jose Monléon, when he mentioned that theatre is a public art oriented towards a 'communal audience', whereas the novel aims at 'solitary readers' (in Corvin and Dichy, *Jean Genet*, p. 967; my translation).

12 I continue to find it astonishing that so many scholars, interested in Genet's politics, ignore his theatre altogether. In three major anthologies to have been published in English in the past decade, Read and Birchall – *Flowers and Revolution*; *Genet: In the Language of the Enemy*, S. Durham (ed.), *Yale French Studies*, 91:1 (1997), 7–27; and Hanrahan *Genet* – a mere handful of the thirty or so essays deal directly with Genet's theatre. There is scant mention of Genet's theatre in the work of Didier Eribon, *Une morale du minoritaire. Variations sur un thème de Jean Genet* (Paris: Fayard, 2001), Pascale Gaitet, *Queens and Revolutionaries: New Readings of Jean Genet* (London: Associated University Press, 2003), and Jeremy Reed, *Jean Genet: Born to Lose: An Illustrated Critical History* (London: Creation, 2005). The edited collection *Jean Genet: Performance and Politics*, Finburgh *et al.* (Basingstoke: Palgrave MacMillan, 2006) was a modest attempt to rectify that. The contributors to that volume all endorsed Bernard Dort's view that 'theatre is at the very centre of [Genet's] work' ('Le théâtre: une féerie sans réplique', *Magazine littéraire*, 313 (1993), 46–50: 46; my translation and modification).

than rupture. Not only does this suggest that Genet's move to activism might be grounded in an expanded notion of aesthetics, it revises, furthermore, the meaning of his late theatre by disclosing the presence in it of revolutionary desires that Genet tried to activate through his own 'oblique' model of committed art. Critics who see Genet as practising a political dramaturgy rather than a revolutionary dramaturgy are unwilling to make that leap.

Spaces of revolution

The subheading of this book, *Spaces of revolution*, is intentionally double-edged. On the one hand, it refers to revolution as a figure or trope within the dramatic space of Genet's theatre; and, on the other hand, it investigates the possibility that theatre, for Genet, has the potential to become a revolutionary space in and by itself. To make such a statement within the context of Genet studies calls out, immediately, for further qualification.[13] Anyone who wants to argue for Genet's revolutionary significance is forced to confront the fact that in each of the late plays revolution is either defeated entirely (*The Balcony*) or else severely compromised (*The Blacks* and *The Screens*). My intention here is not to castigate Genet, as many critics have already done, for refusing to provide a positive image of revolutionary change. Instead, I want to contemplate the failure of revolution as a tactic, a method for transferring political energy from the dramaturgical realm (the space of fiction) to the theatrical realm (the space of corporeality). In doing so, Genet's theatre, in my view, seeks to disarm purposively the spectator and so prevent her from achieving the type of aesthetic and political transparency found in Sartrean and, to a lesser extent, Brechtian theatre.

In this book, theatre is posited as a spatial event, as something that takes place between bodies that are both fictional and real. While a film can be shown in the absence of its performers, theatre cannot: it is, in essence, a public encounter between actors and spectators.

---

13 Within Genet studies, critics often contend that Genet's theatre is devoid of revolutionary hope. See Albert Chesneau, 'Idée de révolution et principe de réversibilité dans *Le balcon* et *Les nègres* de Jean Genet', *PMLA*, 88:5 (1973), 1137–45; Gisèle Bickel, *Jean Genet: criminalité et transcendance* (Saratoga: Anma Libri, 1988), pp. 100–23; Christopher Innes, *Avant Garde Theatre 1892–1992* (London: Routledge, 1993), pp. 108–17; and Richard Schechner, in Finburgh *et al.*, *Performance and Politics*, pp. 213–22.

Furthermore, the fact that it often occurs in a civic or state-sponsored building means that theatre is enmeshed in a network of concrete economic and political relations, the significance of which it can both affect and be affected by. Theatre's relationship with social space is mirrored internally, as well. Theatre audiences assent to a pre-existing set of spatial codes which regulate social behaviour by determining the distribution of bodies and by telling people what they can and cannot do. Looked at in this way, theatre does more than simply reflect social space; it actively produces it. To grasp, fully, how theatre can be considered as a de facto political act on account of its spatiality, it is useful to turn to the theory of spatial production proposed by the Marxian geographer Henri Lefebvre.

Midway through the long introduction to his difficult but seminal book *The Production of Space*, Lefebvre contends that social space is characterised by a trialectical interplay between what he calls 'spatial practice', 'representations of space' and 'spatial representations' (2004: 33).[14] In general, 'spatial practice' orders space; it creates a network of recognisable structures allowing users to navigate their way through a landscape of roads, buildings, rooms, and so on. Spatial practice tells us what things are and how to use them. In turn, a given society's spatial practice is affected by, and composed of, 'representations of space' and 'spatial representations'. Where representations of space (the space of planners, real estate agents and architects) dominate their users by imposing an abstract or conceptual notion of space upon them, spatial representations (the creative spaces produced by artists, children and political militants) disrupt this process by stressing the value of lived experience. This process of active engagement, Lefebvre argues, enables individuals and groups to reappropriate their environment. Since '(social) space', for Lefebvre, 'is a (social) product', it is always open to change from below (*ibid.*: 26). For this to happen, 'spatial representations' – or what Michel Foucault calls 'heterotopias' (1997: 350–1) – need to find a way of challenging and subverting the dominant 'representations of space'. If this appropriation is successful and widespread, as it was during the Paris Commune in 1871 and in May 1968, then the existing spatial practice collapses and a revolutionary situation occurs. This is because, for Lefebvre, social space determines social being.

Even though Lefebvre surprisingly wrote little about theatre, his insights, as a number of recent publications testify, are nevertheless

---

14 Lefebvre sees this trialectic in terms of perceived, conceived and lived space. For an excellent discussion of this, see Edward Soja's study *Thirdspace: Journeys to Los Angeles and Other Real and Imagined Spaces* (Oxford: Blackwell, 1996), pp. 53–70.

highly germane to it.[15] In particular, they suggest that theatre's heterotopic dimension, its ability to reorder the spatiality of the world in the most concrete of ways, means that it is always already a political site, in the extent to which it is always already a mode of spatial production.[16] From this perspective, it is not enough for a politically progressive theatre to represent social contradictions in pre-existing spatial forms; it must seek to activate those contradictions in real time and space. When it does this, theatre has the potential to become a spatial representation, a heterotopia in which new utopic possibilities for collective life can be embodied *and* lived out.[17] The ideas of Lefebvre cast a different light on the politics of Genet's late plays. They imply that the political significance of his theatre is not limited to thematics alone, but rather resides in how it affects the audience, physically, in the heterotopic space of the auditorium.

What space?

If Lefebvre's concept of spatial production provides a new methodology for mapping the politics of Genet's late theatre, the question remains

---

15 This would appear to be borne out by the number of theatre and performance scholars who have turned to his work in recent years. See David Wiles, *A Short History of Western Performance Space* (Cambridge: Cambridge University Press, 2003); Michal Kobialka, 'Theatre and Space: A Historiographic Preamble', *Modern Drama*, 46:4 (2003), 558–79; Jen Harvie, *Staging the UK* (Manchester: Manchester University Press, 2005); Gay McAuley, *Unstable Ground: Performance and the Politics of Place* (Brussels: Peter Lang, 2006); Sophie Nield, 'There is Another World: Space, Theatre and Global Anti-Capitalism', *Contemporary Theatre Review*, 16:1 (2006), 51–61; and Joanne Tompkins, *Unsettling Space: Contestations in Contemporary Australian Theatre* (Basingstoke: Palgrave Macmillan, 2006).
16 Foucault distinguishes between heterotopias and utopias by suggesting that the latter are 'real and effective spaces' that are located within the existing social order itself. By contrast, utopias are u-topoi or non-places, which 'are by their very essence fundamentally unreal'. See 'Of Other Spaces: Utopias and Heterotopias' in N. Leach (ed.), *Rethinking Architecture: A Reader in Cultural Theory* (London: Routledge, 1997), pp. 350–6: 352. What Foucault does not mention, however, is that heterotopias have the possibility of existing as marginal sites where utopic desires can be lived in the here and now. For a good discussion of this, see Kevin Hetherington, *Expressions of Identity: Space, Performance, Politics* (London: Sage, 1998), pp. 123–39; and Tompkins, *Unsettling Space*, pp. 94–5.
17 This idea has much in common with Jill Dolan's notion of the 'utopian performative'. However, where Dolan concentrates on time, I focus on space. My study also differs from hers in that whereas she is interested in *communitas*, I am more concerned with Rancièrian notions such as disidentification and dissensus. See *Utopia in Performance: Finding Hope at the Theater* (Ann Arbor: University of Michigan Press, 2005), p. 5.

as to what aspect of theatrical space this book intends to focus on. As Joanne Tompkins warns in a recent editorial in *Modern Drama*, the concept of space in theatrical circles can say so much that it means virtually nothing:

> [A] central difficulty in analysing any type of space is less the concept itself than its terminology. *Space* is already an over-determined word: [. . .] regarding theatre alone, [it can be used] to describe a play's setting, a theatre venue, scenography, the socio-cultural milieu beyond a theatre building, which nevertheless intersects with theatrical action, and is an elemental aspect of theatre itself [. . .] [S]pace slips between both a literal location and a metaphoric capacity to structure our perceptions of the world: the advantages in capitalizing on this slippage can be outweighed by the potential for confusion. (2003: 538; original italics)

Responding to Tompkins' caution then, space in this book refers, specifically, to the relationship between actor and spectator, and not, as one might expect, perhaps, to scenography, or to environment or site-specificity.[18] I am particularly interested in how Genet blurs the line between the dramatic and theatrical codes of theatre in order to trouble the solidity of the theatrical frame. While this approach has a certain amount in common with earlier semiotic readings of Genet's plays, it also differs from them by focusing on, and speculating about, the phenomenological affects generated by the disorientation that such frame-breaking invariably gives rise to. In this respect, it should come as no surprise that a key concern in this book is with theatre's presentness, the way in which theatrical experience is always, to an extent, real experience. When I use the word presentness, I am not referring to presence in the metaphysical sense of the word, as a form of immediate knowledge that reveals itself to the subject through the magical power of the *logos*. Rather, I take presentness to be the equivalent of a physical 'thereness' which is resistant to all knowledge. Presentness, in my reading, is disruptive; it sets subjectivity reeling.

---

18 I use the words environment and site-specificity here since three of the most innovative stagings of Genet's work – Víctor García's production of *The Balcony* in São Paulo 1969–72; Richard Schechner's interpretation of the same play in New York in 1979–80; and Cornerstone Theatre's and Peter Sellars' Chicano version of *The Screens/Los biombos* in 1998–99 – experimented with theatrical space in accordance with the ways described above. For good descriptions of the stagings, see Ilka Zanotto, 'An Audience-Structure for *The Balcony*', *The Drama Review*, 17:2 (1973), 58–65; Richard Schechner, 'Genet's *The Balcony*: A 1981 Perspective on a 1979/80 Production', *Modern Drama*, 25:1 (1982), 82–104; Michèle Sigal, 'Genet's *The Screens* Directed by Peter Sellars', *Theatre Forum*, 13 (1998), 76–83; and D. J. Hopkins, 'Misunderstanding *Los biombos*: A Response to Irresponsible Press', *Theatre Forum*, 13 (1998), 84–5.

In order to get to grips with the politics involved in Genet's attempts to dislocate the audience, I supplement Lefebvre's ideas with those of the post-Althusserian philosophers Jacques Rancière and Alain Badiou.[19] According to Rancière, becoming a political subject does not mean that we identify with a pre-existing set of ideological roles (say, for instance, signing up as a party member); rather, to use Rancière's terminology, we become political subjects by 'disidentifying' with images and identities that confine us to our proper place in the 'distribution of the sensible' (1999: 36). In Rancière's thought, the sensible refers to the 'primary' aesthetic framework which establishes, in advance, what can be seen, heard and said politically:

> Political subjectification redefines the field of experience that gave to each their identity with their lot. It decomposes and recomposes the relationship between ways of doing, of being, and of saying that define the perceptible organization of the community, the relationships between the places where one does one thing and those where one does something else, the capacities associated with this particular doing and those required for another. (*ibid.*: 40)

Unlike an earlier generation of French thinkers, most notably Jean-François Lyotard, Rancière does not equate disidentification with a moment of sublime unrepresentability; he sees it as a political act allowing the subject to escape from her identity and so reinvent herself. For Rancière, the antithesis to disidentification is 'police logic', a disciplinary mode of aesthetic distribution, which tries to shackle individuals and communities to one identity, and to put them in their proper place:[20]

> A mode of subjectification does not create subjects *ex nihlio*; it creates them by transforming identities defined in the natural order of the allocation of functions and places into instances of experience of a dispute. 'Workers'

---

19 In *The Production of Space*, Lefebvre, for instance, says very little about how the redistribution of space impacts on subjectivity at a micro level. His concern is with macro processes: history, economics, technology, and so on. This means that he neglects to look at the way in which subjects disidentify with prescribed social roles and functions when social space is in the process of being disrupted.

20 Rancière is careful to distinguish between the empirical police and police logic: 'The word *police* normally evokes what is known as the petty police, the truncheon blows of the forces of law and order and the inquisitions of the secret police. But this narrow definition may be deemed contingent [...] The petty police is just a particular form of a more general order that arranges the tangible reality in which bodies are distributed in community [...] The evolution of western societies reveals [...] that the policeman is one element in a social mechanism linking medicine, welfare and culture' (*Disagreement: Politics and Philosophy*, trans. J. Rose (Minneapolis: University of Minnesota Press, 1999) p. 28).

or 'women' are identities that apparently hold no mystery. Anyone can tell *who* is meant. But political subjectification forces them out of such obviousness by questioning the relationship between a *who* and a *what* in the apparent redundancy of the positing of an existence. (*ibid.*: 36; original italics)

Rancière's commitment to undoing identity underscores the importance that theatre plays as both trope and practice in his thought.[21] Against Plato who famously rejected the clapping of what he sarcastically named 'the theatrocacy' as mere babble, Rancière embraces theatre as a democratic machine for the way in which the actor shows that identity can be (at least) always double. Both for the actor and the audience, theatre is, as the UK philosopher Peter Hallward explains in an insightful article on Rancière, the 'privileged site of a more general displacement – a place for the out of place' (2006: 118). What theatre does is to expose reality's lack of foundation. It institutes a different world by *showing* appearance:

> The democratic distribution of the sensible makes the worker into a double being. It removes the artisan from 'his' place, the domestic space of work, and gives him 'time' to occupy the space of public discussions and take on the identity of a deliberative citizen. The mimetic act of splitting in two, which is at work in theatrical space, consecrates this duality and makes it visible. The exclusion of the mimetician, from the Platonic point of view, goes hand in hand with the formation of a community where work is in its place. (Rancière, 2006: 43)

Rancière's notion of disidentification highlights, with some accuracy, the heterotopic and utopic terrain on which the spatial politics of Genet's late theatre play themselves out.[22] By showing oppressed subjects flaunting the falsity of identity, and refusing to remain in their proper place, Genet upsets, profoundly, the existing distribution of sensible experience. The painful 'shock' or wound produced by this act of dislocation permits, as I argue in the book, the spectator to disidentify with her role as a proper French subject, and, in the process, to open herself to those who embody what Rancière calls the 'wrong' or disagreement.[23] This

---

21 The trope of the stage runs throughout Ranciere's work. Particular texts that concentrate, specifically, on theatre as an actual practice are *Les scènes du peuple: les révoltes logiques 1975–85* (Lyon: Horlieu, 2003); *The Politics of Aesthetics: The Distribution of the Sensible*, trans. G. Rockhill (London: Continuum, 2006), pp. 42–5; and 'The Emancipated Spectator', *Artforum*, 65:7 (2007), 270–81.
22 Alan Read's analysis of how Rancière's ideas transform existing notions of political theatre is pertinent here, see *Theatre, Intimacy and Engagement: The Last Human Venue* (Basingstoke: Palgrave Macmillan, 2008), pp. 175–86.
23 Importantly, for Rancière, the 'wrong' is not something that can be righted through discussion or debate; it can only be addressed by intervening and disputing

mention of disidentification seems an appropriate moment to discuss what I mean by the term 'French spectator'. When I refer to the spectator in Chapters 4, 5 and 6, I think of her, primarily, in terms of the spectacular notion of Frenchness manufactured by the French State in the 1950s and 1960s. That is to say, as a subject whose identity, irrespective of the specifics of gender, sexuality and class, was configured as white, and whose destiny was irremediably linked to France's ability to transform itself into a modernised, capitalist nation.[24]

Where Rancière allows us to understand the politics of Genet's late theatre, Alain Badiou's theory of the event helps us to account for its origins and consequences. In linguistic terms, the event can be loosely defined as a moment of rupture which shatters the existing 'state of the situation' and discloses the capacity for bringing a different world into being.[25] According to Badiou, the truth of the event resides in the subject's fidelity to the gap in knowledge it has opened up: '[a] fidelity. . .is not a matter of knowledge. It is not the work of an expert: it is the work of a militant' (2007: 329). Within the domain of politics, the event is a moment which discloses the very thing which the political State is concerned to repress: the fact that all people, regardless of where they come from, are equal: '[t]his idea must be understood: the essence of the State is that of not being obliged to recognize individuals' (*ibid.*: 105). As Badiou explains it, the State, like the more generalised 'state of the situation', exists to uphold pre-existing class interests and to prevent any

consensus. Nick Hewlett notes that politics, in Rancière's thought, 'is never a rational debate' but a battle to make one's voice count as one that is recognized as legitimate' (*Badiou, Balibar, Rancière: Re-thinking Emancipation* (London: Continuum, 2007), p. 98)

24 I realise, of course, that my notion of the French spectator above does not account for differences between audience members. Nevertheless, if one examines Genet's prefaces and essays on theatre, in particular the 'Avertissement' to *The Balcony* and 'Preface to *The Blacks*', this is the spectator he has in mind. At the time same, it is also worth pointing out that although Genet's notion of the 'white bourgeois spectator' is confined, in this study, to France, it is possible to apply it to other national contexts, too. One thinks, for instance, of the scandalous impact Víctor García's production of *The Maids /Las criadas* had in Spain in the late 1960s; or, for that matter, the political passions aroused in Brazil when García staged *The Balcony* at the Ruth Escobar Theatre in São Paulo between 1969 and 1972. Yet to grasp in detail how and why these productions affected Spanish and Brazilian spectators, it would be necessary to supply a detailed account of the specific social and political factors pertaining to both countries at the precise historical moment(s) during which the productions cited above were performed.

25 Badiou's theory of the event is thought through and expressed as a mathematical equation. See for instance his 'matheme of the event' in *Being and Event*, trans. O. Feltham (London: Continuum, 2007), pp. 178–83. For the sake of readability, I have decided to leave the mathematical intricacies of set theory behind in this study, and to express the logic of the event in everyday language instead.

possibility of a different, more equitable reality from emerging, 'the *State always represents what has already been presented*' (*ibid.*: 106; original italics).[26] In contrast to this, the militant of the event, claims Badiou, is committed to the excessive equality that the state cannot represent, and which he defines, like Genet, in terms of the void:

> [P]olitics stakes its existence on its capacity to establish a relation to both the void and excess which is essentially different from that of the State; it is this difference alone that subtracts politics from one of statist re-insurance. Rather than a warrior beneath the walls of the State, a political activist is a patient watchman of the void instructed by the event [...] There the activist constructs the means to sound, if only for an instant, the site of the unrepresentable, and the means to be thenceforth faithful to the proper name that, afterwards, he or she will have been able to give to – or to hear, one cannot decide – this non-place of place, the void. (*ibid.*: 110–11)

The importance of Badiou's theory of the event to this study is twofold. Initially, it allows me to theorise the political transformation that occurred in Genet's theatre in terms of a radical fidelity to the wound. Second, it provides a valuable tool for thinking through the concrete political impact of Roger's Blin production of *The Screens* at the Odéon-Théâtre de France in 1966. For, as I argue in Chapter 6, the play deserves to be considered as a political event in and by itself, in the extent to which the street battles and scandal it provoked contributed to the growing sense of social disaffection that ultimately resulted in the revolutionary situation of May 1968.

Reading history

Given the emphasis I place on presentness, it might come as a surprise to learn that this monograph is largely textual in nature. With the exception of Chapter 6, I concentrate, for the most part, on interrogating the political potential residing in the dramaturgy of Genet's scripts. My concern is to show how Genet's approach to theatre is fuelled by a desire to disturb spectators by subverting existing genres of performance and deconstructing the theatrical frame itself. To achieve this, I supplement

---

26 In Badiou's philosophy, the concept of the 'state of the situation' resonates, intentionally, with the sense of the State. In both instances, the point of the state /State is to include certain elements while excluding others.

my interest in space with a series of readings that borrow from Walter Benjamin's notion of allegory, Guy Debord's theory of *détournement* and Hans-Thies Lehmann's postdramatic ideas about the theatrical gaze.

Regardless of what some might say, I do not think that my reluctance to 'reconstruct' actual productions, in any great detail, is at odds with my concern for phenomenological experience.[27] As I see it, the dramatic text possesses an experiential potentiality that transcends the meaning of any specific production, no matter how successful this production may (or may not) have been in engaging its actual audience at the time. A major reason for this is due to the rhetorical quality of Genet's language itself, the power of which allows the reader to imagine, vividly, how the work might be staged. The theatre phenomenologist Stanton B. Garner provides an articulate defence for my position in *Bodied Spaces: Phenomenology and Performance in Contemporary Drama*:

> Unlike a specific performance event (or its description), the dramatic text deals with the actual in its possible manifestations [. . .] In this sense, the dramatic text effects a version of the *epoche* or 'reduction', whereby phenomenology suspends awareness of the object's actual existence in one place and one time in order to disclose this actuality in its own parameters and tolerances, its dialectic of the variable and invariable. Drama, in short, presents the 'thing in itself' as a bounded (or floating) facticity, available to a variety of specific actualizations. (1994: 6)

For Garner, it is too simplistic to see the dramatic text as being somehow opposed to the real stuff of theatrical practice. Rather, because the script is always rooted in a '*possible actuality*', it is axiomatic that it should exist as a basis for practice (*ibid.*: 7; original italics). Widening Garner's notion of 'possible actuality' to include historical context encourages an imaginative engagement with the past from the standpoint of the present and permits phenomenology to be historicised and vice versa. This is crucial when it comes to gauging the political implications of Genet's late plays.

27 For good descriptive accounts of actual productions of Genet's work, see Odette Aslan, 'Les paravents de Jean Genet', in D. Bablet and J. Jacquot (eds), *Les voies de la création* théâtrale, 3 (Paris: CNRS, 1972), pp. 11–105 and '*Les paravents*', in D. Bablet and J. Jacquot (eds), *Les voies de la création théâtrale*, 14 (Paris: CNRS, 1986) pp. 295–316; Walter Donohue, 'Genet's *The Screens* at Bristol', *Theatre Quarterly*, 4:1 (1974), 74–90; David Bradby, 'Blacking Up: Three Productions by Peter Stein', in W. G. Sebald (ed.), *A Radical Stage: Theatre in Germany in the 1970s and 1980s* (Oxford: Berg, 1988), pp. 18–30; Michel Corvin in Corvin and Dichy, *Jean Genet*; and Maria Delgado, *'Other' Spanish Stages: Erasure and Inscription on the Twentieth Century Spanish Stage* (Manchester: Manchester University Press, 2003) pp. 192–4 and '*Las criadas*, Genet and Spain', in Finburgh *et al.*, *Performance and Politics*, pp. 143–57.

That critics or directors at the time neglected to *discuss* his work in terms of decolonisation and modernisation does not rule out the possibility that these are indeed what they were about, or that spectators might have *experienced* them in these terms. Although I do not dispense with the opinions of reviewers or neglect relevant productions altogether, my approach to historiography in this book is conditioned by the wager of 'possible actuality'. By reading his texts in tandem with his prefaces and instructions for performance, I propose to think about the possible affects that Genet's theatre might have had on French audiences in the 1950s and 1960s. As well as reassessing the meaning of Genet's theatre in the past, this hypothetical excavation highlights its significance to our present.[28] It establishes a sense of historical continuity between then and now, and demonstrates the extent to which Genet is our contemporary. As the US cultural historian Kristin Ross reminds us in her exemplary study *Fast Cars and Clean Bodies: Decolonization and the Reordering of French Culture*, the neo-racist consensus 'haunting the collective fantasies of French society today is the old accomplice to the accelerated growth of French society in the 1950s and 1960s' (1995: 9).

Structure

This book is divided into three parts. Part I explores the relationship between politics and aesthetics in Genet's theatre and political writing in the period 1955 to 1986; Part II focuses on the spatial politics of *The Balcony*, *The Blacks* and *The Screens* by historicising them within the processes of modernisation and decolonisation in France of the 1950s and 1960s; and Part III analyses how Genet's radical spatiality works in practice by interviewing key contemporary practitioners, Lluís Pasqual, JoAnne Akalaitis, and Ultz and Excalibah. The rationale behind these interviews is to find a way of merging past and present, and so explore why Genet's late theatre, although firmly rooted within its own political and historical landscape, retains its relevance for practitioners working within different geographical and historical contexts today. As I argue in the book's conclusion, the happy paradox of this study (and, to speak more broadly, of theatre in general) is that any attempt to historicise

---

28 This also explains why, in this book, I have kept the word theatre in the title. Reading a dramatic text phenomenologically does not automatically reduce that text to a subset of dramatic literature; on the contrary, to read a dramatic text is to imagine, necessarily, how that text might be staged.

Genet, as I have done, is always partial and forever contingent. The future always has the last word on the past.

The book's appendix, brilliantly translated by Clare Finburgh, contains the first full-length English translation of 'Preface to *The Blacks*', and allows anglophone readers to access a very different Genet, a Genet hugely interested in questions of politics, aesthetics and theatrical representation. Two very different historiographical methods are at work in the book. In Chapters 4 and 5, the onus is on reading *The Balcony* and *The Blacks* historically, that is to say, by placing them within a specific historical context. In Chapter 6, by contrast, I am concerned with piecing together, through a more empirical-based study of Roger Blin's production of *The Screens*, how theatre can sometimes produce history by setting a new political sequence in motion.

A more precise chapter breakdown is as follows: Chapter 1 describes what Genet's post-1968 commitment consisted of, and explains how his emphasis shifted in that period from aesthetic politics to political aesthetics. Chapter 2 accounts for the political transformation that occurred in Genet's work in the mid-1950s by reflecting on the pivotal role played by the wound in his thought. Chapter 3 examines the influence that the wound had on Genet's theory and practice of aesthetic politics. Chapter 4 reads *The Balcony* as an allegorical and spatial critique of the society of the spectacle. Chapter 5 looks at how *The Blacks* plays on French fears about mass immigration into the country from the ex-colonies by exploring the dynamic interplay between *détournement*, abjection and disidentification. Chapter 6 proposes that Roger Blin's production of *The Screens* is best read as a political event in the extent to which it allowed militant students the opportunity to dissent from the Gaullist consensus on French identity and to pursue a different, more internationalist politics. As I mentioned above, the interviews with Lluís Pasqual, JoAnne Akalaitis, and Ultz and Excalibah are attempts to make what Walter Benjamin calls 'a tiger's leap into the past' (1969: 261), and to gauge how living theatre directors try to activate the politics of Genet's theatre for contemporary European and US spectators.

This last sentence articulates what is at stake in this monograph. In addition to expanding the field of Genet studies by presenting a fresh historical perspective on his late theatre, my ambition for this book is that it will contribute, more generally, to debates and practices about what political performance can, and should, be doing now. For me, Genet's late theatre is at the heart of this debate, both for its impact upon theatrical and political structures in the recent past, and for its continued influence on so many contemporary practitioners working in the present. So while this study makes no excuses about locating itself within a tightly circumscribed historical époque, its eye is restless and focused elsewhere on different historical and geographical contexts. This is necessary, I believe, for two reasons. First, because in the countries that constitute the global North, we are still attempting to come to terms with the processes of decolonisation and modernisation that Genet's theatre sought to make visible to French audiences in the 1950s and 1960s; and second, because theatre, as the theorist and historian Freddie Rokem suggests, is always radically anachronistic, in so far as the performance of history is necessarily 'redoing something which has already been done in the past, creating a secondary elaboration of historical event[s]' (2000: 6; citation modified). By that token, any historical study about Genet can only ever exist as a study about the present, as well as escaping its specific mooring, and becoming, in the process, an investigation into the politics of theatre in general.

ID # 1

Genet and commitment: politics and aesthetics

Perhaps we ought to recognize that the end pursued [...] by revolutions or liberations is the discovery or rediscovery of beauty, that is, something that is impalpable and unnameable except by this word. (Genet, 2004: 225)

Introduction

Given the focus of this book – the fact that it concentrates so intensely on Genet's theatre between 1955 to 1961 – it might seem illogical to start with an analysis of the years 1968 to 1986, the period when theatre was replaced in Genet's life with a more direct style of political interventionism and committed writing. However, as the forthcoming chapters make clear, it is ultimately impossible to separate the politics of Genet's theatre from his thinking about politics per se. To do so is not only to fall into the naïve trap of believing that Genet's political commitment was synonymous with a total abandonment of art.[1] More seriously still, it misjudges the complex relationship between aesthetics and politics that

---

1   Much of this misunderstanding is caused by Genet himself. In an interview with Rüdiger Wischenbart and Layla Shahid Barrada, he said that his time with the Black Panthers and the Palestinians delivered him from 'the daydream' of writing. See *The*

became a key theoretical and practical concern in his work after 1955. In order to avoid this situation, this chapter unveils the utopian elements in Genet's post-1968 revolutionary thought, before going on how to show how they were already anticipated by the themes and practices of his late theatre.

A caution

In 1961, Genet finished his last play *The Screens*, and fell into a debilitating bout of writer's block that was compounded by a lengthy depression caused by the death of his lover Abdallah in 1964, and by his own bungled suicide attempt in the Italian border city of Domodossola in 1967. As a consequence, he never managed to complete his masterpiece *Le bagne*, or indeed any of the other works that supposedly comprised the ambitious seven-play cycle *La mort*, which had been announced on numerous occasions from the late 1950s onwards.[2] Although Genet's experience of working closely with both Roger Blin on *The Screens* in 1966 and Víctor García on *The Maids/Las criadas* in Barcelona in 1969 galvanised him aesthetically, he was never to return, at least not in any sustained sense, to the theatre. In fact, from 1961 until his death in April 1986, his creative output was severely curtailed, and he was reluctant to release any of the numerous projects, including screenplays and operas, which he continued to work on throughout the 1970s and 1980s. It is surely no coincidence, in this regard, that *Prisoner of Love* was published posthumously; and indeed it is perfectly plausible to surmise that without Genet's death, the book might not have appeared in Gallimard's catalogue in 1986 at all, despite its supposedly imminent publication date.[3]

Within Genet studies, there has been a strong temptation to see the revolutionary events of May 1968 in Paris as heralding the start of

---

Declared Enemy: Texts and Interviews, A. Dichy (ed.), trans. J. Fort (Stanford: Stanford University Press, 2004), pp. 239–40.
2 For a comprehensive discussion of Genet's posthumously published and unpublished plays, see Brian Kennelly, 'A paraître/apparaître, Genet and his press', *French Review*, 68:3 (1995), 466–76,
3 According to Albert Dichy, Genet had submitted the completed manuscript for *Prisoner of Love* to Gallimard in November 1985. Given Genet's track record in the 1970s and 1980s, however, there is no guarantee that he would have been satisfied with the finished product. See Corvin and Dichy, *Jean Genet*, p. xciv.

Genet's existential and emotional rebirth, the moment when he turned his back on art and transformed himself into a pragmatic political militant. According to the critic Robert Sandarg, for instance, Genet had 'by 1970 subsequently abandoned literature and turned directly to revolutionary politics' (1986: 270). However, while there is no doubt, as Edmund White has shown (1993: 578), that the actions of the students and workers in France in 1968 affected Genet profoundly, we must guard against Sandarg's neo-Sartrean analysis of Genet's career. Not only did Genet continue to write creatively until his death, but his notion of revolutionary politics was predicated upon enlarging the aesthetic possibilities of everyday life itself. Instead then of seeing Genet's response to May 1968 in terms of some Sartrean rejection of the aesthetic for the authenticity of history, it is more accurate to regard it as an event that promised to realise, concretely, the political possibilities that his theatre of the 1950s and 1960s had merely gestured towards. In other words, Genet's renunciation of theatre and subsequent commitment to revolutionary politics allowed him to continue his aesthetic project by other means. My intention in proposing this is not to suggest that Genet's relationship to art was without transformation or change, but simply to stress the sense of both continuity and difference in his approach to the political dimension of the aesthetic.

1968 and after

In an ironic twist that would have surprised Jean-Paul Sartre, his earliest biographer, Genet was, from 1968 until his death in 1986, the consummate political activist.[4] Some of the causes and movements which he supported were (in no particular order): the Viet-Cong, the Algerian Liberation Front (FLN), the Black Panther Party, the Palestinian Liberation Organization (PLO), the Red Army Faction,

---

4 Sartre claimed that Genet, because of his peasant upbringing and illegitimacy, was unable to identify with collective revolutionary movements. For Sartre, Genet is an ethical writer, not a political one. See *Saint Genet: Actor and Martyr*, trans. B. Frechtman (London: Heinemann, 1988), pp. 544–83. Similarly Sartre argued that Genet's plays, especially *The Screens*, offered little in the way of political hope. See *Sartre on Theater*, M. Contat and M. Rybalka (eds), trans. F. Jellinek (London: Quartet, 1976) p. 122. As I have argued elsewhere, Sartre's reading of Genet's theatrical politics is flawed by the limitations inherent in his own notion of political theatre. See Carl Lavery, 'Between Negativity and Resistance: Genet and Committed Theatre', *Contemporary Theatre Review*, 16:2 (2006), 220–34: 224–5.

disaffected students and anti-Vietnam war protesters in Japan, France and the USA, Michel Foucault's Group d'Information sur les Prisons (GIP) and the Committee Djali in France who campaigned against the racist treatment suffered by immigrant workers. Investing in what Keith Reader, in a different context, has called a Maoist imperative 'to serve the people' through real acts as opposed to simply speaking on their part, Genet was tireless in his support of oppressed peoples and individuals, both globally and within a specifically French context (1987: 32).

May 1968 is the moment when Genet broke his political silence (after much soul-searching he had neglected to sign the 121 Manifesto against the war in Algeria in 1960) and entered the public realm as a fully committed intellectual.[5] 'Lenin's Mistresses' was published on 30 May 1968 in a special edition of the popular weekly magazine *Le Nouvel Observateur*. In it, Genet defended the student leader, Daniel Cohn-Bendit, from anti-Semitic slurs made by the newspaper *L'Humanité*, the official organ of the Parti Communiste Français (PCF). The title of the article is both provocative and ironic. By comparing the treatment of Cohn-Bendit in the pages of *L'Humanité* to the treatment of Lenin in those of the reactionary newspaper, *Le Matin* in 1920, Genet confirmed what many on the alternative left (*le gauchisme*), especially the young, had been thinking since the outbreak of the Algerian War in 1954: that the PCF had degenerated into another bourgeois party. This accounts for the statement made by Genet midway through the article when he claims that Cohn-Bendit and the student revolutionaries embody 'a third force more radical than the two opposing forces: Gaullism and the Communist Party' (2004: 19). For Genet, this third force had little in common with the accord signed between the reconfigured Parti Socialiste (PS) and PCF in the early 1970s; rather, it was a return to authentic revolutionary politics, which, for him, as for other *gauchiste* groups of the period had more to do with sexual and gender equality, Third Worldism and avant-garde aesthetics than with economics and ideology.

Genet's *gauchiste* desire for a ludic, poetic mode of revolt that would put an end to alienation explains his equally enthusiastic response

5 The 121 Manifesto was a protest against the French military presence in Algeria made by prominent intellectuals and cultural figures such as Jean-Paul Sartre, Alain Resnais and François Truffaut. More specifically, it called upon French youth to refuse the draft. Genet gives his reasons for not signing the 121 Manifesto in a 1960 letter to Bernard Frechtman. To a certain extent it seems that his silence was caused by a desire to protect the meaning of *The Screens*; he did not want the play to be deciphered, and thus neutralised, as a straightforward political play. See Corvin and Dichy, *Jean Genet*, pp. 939–41.

to the aims of the US hippies and anti-war protesters of the late 1960s. Commissioned by *Esquire* magazine to report on the infamous Democratic convention held in Chicago in late August 1968, Genet was amazed to find that a new culture was on the verge of coming into being in the most developed of capitalist economies. The lyricism and *éloge* of sensuality inherent in the passage below give a good indication of where his priorities lay:

> I believe [in the USA] there was a sort of world flowering or spring: defeats in North Vietnam burgeoned in long hair, unisex jeans, single diamond ear-rings, Berber bracelets and necklaces, bare feet, Afro haircuts, boys with long hair and beards kissing one another in the street, marijuana and LSD smoked in public, one joint between nine or ten people, with long coils of smoke passing from one's person's stomach to the open mouth of his lover and scarcely diminishing from mouth to mouth and stomach to stomach. (1992: 158)

Genet was drawn to the radical left in the USA because, like the students in France, it embraced different notions of race, gender and sexuality, and rejected long-established ideas about work and the family. Tellingly, in the 1982 essay, 'Four Hours in Shatila', Genet cites Hannah Arendt's distinction between 'revolutions that aspire to freedom and those that aspire to virtue – and therefore to work' (2004: 225), and pledges his support, as one might expect, to the first model.[6] Genet's experience of the street battles in Chicago and Paris altered, for ever, his own views on politics and communal action. It left him, as Jean-Bernard Moraly speculates, with a 'taste for feverish atmospheres' and acted as a catalyst for his engagement throughout the 1970s and 1980s (1988a: 131; my translation).

Although Genet was later to criticise the theatricalised nature of the student revolution, it is notable that unlike many *ex-gauchistes* in France he felt no compulsion to disown his enthusiasm for May 1968.[7] In his writings, May features, as it does in the work of the French gay historian Guy Hocquenghem (1986), as a rare beacon of hope, a time when the nowhere space (the *utopos*) of utopia was, paradoxically, grounded in

---

6 The theatre director Roger Blin confirms the energising affect that the students and hippies had on Genet: 'He told me he went because that was where things were happening. That's what he wanted to feel alive again. It was like a sexual rejuvenation' (in Edmund White, *Genet*, p. 581).
7 Kristin Ross is particularly scathing about the desire of prominent French intellectuals to deny their involvement in May 1968. See *May '68 and Its Afterlives* (Chicago: University of Chicago Press, 2002) and 'Managing the Present', *Radical Philosophy*, 149 (2008), 2–5.

history.[8] The importance that Genet attached to May, along with his repeated references to progressive elements of the US public in his writings for the Black Panther Party, shows that it is too simple to equate his revolutionary politics with a complete rejection of what he himself termed as 'the white world' (2004: 42). A more accurate formulation is to say that he was interested in overturning the violence inherent to what Derrida, in *Glas*, refers to as his rejection of 'the absolute knowing of Europe' (1990: 36). His 'joy' in seeing cities like Paris and Chicago reclaimed by students and hippies proves that Genet's revolution was against a certain idea of the West, and not against all western people *in toto*.

Yet for all his sympathies with the eclectic brand of Romantic humanism and Third Worldism that radicalised bodies and minds in the streets of Paris in 1968, Genet's notion of revolutionary change did not, completely, coincide with the one(s) offered by *gauchiste* groups such as the critics and writers associated with the journal *Tel Quel*, Trotskyite and Maoist students, the Situationist International or Socialisme ou Barbarie. Rather, as I explain below, Genet's politics remained consistent with the sophisticated and open-ended view of revolution that he proposed in his late theatre. In both his theatre and militancy, Genet always insists on the necessity for social change, without, for all that, being willing to invest in what Jacques Rancière would call metapolitical solutions.[9] For Genet, the social is an open wound that resists healing, and both aesthetics and revolutionary politics are instances of permanent rawness: they keep *la plaie ouverte*. This reluctance on Genet's part to assent to Marxian notions of post-revolutionary social harmony creates the curious situation whereby his politics of emancipation have as much (if not more) in common with the ideas of current political philosophers like Badiou and Rancière as they do with pre-1968 leftist thinkers such as Lefebvre, Debord and Herbert Marcuse.

This reference to the affinities existing between Genet and the two philosophers mentioned above is not fortuitous, a simple matter of coincidence between three thinkers whose modus operandi was changed by the events of May. Rather, as I show in this book, reading Genet with

---

8 In his 1986 text *Lettre ouverte à ceux qui sont passés du col du Mao au Rotary*, Hocquenghem delivered a devastating riposte to all those thinkers, ministers and media celebrities who found it convenient to denounce their involvement in May 1968. Kristin Ross offers an excellent synopsis of Hocquenghem's argument. See *May '68*, pp. 163–9.

9 For Rancière, democratic politics are groundless. In democracy, no one can lay claim to a legitimate right to power. Metapolitics, which Rancière associates with Marxism, is an attempt to resolve or fill in the hole at the heart of democracy. In Rancière's view, democratic politics are anarchic politics: they have no origin or end.

Rancière and Badiou in mind offers a very different interpretation of his politics from those advanced by Derridean and Deleuzian scholars in the 1990s. For Derrideans such as Patrice Bougon and Jean-Michel Rabaté, Genet's reluctance to identify, totally, with any pre-existing political position is conditioned by a need to exist as a 'friendly enemy', an enemy who, as they say, provokes 'thought, action and writing' (1995: 105; my translation). More significantly, however, the troubling contradiction that the 'friendly enemy' provokes and embraces, in their opinion, evades the dangerous return to binary oppositions that all too often lead revolutions to transform into reaction. Applying the deferred logic implicit in Derrida's 1994 text *The Politics of Friendship* to Genet's writing, Bougon and Rabaté claim that his desire to suspend essentialist categories of being and truth, evinced so famously in his candid assertions about betraying the Palestinians in *Prisoner of Love*, is determined by a quest to remain truthful to the infinite demands of spectral justice (*ibid.*: 106). That is to say, to a promise of justice which can never be ontologised in history or wholly satisfied. For them, this is where Genet's utopianism resides – in its insistence on deferral.

The Deleuzian-inspired criticism of Michael Hardt and Scott Durham, by contrast, does not view Genetian utopianism in terms of infinite suspension, but rather as an attempt to produce a new life from the 'incompossible' flows and assemblages that lie dormant within the situation at hand. As Durham notes, 'the divided logic which emerges from the ruins of the dialectic [in Genet's work] does not so much turn away from the social as articulate the forms in which a different sociality is already beginning to be imagined' (2004: 72). In Durham's view, this new sociality, or what he also calls a 'phantom collective', is brought into being through the 'powers of the false'. This Nietzchean appeal to simulation or counter-actualisation reconfigures the world via an aesthetic negation of the status quo. Describing the character of Saïd in *The Screens* as a spontaneous simulator, Durham remarks:

> The truth of the *spontané simulateur* [spontaneous simulator] is like that of Saïd: it lies neither in the image nor in its negative, neither in its glory nor in its power of abjection. It lies, rather, in the powers of the false – the power of the engraver, artist, or writer – for which the nonbeing of the depths serves paradoxically to ground the dazzling image on the surface. (1997: 175)

For Durham, Genet's politics are utopian in so far as they offer, from the depths of non-being, images and tropes that produce a phantom people through a process of performative play. One of the examples he gives is of exiled Palestinian women in *Prisoner of Love* returning to their demolished homes in a village called Maaloul in the Occupied Territories and keeping the idea of Palestine alive by acting *as if* the houses were still there:

> The former villagers reinvent the vanished collective through a dream image [...] but in doing so they incorporate into the space of phantasy the very figure of the collective's disappearance. The image that mediates their experience of this historically over-determined space is thus a dialectical one. On the one hand, it extracts from the image of the vanished village a utopian power it had never realized in any present, thus marking the potential point of emergence for a new collective. On the other hand, even as it asserts the claims of a thwarted wish on collective memory, it awakens the resurrected village to itself as a dream. (1995: 50–1)

Hardt makes a similar point when he describes how Genet's imaginative and masturbatory fantasies in prison allowed him to discover an alternative time schema, in which past, present and future merged in a dizzying nexus. According to Hardt, Genet's experiments with 'prison time' sensitised him to the way in which 'every revolution', as Walter Benjamin famously said, 'arrives as an event that blasts open the continuum of history' (1997: 77). Hence Hardt's claim that Genet's desire to betray the Palestinians (if and when they come to power) is motivated by a fidelity to the utopian openness of 'revolutionary time':

> Genet may betray a constituted State but he will never deny the revolutionary force of things. He may betray any identity (in fact, he would happily betray all identities) but he will continuously, without fail, abandon himself to the constituent time, the ceremonial time, the revolutionary time that always remains open and exposed. This revolutionary time is the time of love. (*ibid.*: 79)

While it has a certain amount in common with these interpretations, the utopianism that I am interested in exploring is ultimately more focused on what Badiou calls the 'axiom of equality' (2005: 98–9) and Rancière 'the wrong' (1999: 21) than on deferral or phantom communities. For me, Genet's notion of revolution, although always bound up with questions of aesthetics and justice, is conditioned by the attempt to remain faithful to, and to act upon, the unspeakable truth that was revealed to him through the experience of wounding he narrates undergoing in the early 1950s. Genet's politics insist upon a mode of action which is simultaneously immediate and egalitarian. To legislate for one is to legislate for all. As I explain in Chapter 2, the wound that threatens to dissolve all epistemology and ontology is, for Genet, the very thing which makes politics possible: its disclosure of the void reveals a potentially utopian space where subjectivity pledges itself, impossibly, to what Rancière defines as 'the cause of the Other' (1998), and wagers on accomplishing that task in the here and now.

The Black Panthers and the Palestinians

The two movements that exerted the greatest influence on Genet in the 1970s and 1980s were the Black Panther Party and the Palestinians. Genet first encountered the Black Panthers in Paris in February 1970 when two of their members asked him to help their cause, which at that time was under considerable pressure in the USA because of the arrests and exile of their founding members: Huey P. Newton, Bobby Seale and Eldridge Cleaver.[10] Genet's decision was immediate. Several days later he had entered the USA illegally (he was denied a visa on the grounds of his homosexuality) and from March to May of that year criss-crossed the country on a frantic fundraising tour, speaking at fifteen university rallies.[11] In the published transcript to the 'May Day Speech' given at Yale University in 1970, Genet accuses US society of being fascistic and racist, and, in an utterance that echoes Irma's accusation in the final moment of *The Balcony*, calls for a concrete type of revolutionary praxis that would replace gestures with real acts: 'I think we can say that a symbolic attitude is both the good conscience of the liberal and a situation that makes it possible to believe that every effort has been made for the revolution. It is much better to carry out real acts on a seemingly small scale than to indulge in vain and theatrical manifestations' (2004: 37).

In addition to fundraising for the Panthers, Genet gave a number of interviews pleading their cause in the French media and published a series of articles on them, the most important of which was the foreword to George Jackson's 1970 text *Soledad Brother: The Prison Letters of George Jackson*.[12] Genet sympathised with Jackson not only because he was a member of the Black Panther Party, but, because, like him, he was

---

10 For a good account of how the Panthers were targeted and repressed by the police and FBI, see Huey P. Newton, *War against the Panthers: A Study of Repression in America* (New York: Harlem River Press, 1996).
11 See Edmund White, *Genet*, p. 604.
12 Robert Sandarg offers a detailed account of Genet's relations with the Black Panther Party. See 'Jean Genet and the Black Panther Party', *Journal of Black Studies*, 16:3 (1986), 269–82.

a poet and writer. (Jackson was serving a sentence for armed robbery at Soledad prison, California, and while there was accused of murdering a white prison guard.) Genet's preface to Jackson's letters is striking for the way it rejects his earlier glorification of prison life in works such as *Miracle of the Rose, Un chant d'amour* and the abandoned film-script and play *Le bagne*. Looking forward to the more critical attitude he was to adopt in the (still unreleased) documentary film *Le langage de la muraille* written in 1981 about his experiences at Mettray, his primary concern is to highlight the racism and oppression endemic in the US penal system:

> It is all too evident that the legislative and judicial systems in the United States were established to protect a capitalist minority and, with some reluctance, the whole of the White population; but these infernal systems are still erected against Blacks. We have known for a long time that the black man is from the start, natively, the guilty man. (*ibid.*: 55)

Despite his deep love for the Black Panthers, Genet's most profound political attachment was to the Palestinians, who had been evicted from their land to make room for the newly formed Israeli State in 1948. Genet was aware of the Palestinian resistance movement from as early as 1968, but his engagement to them did not start until late 1970. In October of that year, Genet flew to Amman on the invitation of Yasser Arafat and the PLO, to witness the difficulties faced by the Palestinian people after they had lost the fight for the Jordanian capital in 'Black September'. Genet was expected to stay with the Palestinians for about eight days: he ended up staying for nearly two years. During that time, which he repeatedly defines as the happiest of his life, Genet lived with Palestinian refugees in the camps at Irbid, Jerash, Salt and Baqa, and accompanied the *fedayeen* (freedom fighters) in manoeuvres in the hills and deserts of north-west Jordan.

Genet's initial stay with the Palestinians ended in 1972 when he was advised to leave Jordan for his own safety; he did not revisit the Middle East until September 1982. Like his early journeys to Amman and the US, Genet's decision to rejoin the Palestinians was a matter of urgency. September 1982 was a month of crisis for Arafat and the PLO, which resulted, tragically, in the massacres of Sabra and Shatila on 16 September. The next morning, Genet entered the camps. He was one of the first Europeans to witness the carnage carried out there. In the crucial text 'Four Hours in Shatila', published in 1983, Genet produced a powerful and emotive literature of testimony, which fuses poetic images, documentary reportage and complex narratological shifts for startling political purposes. A good example of his technique is found in the way in which, after producing a graphic description of the corpses laying abandoned and rotting in the streets, he starts to doubt the veracity of what he has seen: '[t]his city that I saw crumbled and scattered on the ground, or thought I saw, that I walked through, lifted and carried by the powerful stench of the dead – had all that taken place?' (*ibid.*: 227). In this passage, Genet puts the very notion of aesthetic commitment *sous rature*; he shows that writing is a form of hallucination, which fabricates the truth as much as recording it. However, despite language's inability to express the stuff of real experience, Genet believes that it is imperative to record and witness. Political writing, in other words, is an impossible task which insists on being realised.

Writing 'Four Hours in Shatila' reinvigorated Genet as a creative artist and resulted three years later in the publication of *Prisoner of Love*, his *mémoire* about the Palestinians and Black Panthers. *Prisoner of Love* was the first fictional work that Genet had published since *The Screens* in 1961, and while the tone of the book is infused with a profound sense of political disappointment at the loss of revolutionary hope, at no point in it does he ever question the essential rightness of either the Palestinians' or the Black Panther Party's struggle for justice.[13]

Immigrant workers

As well as supporting oppressed peoples in the USA and Middle East, Genet was also committed to the plight of immigrant workers in France, who, since their arrival *en masse* in the late 1950s and 1960s, had been subjected, constantly, to acts of institutionalised racism and casual miscarriages of justice.[14] In the article 'Yet Another Effort Frenchman', written in defence of the activist lawyer Roland Castro, on trial for protesting against the deaths of five African workers in Aubervilliers in 1970, Genet wrote:

> The impression we're left with, after the death of so many immigrant workers, is that this winter the French employers killed them coldly [. . .]

---

13 Genet is particularly critical of some Palestinian leaders, who, he contends, 'sold out' the revolution in order become 'dollar millionaires' see *Prisoner of Love* [1986], trans. B. Bray (Hanover, MA: University of New England Press, 1992), (p. 20).
14 In this context, see Maxim Silverman, *Deconstructing the Nation: Immigration, Racism and Citizenship in Modern France* (London: Routledge, 1992); and Jane Freedman, *Immigration and Insecurity in France* (Aldershot: Ashgate, 2004).

And no doubt French employers have no need to worry, French-speaking Africa is a practically inexhaustible reservoir of manual labour for Citröen, Simca, the mines and the factories. (*ibid.*: 25)

Genet's interest in immigrant workers intensified in the mid-1970s as economic recession, provoked by the oil crisis in 1973, led the French President Valéry Giscard d'Estaing to institute tighter immigration controls, and to introduce, through the offices of Lionel Stoléru, the Minister for Labour, the controversial mass repatriation scheme for workers born outside of the European Community.[15] In a series of angry articles, Genet criticised France for its hypocritical attitude towards immigrants:

The aggression of the French during the colonial conquests was intensified by an almost natural racism. Now that this aggression has come to appear ridiculous, what remains is a racism concerned with exploitation by the stupidest means possible. After 'Let's use this starving labour power' comes 'Let's get rid of these darkies'. (*ibid.*: 181)

Genet's writings on migrant workers in the 1970s are prophetic.[16] In addition to anticipating the immigration policies that continue to blight France today, they predict the ways in which empire with a small 'e' became what the philosophers Antonio Negri and Michael Hardt have more recently called Empire with a capital 'E' (2001: xi). For Hardt and Negri, imperialism is no longer the prerogative of European nation-States, as it was from the nineteenth century to (roughly) the mid-1950s. It is now synonymous with the deterritorialised flows of capital itself, which work to undo borders and national sovereignty. What makes Genet's critique so compelling is that he realised how colonialism, in a modernised neo-liberal world, is a form of political economy that exploits the underprivileged on a global scale, and in such a way as to eradicate binary distinctions between the West and 'developing' countries.

Genet's commitment to immigrant communities in France is consistent with his support for the causes of May 1968, the Black Panther Party and the Palestinians. In all cases, the goal was to attack and

15 For a detailed account of the French government's drastic change of direction on immigration policy in the 1970s, see Alec Hargreaves, *Immigration, 'Race' and Ethnicity in Contemporary France* (London: Routledge, 1995). France was particularly reliant on immigrant labour because of the shortage of labour power in the country following the First World War. Additionally, French governments were exercised by the spectre of under-population, as they thought this left the country vulnerable to invasion from Germany.
16 Genet's screenplay for the unmade film *Le bleu d'œil* also deals with the injustices suffered in France by a Moroccan immigrant worker.

overthrow the alienating structures of capital. In Genet's view, capitalism institutionalises racism; the aim being to provide western employers and consumers with an essentialist alibi for taking advantage of the labour of the oppressed: 'displaced Africans have been designated once and for all as immigrant workers, which amounts to saying that they belong to an underclass, an essence assigned to them and which they cannot shake off, for the administration is watching' (2004: 179).

Genet's rejection of 'neo-imperialism' in France in the 1970s is not a new development in his thought, a consequence of his greater political interest in the world. On the contrary, his concern with the plight of immigrant workers is one of the great themes of his late theatre, and highlights just how politically salient and engaged it was. Read historically and in retrospect, we can see how the immigrant worker occupies a central role in Genet's theatre of the 1950s and 1960s; she is the figure who bears the 'the wrong', the one whose cause needs to be heard and supported. In my readings of *The Blacks* and *The Screens* in Chapters 5 and 6, I explain how Genet's plays are not so much about revolution in Africa or Algeria, as many critics have claimed; on the contrary, I see them, like Bernard-Marie Koltès' plays of the 1970s and 1980s, as performative barometers, devices for gauging the French reaction to the presence of Caribbean and North and West African workers in France itself. By putting Blacks and Arabs on the French stage, and thus by rendering them visible in the *métropole* itself, Genet's theatre subverted official governmental policy towards ex-colonial immigrants in the 1950s and 1960s, which insisted on excluding them from public space and denying them their rights to the city. To this extent, Genet's project from the mid-1950s onwards can be accurately defined as a concerted attempt, both aesthetically and politically, to stage an encounter with what the historians Tyler Stovall and Georges Van den Abbeele have termed the 'discontents' of French modernisation (2003). The motivation behind Genet's desire to confront France with a return of the historical repressed is ostensibly the same as in his revolutionary politics: to reveal the fundamental equality of all human beings, and to show that the existence of one world is dependent upon an acceptance of non-belonging and radical contingency.

Anti-imperialist politics

As much as he was interested in ethics and aesthetics, Genet was not, in any way, a pacifist. In his writings on the Black Panthers and Palestinians, he insists, like Sartre, Frantz Fanon and Mao Zedong that violence is a necessary element in any revolutionary struggle: '[t]he Black Panther Party seeks to be armed [...] with real weapons. To speak to its members of pacifism and non-violence would be criminal' (2004: 37). Without the threat of violence, political protest is, according to Genet, mere dilettantism. Reflecting critically on the failure of the student revolution to seize power in May 1968, Genet stated that if they had been authentic revolutionaries they would have occupied 'the Parisian law courts' rather than the Odéon theatre, 'a place from which power [had] been evacuated'(*ibid*.: 132).

While it is impossible in this book to explore the issues raised by Genet's commitment to violence in the depth that they merit, it is crucial to point out that he was not, as some commentators have unfairly accused him of being, 'a fascist nihilist', obsessed with a desire to destroy western civilisation and culture. Neither was his support for the Palestinians and the Black Panthers, as other critics have alleged, a symptom of anti-Semitism.[17] Genet's politics defy hysterical and simplistic responses. In addition to addressing what is arguably the fundamental political question of the early twenty-first century – what is the difference between State and terrorist violence? – they expose, as Rancière (2004) and Badiou (2005) have recently pointed out, the limitations inherent in recent philosophical attempts to reconfigure politics in terms of an ethics of difference.[18] To this extent, any attempt to deal with Genet's politics is obliged to reflect on what he means by the political, and to pose questions about why he is so vehemently opposed to the European nation-State as a governmental apparatus.[19]

For all the onus placed on pragmatism, Genet's politics are perhaps best categorised as anarchic or utopian politics. In common with nineteenth-century, anarcho-socialist thinkers such as Pierre-Joseph Proudhon and Paul Lafargue, Genet is committed to transcendent and universalist notions of freedom and equality. His critique of 'social function' provides a clear illustration of this:

17 See Harry Stewart and Rob Roy McGregor, *Jean Genet: From Fascism to Nihilism* (New York: Peter Lang, 1993); and Eric Marty, *Bref séjour à Jérusalem* (Paris: Gallimard, 2003).
18 The problem with the notion of difference is that while it compels us to recognise the Other's suffering, it does not, necessarily, lead us to share her cause. Rancière articulates this well in his criticism of Lars von Trier's film *Dogville*. See *Malaise dans l'esthéthique* (Paris: Galilée, 2004), pp. 125–53. For a more balanced study of Genet's acceptance of violence, see Clare Finburgh, '"Micro-Treatise or a Mini-Politics": Genet, Individualism and Collectivity', in Finburgh *et al.*, *Performance and Politics*, pp. 79–91.
19 In addition to Neutre's study, Edmund White's analysis of Genet's rejection of Europe is pertinent here. See 'Genet and Europe', Bougon (ed.), *L'Esprit Créateur*, 35:1 (1995), 5–10.

> In Europe, out of innate indolence, I used to consider the function and not the man [...] This happened at all levels and with all functions: every man was exchangeable within the framework of his function [...] In the Palestinian bases the opposite happened [...] no man was exchangeable; we noticed only the man, regardless of the function. (1973b: 8)

As one might expect from a utopian anarchist, Genet has little time for juridical notions of the political based on social contract theories.[20] On the contrary, he believes that alternative notions of community burst forth spontaneously, when the laws and customs of society – those codes which force individuals to identify themselves, exclusively, with a single function or identity – have been transgressed. In his analysis of the Palestinian revolution, he is quick to point out how the Palestinian women reinvented themselves in a space beyond the law:

> Even more than the men, more than the fedayeen in combat, the Palestinian women appeared strong enough to maintain resistance and to accept the changes brought about by a revolution. They had already disobeyed the customs: by looking men straight in the eye, by refusing to wear the veil, by leaving their hair visible and sometimes completely uncovered, by speaking with a firm voice. Even the briefest and most prosaic of their acts were the fragments of a confident movement toward a new order [...] in which they sensed a freedom that would be, for them, like a cleansing bath. (2004: 216)

The antithesis of the creative and democratic energy that Genet associates with revolution is found in colonialism.[21] Colonialism in Genet's thought has three distinct forms or phases: imperialism, neo-imperialism and the 'colonisation of everyday life'. For Genet, imperialism describes the historical and geographical process that started in the nineteenth century when European nation-States appropriated the land, labour and natural resources of countries in Asia, Africa and South America. Genet's rejection of imperialism accounts for his support for national independence movements in the Third World in the 1950s and 1960s, and also explains his commitment to the Palestinians in the 1970s and 1980s. In Genet's view, Zionism is essentially a new form of European imperialism:

---

20 For philosophers such as Hobbes and Rousseau, and more recently John Rawls, equality is not axiomatic; it is produced through respecting the rules drawn up by a legally constituted community. The problem, of course, is that those subjects who do not belong to a community or who might reject it by breaking the contract are deprived of all rights.

21 Hadrien Laroche, *Le dernier Genet* (Paris: Editions du Seuil,1997); and Jérôme Neutre, *Genet*, offer two excellent accounts of Genet's critique of imperialism and neo-imperialism.

> [I]t should not be forgotten that Zionism is a nineteenth-century phenomenon, which is an exact copy of its model, colonialism. And since its beginnings Zionism has displayed just as total a lack of good faith as colonialism. Colonialism claimed to propagate throughout the world the revolutionary values of 1789, but in fact it initiated a system of slavery calculated to increase its profits. The ostensible task of Zionism was to maintain a refuge against Western anti-Semitism and to recover the promised land, but in fact it built a theocratic state by driving out a whole people. (1973b: 30)

Neo-imperialism, on the other hand, is synonymous, in Genet's thinking, with a more abstract and insidious form of economic exploitation that uses democracy as both front and weapon. Differently from imperialism, it occurs, claims Genet, when previously colonised peoples are exploited both in the developed world and in western countries which purport to uphold the values of liberty and equality. In France, for instance, it was – is – reflected in the poor standard of living and racism experienced by the immigrant workforce that had been invited into the country to work in factories, or to rebuild Paris in the 1950s and 1960s. Unlike imperialism which exploited, mercilessly, the colonised, neo-imperialism proclaims that immigrants in Europe and African-Americans in the USA have the same opportunities as indigenous subjects. In Genet's view, this is a sham. The institutionalised racism endemic to neo-imperialism (what we might also call postcolonial colonialism) deprives the 'poor' of a voice, and does its utmost to make their presence invisible, or else to control their freedom of movement. In his 'Letter to American Intellectuals', delivered at the University of Connecticut in 1970, Genet explained, in concepts borrowed from *The Blacks*, that blackness in the USA is either rendered invisible or theatricalised:

> The reality of the black colony in the United States is very complex [. . .] The majority of Blacks live in poverty and deprivation [. . .] But we close our eyes and stop up our ears, so as not to be too troubled by the poverty and misery of black people [. . .] In order to complete the scenario, we have perfected an imposture in the grand style: to a few carefully chosen Blacks we have granted celebrity status, and we have multiplied their image, but only so that they will remain what we ask them to be: actors and comedians. (2004: 30–1)

Where neo-imperialism exploits the labour and culture of immigrant workers within the metropolitan centres of Europe, 'the colonisation of everyday life' impacts on all social classes in developed countries, and is associated with the triumph of the commodity. Henri Lefebvre, one of the principal theorists of the term, is particularly eloquent about this. Looking back on his project in the third volume of the *Critique of Everyday Life* published at the start of François Mitterrand's Socialist presidency in 1981, Lefebvre states:

> According to this theory, daily life replaces the colonies. Incapable of maintaining the old imperialism, searching for new tools of domination, and having decided to bank on the home market, capitalist leaders treat daily life as they once treated the colonized territories; massive trading posts (supermarkets and shopping centres); absolute predominance of exchange over use; dual exploitation of the dominated in their capacity as producers and consumers [. . .] No particular feature – consumption as such, the spectacle and spectacularization, the abuse of images, the overwhelming abundance and redundancy of information – suffices to define this society; all of them are involved in daily life. (2005: 26)

Lefebvre's ideas are echoed by Genet in his most controversial essay 'Violence and Brutality', written in support of the Red Army Faction in 1977. In addition to criticising the German Democratic Republic for its brutal and hypocritical treatment of Andreas Baader and Ulrike Meinhoff, Genet extends his notion of State brutality to encompass everything that prevents people from living a sensual and creative life. This includes architecture, housing, technology and bureaucracy:

> Brutality thus takes the most unexpected forms, often not immediately discernable as brutality: the architecture of public housing projects; bureaucracy; the substitution of a word – proper or familiar – by a number; the priority in traffic, given to speed over the slow rhythm of the pedestrian; the authority of the machine over the man who serves it; the codification of laws that prevent custom; the numerical progression of prison sentences. (2004: 172)

From this perspective, the huge influence that the revolt of May 1968 had on Genet can be explained in terms of its aesthetic revolt against what Guy Debord termed 'the fraud of [spectacular] satisfaction' (1983: 70).[22] Refusing to betray the utopian promise he glimpsed in 1968, Genet demands that revolutionary movements ought to produce a properly decolonised mode of living, in which poetry, sexuality and the body are accorded a central place. Genet's aesthetic desire to revolutionise everyday life is evident in his Nietzschean-inspired address to the US counter-culture which he encouraged to build 'a new continent, an earth of flowers' (2004: 273–4).

The consequence of Genet's distrust of imperialism (in all its forms)

22 The reference to Debord is to the maxim not to the page number.

is a rejection of the form of government that brought it into being: the European nation-State. In the penultimate pages of *Prisoner of Love*, he laments the failure of the Palestinians to imagine a different form of social organisation:

> Like Algeria and other countries that forgot the revolution in the Arab world, my Palestine thought only of the territory out of which a twenty-second state might be born, bringing with it the law and order expected of a newcomer. But did this revolt, that had been an outlaw for so long, really want a law that would have Europe for its Heaven? (1992: 373)

Although he might be criticised here for practising his own form of imperialism, Genet's comments get to the very heart of his notion of the political. For him, revolutionary politics should reject old repressive forms and seek to invent something radically new, a utopian community where the commitment to freedom and equality wins out over ideology and propriety. Importantly (as we shall see in the forthcoming chapters) the utopian community that Genet aims at is neither fixed in representation nor closed spatially; rather, it exists as an essentially processual and open-ended project. There are no boundaries to hem it in, no pristine island State that would put an end to the dissensual workings of border crossing. In Genet's view, politics are always immediate; they take place in the here and now and have no need of ideology or theory. As Badiou would have it, they are axiomatic and transcend any need for justification. His approval of the Black Panther Party's globalised revolutionary agenda exemplifies, perfectly, the type of politics he was committed to: '[t]o say the Party had no ideology because its "Ten Points" were either vague or inconsistent, and its Marxism-Leninism was unorthodox is neither here nor there. The main object of a revolution is the liberation of man – in this case the American Black – not the interpretation of some transcendental ideology' (*ibid.*: 41).

Genet's rejection of the imperialist tendencies of the nation-State elucidates the politics of his late theatre. It allows us to understand why his plays support revolutions while they are in process, but then disown them when they come to power. In *The Blacks*, the anti-colonial revolution runs into problems when it attempts to invest in the same governmental structures at the white oppressor '[a]nd what about your darkies? Your slaves? Where will you get them?. . .You'll need them you know. . .' (1973a: 82). Likewise in *The Screens*, the democratic energy, which saw the brothel dismantled and the Nettle family accepted by the village, is dispersed once the revolution degenerates into a State where everyone and everything is consigned to its proper place.[23] In this respect, it is no coincidence that Saïd's murder at the hands of the new revolutionary guard is a decisive moment in the play. As long as Saïd is left to wander aimlessly in the desert, the hope remains that the revolution will reconcile itself to alterity and leave itself open to the claims of those deprived of visibility and justice. Once Saïd is shot, however, the utopian dream dies; his disappearance marks the end of the revolution as a creative *and* egalitarian force. Regardless of Genet's melancholy, however, it would be an error to interpret the ending of the play, as many critics have done, as being somehow indicative of political confusion or nihilism on his part (see Chapter 6 for a more detailed discussion of this). The play is not an exercise in revolutionary defeatism but a demand, as Edward Said realised (1995: 240), for existing revolutionary regimes, such as the FLN, to be more inventive and daring in their attempts to create new forms of being together. To claim that such a position is hopelessly utopian is justified, but to argue that it is intellectually botched or nihilistic is to misunderstand, wilfully, Genet's anarchist notion of the political. Just as importantly, it misinterprets the sense of political possibility on offer at the time, the sense in which, in the 1950s and 1960s, a new revolutionary dawn seemed to be on the point of breaking in the Third World, Eastern and Western Europe and the USA.

The aesthetics of revolution

Aesthetics, or to use Genet's term 'poetry', has a crucial role to play in the struggle against imperialism. Whereas imperialism works to oppress and exclude by imposing stereotypical roles, poetry, proposes Genet, emancipates through the production of new images and identities. Distancing himself from Sartre's manifesto for prose in the 1947 text *What is Literature?*, Genet bases his utopian agenda on a poetic reconfiguration of the world. In the 'Preface to *Soledad Brother*', he claims that: '[if] we accept the idea that the revolutionary enterprise of a man or a people has its source in their poetic genius, or more precisely, that this enterprise is the inevitable conclusion of poetic genius, we must reject nothing that makes poetic exaltation possible' (2004: 54).

23 Two critics who explore the utopian nature of *The Screens* are Margaret Scarborough, 'The Radical Idealism of Genet's *The Screens*', *Modern Drama*, 15:4 (1973), 355–68; and Pierre-Luc Bélanger, 'L'Ethique de la trahison. *Les paravents* de Jean Genet', in G. Sicotte and P. Popovic (eds), *Misères de la littérature* (Montréal: Université de Montréal, 1995), pp. 11–31.

In this passage, Genet is doing more than simply suggesting that revolutionary politics ought to encourage poetry; he is proposing that poetry is the alpha and omega of the revolutionary spirit, a transcendent form of energy that sets the drive for liberation in motion, and, critically, keeps it alive. Accordingly, then, for Genet, the task of the revolution is to create the optimum conditions for poetry to take place. Genet underlines the pivotal role played by aesthetics in his analysis of the effects of the Algerian revolution:

> In France, before the Algerian War, the Arabs were not beautiful, they seemed odd and heavy, slow-moving, with skewed, oblique faces, and then almost at once victory made them beautiful [. . .] We had to admit the obvious: they had liberated themselves politically, in order to appear as they had to be seen: very beautiful. (*ibid*.: 225)

Genet's comments here reverse the standard notion of artistic engagement in which art is conventionally placed in the service of politics.[24] In his argument, the Algerian revolution occurred because the Algerians were starved of poetic self-expression. Consequently, the Algerian revolution is best interpreted in Genet's thought, contra the logic of committed art, as a revolt into style; or, as he puts it, a revolt for the sake of beauty.

Genet's view of poetry, like so much avant-garde thinking, can be traced back to Immanuel Kant's original notion of the aesthetic.[25] In *The Critique of Judgement*, Kant posited the aesthetic as an autonomous realm where oppositions and antinomies between self–Other, part–whole and equality–freedom are reconciled and overcome. For Kant, this is because aesthetic judgement, as Terry Eagleton notes, is essentially intuitive and beyond the law: '[T]he aesthetic is in no way cognitive, but it has about it something of the form and structure of the rational; it thus unites us with all the authority of a law, but at a more affective and intuitive level. What brings us together as subjects is not knowledge but an ineffable reciprocity of feeling' (1990: 75).

Faced with the work of art, the spectator renounces, contends Kant, the desire to understand or grasp the object through practical reason alone, and instead engages in an imaginative act which allows her to know 'the object' without lapsing into the nightmare of solipsism:

---

24 I am thinking here, in particular, of the models of engaged art upheld by Sartre and Bertolt Brecht and by various forms of applied or community-based theatre.
25 See Rancière 'The Aesthetic Revolution and Its Outcomes', *New Left Review*, 14 (2002), 133–51; *Malaise dans l'esthéthique*; 'From Politics to Aesthetics?', in M. Robson (ed.), *Jacques Rancière: Aesthetics, Politics and Philosophy* (Edinburgh: Edinburgh University Press), pp. 13–25; and *The Politics of Aesthetics*.

Now a representation, whereby an object is given, involves, in order that it may become a source of cognition at all, *imagination* for bringing together the manifold intuition, and *understanding* for the unity of the concept uniting the representations. The state of *free play* of the cognitive faculties attending a representation by which an object is given must admit of universal communication; because cognition as a definition of the Object with which given representations (in any Subject whatever) are to accord, is the one and only representation which is valid for everyone. (1978: 58; original italics)

Aesthetic judgement or taste in Kant's philosophy assumes, on the one hand, that the subject and object are autonomous entities, and, on the other hand, that the 'truth' involved in aesthetic experience, although wholly private, is also universal and available to everybody else in a non-coercive manner: '*[t]he beautiful* is that which, apart from a concept, pleases universally' (*ibid.*: 60; original italics). Theodor Adorno extracts the democratic potential of Kantian aesthetics in the posthumously published *Aesthetic Theory* by insisting on the artwork's capacity for evading the general concept (the Hegelian idea) that violently reduces difference to sameness: '[t]he artwork is a process essentially in the relation of its whole and parts. Without being reducible to one side or the other, it is the relation itself that is a process of becoming. Whatever may in the artwork be called totality is not a structure that integrates the sum of its parts' (2004: 235).

The impossible totality that Adorno, in reference to Kant, locates in the artwork has its equivalent form in life itself, Genet contends, in the struggle for revolutionary freedom. In the revolutionary community, individuals, like the monadic parts which make up the totality of aesthetic experience, are both self *and* other, equal *and* autonomous. Recalling his time with the Palestinians in the early 1970s in *Prisoner of Love*, Genet observes:

> No one, nothing, no narrative technique can tell what they were like – those six months the *fedayeen* went through in the mountains of Jerash and Ajloun. [. . .] They were prisoners, but to look at them, you'd think they were on parole. There under the trees everything and everyone was quivering, laughing, filled with wonder at life so new to them, and to me too. Everyone belonged to everyone else yet each was alone in himself. (1992: 222)

Like the Kantian aesthetic, revolution, for Genet, creates a utopian space where alienation is overcome, freedom restored and people treated as ends and not means. However, where Kant famously put the aesthetic outside of the practical world in the realm of disinterested experience, Genet infuses it with a strong dosage of Romantic vitality. For him, the aesthetic is to be realised. The goal of the revolution is to infuse everyday life with beauty, equality and freedom. Importantly, the sense of political transcendence expressed in the above citation is necessarily temporary; it can only continue as long as the revolution is in process. As soon as the revolution settles down, economic and social inequalities – the stuff of alienation – reassert themselves and a new revolutionary movement is required to keep the fires of dissensus alive.

Leaving aside the emphasis that he attaches to permanent revolt, it becomes possible to see how Genet's politics have much in common with the model of aesthetic revolution proposed by the idealist philosopher Friedrich Schiller. In *On the Aesthetic Education of Man*, Schiller offered a deliberately complex and twofold account of aesthetics. In his formulation, the aesthetic is associated with the production of autonomous artworks and, at the same time, with life itself:

> For, to declare it once and for all, Man plays only when he is in the full sense of the word a man, and *he is only wholly a Man when he is playing*. This proposition, which at the moment seems paradoxical, will assume great and deep significance when we have once reached the point of applying it to the twofold seriousness of duty and of destiny; it will, I promise you, support the whole fabric of aesthetic art, and the still more difficult art of living. (1977: 80; original italics)

For Schiller, both of these modalities of the aesthetic were ultimately dependent on what he called the *Spieltrieb*, or the drive to play (which, in his view, was the human activity *par excellence*). By stating that the individual is 'only fully a human being when he plays' (*ibid.*: 106–9), Schiller equated aesthetics with ontology, and, at the same time, transformed playfulness into a political category. As Rancière points out, Schiller's *Spieltrieb* was designed to correct the ills of the French Revolution of 1789 by promoting an aesthetic education which, 'train[ed] men susceptible to live in a free political community' (2006: 27). This is because, for Schiller, aesthetic experience produces transcendent notions of equality and freedom by suspending distinctions between activity and passivity, abstraction and reason, and collective and individual bodies:

> All improvement in the political sphere is to proceed from the ennobling of the character – but how, under the influence of a barbarous constitution, can the character become ennobled? We should need, for this end, to seek out some instrument which the State does not afford us, and with

it open up well-springs which will keep pure and clear throughout every corruption.

I have now reached the point to which all the foregoing considerations have been directed. This instrument is the Fine Arts and these well-springs are opened up in their immortal examples. (1977: 50–1)

In spite of Schiller's language of purity, his ideas offer a beneficial perspective from which to study Genet's radical politics. Unlike Walter Benjamin who considered the aestheticisation of politics to be synonymous with Fascism (1969: 241–2), Genet believes that emancipatory politics are always already aestheticised: the struggle for a new life is a poetic demand that insists on being concretised.[26] Notwithstanding his interest in aesthetics, Genet is careful not to reduce revolutionary politics to a mere game. Throughout his political writings, he criticises the Black Panthers and *fedayeen* for replacing reality with images:[27] '[the Black Panther Party] grew weak through [. . .] the quantity and inevitable evanescence of its TV images, its use of a rough yet moving rhetoric not backed up by rigorous thought, its empty theatricality – or theatricality *tout court*! – and its rapidly exhausted symbolism' (1992: 42). Genet's critique of 'empty theatricality' shows that if the aesthetic revolution is to succeed, poetic images and tropes need to be backed up with real acts and constantly renewed and interrogated. They must not become clichés. And, in this context, it is surely worth noting that Genet qualified the citation above by asserting, in the next paragraph, that the aesthetic play of the Black Panther Party 'carried away shame' from the black ghettoes of the USA (*ibid.*: 43).

Genet's commitment to an endless view of aesthetic revolt encourages a radical reassessment of the trajectory commonly associated with his career. It intimates that his abandonment of theatre was not synonymous with a rejection of the aesthetic, but rather predicated upon a change in aesthetic emphasis. Although Genet continued to produce autonomous artworks, the focus, increasingly, was on poeticising life itself – what Schiller calls 'the difficult art of living'. Whether or not we agree with the correctness of his choice, and there are many who would certainly take issue with the Idealist view of the aesthetic for its inherent universalism, the fact remains that the aesthetic is the bridge where Genet's militant politics and late theatre meet; it is the site, in both art *and* life, where freedom and equality disclose themselves (see Chapter 3, pp. 84–8, in this book).

26 For a critique of Benjamin's argument, see Rancière, *Politics of Aesthetics*, p. 13.
27 Scott Durham, offers an excellent distinction between these two different types of revolutionary aesthetic. See 'Genet's Deaths', Durham, *Genet*, 158–84: 163–5.

A useful way of thinking about this complex idea is to borrow Rancière's language, and to differentiate between 'aesthetic politics' (the political play of the artwork) and 'political aesthetics' (the political play of life) (2004: 39; my translation). According to Rancière, political reality is inherently aestheticised, since it is produced through images, tropes and experiences, 'that create new modes of sense perception and induce novel forms of political subjectivity' (2005: 9). As such, to change reality is to bring a new aesthetic configuration into being: '[a]t the core of the emancipation of the workers was an aesthetic revolution' (*ibid.*: 14). Rancière calls this form of redistribution political aesthetics. Conversely, aesthetic politics, in Rancière's thinking, are a specific mode of politics belonging to the artwork itself: '[a] sensible politicity exists that is immediately attributed to the major forms of aesthetic distribution such as the theatre, the page or the chorus. These "politics" obey their own logic, and they offer their services in very different contexts and time periods' (2006: 15). For Rancière, the artwork has no need to step outside of itself to be political; it is political because it is always already bound up with the distribution of the sensible. Although Rancière's notion of aesthetics, like Schiller's, posits a space where art and life converge, he nevertheless insists that aesthetics politics and political aesthetics are not the same thing. Art belongs to its own specific *sensorium*. To erase that *sensorium* is to lose art's political dimension, which, according to Rancière, is found in its ability to reconfigure the world in any way it sees fit.[28]

Interpreting Genet's revolutionary politics through Schiller and Rancière both complements and differs from the utopianism that Durham and Hardt have so skilfully teased out (see pp. 27–8). Such an exegesis shows that the aesthetic is not simply about reinventing life through the (false) powers of simulation; rather it is a reinvention that demands an impossible commitment to equality. For if the essence of politics is equality, then aesthetic experience by simultaneously assuming and disclosing that equality is politicised to its very core. Or to put this another way: the aesthetic is not virtual but actual; it discloses justice by rearranging the parameters of sensible experience in the present.

---

28 Rancière's insistence upon the need to keep the tension of the aesthetic in place is predicated upon what he sees as the 'aesthetic revolution' that occurred in the early years of the nineteenth century. The aesthetic revolution is important because it 'asserts the absolute singularity of art, and at the same time, destroys any pragmatic criterion for isolating this singularity' (*Politics of Aesthetics*, p. 23). For Rancière, the aesthetic regime is inherently democratic since it refuses to exclude anything from the realm of art. This indifference impacts on life itself, in the extent to which it presupposes the equality of human beings.

The production of revolutionary space

Like political geographers, such as Derek Gregory (1994), David Harvey (1995) and Arjun Appadurai (1996), Genet realises that colonialism, in all of its forms, is primarily spatial. Whether it is in Paris, the USA or the Middle East, the objective of imperialism is to appropriate and exploit territory for its own ends. As a consequence, there is little room left for play or improvisation; the key function of imperialist planning is to control bodies and minds. Against imperialism's abstract and incarcerating production of space, Genet posits the transgressive force of the *Spieltrieb*. In his analysis of the urban poetry of the Black Panthers in *Prisoner of Love*, it is notable that Genet should emphasise their politics of visibility, their desire to be seen: 'the Black Panthers attacked first by sight. They were immediately recognizable' (1992: 214). Visibility, for the Panthers, was, as Genet understood, a sign of their refusal to submit to the exclusionary politics of US society. By becoming corporeal sign-systems, realised poetry, the Panthers asserted, actively and aggressively, their right to occupy public space. Their performance was constructed to 'look back' and so disorientate Whites:

> When the Panthers' Afro haircuts hit the Whites in the eye, the ear, the nostril and the neck, and even got under their tongues, they were panic-stricken. How could they defend themselves in the subway, the bus, the office and the lift against all this vegetation, this springing electric, elastic growth like an extension of pubic hair? (*ibid.*: 218)

The same desire to re-appropriate public space characterises Genet's commitment to immigrant workers in Paris. In the essay, 'On Two or Three Books No One Has Ever Talked About', Genet proposes that in France the immigrant worker is like a figure in a landscape painting: '[e]very thing happens here as if the formerly colonized were still a part of the exotic scenery: the Arab woman hard at work or the black man walking along the path take their place within the restful scenery upon which the rich man gazes from his window' (2004: 100–1). The onus that Genet places on aesthetic form underlines how the laws of classical perspective simply reinforce the power of capital to organise social space by placing the viewer centre stage, so to speak. As a result of being positioned in this way, the spectator controls the 'prospect', becoming, in the process, a master of all that she surveys.

In order to prevent the immigrant worker from being consumed as a spectacle, Genet posits a disruptive form of urban aesthetics, an aesthetics where the rules and spaces of classical spectatorship are challenged, and where the colonial voyeur is decentred and dethroned. As the tactics of the Black Panthers demonstrated, this is to be achieved through a process of overt theatricalisation. Theatricality here is a spatial weapon; its excessive display, along with its commitment to appearance, overturns the laws of perspective, and allows the subaltern to escape the disciplinary gaze of the white spectator.

Genet's desire to think space differently also accounts for his reluctance to endorse the territorial aims of the Palestinians, and subsequent promise to betray them if their right to return was ever achieved: '[t]he day the Palestinians become an institution, I will no longer be on their side. The day the Palestinians become a nation, like other nations, I won't be there anymore' (*ibid.*: 244). Genet's comments are neither perverse nor nihilistic. For him, the organisation of capital and labour is dependent upon the management of territory, which invariably results in the exclusion and oppression of individuals and communities who are perceived not to fit in. As Hardt and Negri put it in *Empire*: '[w]ith national "liberation" and the construction of the nation-State, all of the oppressive functions of modern sovereignty inevitably blossom in full force' (2001: 109).[29]

For Genet, revolutionary space, unlike colonialist space, is always on the verge of becoming other than what it is. In this way, Genet departs, radically, from the desire for sovereignty that is both the spatial origin and goal of imperialism. By equating sovereignty with a privileged place or origin, imperialism denies the contingency inherent in the very idea of democracy, which, as Rancière reminds us, assumes that people are equal regardless of their place of birth. In order to tap the revolutionary potential inherent in democracy's 'homelessness', Genet affirms, like Deleuze and Guattari, a deterritorialised geography that erases all ideas of naturalness and propriety. At this point in Genet's thought, spatial deterritorialisation and poetic invention fuse to become part of the same process. Both are committed to dislocating and reconfiguring space endlessly. Challenged by this infinite rewriting of space, colonialism's desire to distribute fixed roles and to attribute proper places is rendered impossible. For how can one assert one's right to a space that is, by implication, the property of all?

Yet, if the desire for utopia, in Genet's thinking is an endless quest, this does not mean that it is necessarily always spectral, without body.

---

29 Hardt and Negri cite Genet as an exemplary proponent of deterritorialised politics in *Empire* (Cambridge, MA: Harvard University Press, 2001), p. 109.

His commitment to eternal *errance* is based on empirical experience, and coincides with those moments in contemporary history when social order was dislocated and new festive communities came into being: May 1968 in Paris; Palestine in the early 1970s.[30] In these no-spaces or *u-topoi*, politics and aesthetics momentarily coincided to produce what, for Genet, is the very essence of revolutionary praxis: the challenge to live poetically.

Genet's critique of neo-imperialist geography – and subsequent commitment to the no-place – establishes yet another parallel between his post-1968 politics and his late theatre. On this occasion, however, the relationship has more to do with form than it does with content. In plays such as *The Balcony* and *The Blacks*, Genet consciously set out to dismantle the spectator's sense of perspective by transgressing the conventional spatial codes of theatre. By exploiting the presentness of the theatrical event, Genet sought to create a troubling atmosphere of ambiguity and doubt in the auditorium: the aim being to compel the French spectator to exist as a stranger in her own house, to experience herself as a person without a place.[31] In this way, Genet's late theatre utilised the heterotopic aspects of theatre for distinctly utopian ends. As I show in Chapters 4, 5 and 6, this utopic 'neutralization' of reality was not simply a vague longing for a better world. On the contrary, it was targeted at subverting the injustices involved in the Gaullist consensus on French identity, which, in the wake of decolonisation, was 'racially' reconfigured and spatially confined within the borders of its own hexagon.

Conclusion

This investigation into Genet's politics offers alternative insights into the conventional trajectory associated with his career. It shows that his abandonment of theatre was, in no way, synonymous with an abandonment

---

30 This of course conflicts with Derrida's spectral notion of messianism developed in works such as *Spectres of Marx: The State of the Debt, the Work of Mourning and the New International*, trans. P. Kamuf (London: Routledge, 1994).
31 There is much in common here with Fredric Jameson's notion of utopian discourse as the 'neutralization' of what exists now. For Jameson, 'the force of the utopian text', as Philip Wegner says, 'is not to bring into focus the future that is coming to be, but rather to make us conscious precisely of the horizons or outer limits of what can be thought of and imagined in the present' ('Horizons, Figures and Machines: The Dialectic of Hope in the Work of Fredric Jameson', *Utopian Studies* 9:2 (1998), 58–74: 61).

of the aesthetic in its expanded sense. Rather revolution, for him, was the best method for integrating aesthetics into life itself. Such a reversal establishes, as one might expect, a very different relationship between Genet's late theatre and his political militancy, since it underlines the extent to which they share the same utopian trajectory. But care needs to be taken here. I am not suggesting that aesthetic politics are the same as political aesthetics, irrespective of the obvious overlap between them. In Genet's late theatre, politics are to do with the formal and spatial redistribution of the spectator's experience, not with the execution of real acts. Paradoxically, theatre is a revolutionary space, for Genet, precisely because, as I argue in Chapter 3, it is unable to realise the revolutionary promise that it has uttered.

2

Tracing the shift: the event of the wound

About four years ago, I was on a train. Opposite me in the compartment an appalling old man was sitting [. . .] His gaze crossed, as they say, mine and, although I no longer know if it was short or drawn-out, I suddenly knew the painful – yes, painful feeling that any man was exactly – sorry but I want to emphasize 'exactly' – 'worth' any other man. 'Anyone at all', I told myself, 'can be loved beyond his ugliness, his stupidity, his meanness'. (Genet, 2003: 49)

Introduction

In the previous chapter, I looked at Genet's post-1968 militancy, and argued that his concept of revolution is prefigured in the themes and forms of his late plays. In this chapter, I backtrack a little by attempting to account for the critical aesthetico-political shift that occurred in his theatre from *The Balcony* onwards. Appropriating a word from Sartre, I locate this 'metamorphosis' within Genet's work as a whole (1988: 1), before attempting to think through the reasons behind it by focusing on both historical and personal experience. Special attention is given to a painful existential event that Genet recounts undergoing in the early

1950s, and which he was later to describe in several important essays on Rembrandt and Giacometti as '*la blessure*', or wound. While poststructuralist scholars, especially those steeped in *Glas*, Derrida's formidable reading of Genet's texts, might see this recourse to biography as a spurious quest for authenticity, an attempt to stem the flow of *différance*, to fail to engage with the 'wound' is to posit Genet's *œuvre* as a homogeneous system of writing. This, for me, is problematic, since it ignores the specificity or difference of theatrical signification, while also remaining silent about the complex reasons behind his move from a politics of resistance to a more collective approach to revolution.[1]

The novels: resistance

One of the dangers of reflecting uniquely, as this book does, on Genet's late theatre is that it might give the impression that his aesthetic politics suddenly arrived, as if from nowhere, in the mid-1950s. Of course, this is not the case, and neither is it my intention to argue for that. Instead of thinking of Genet's work prior to *The Balcony* as being devoid of politics, I intend to reflect on its transformations and mutations. In doing so, I want to argue that Genet's late theatre, unlike his novels and early dramas which practise a largely individualistic politics of resistance, look to build what the queer and gender theorist Judith Butler has called different 'coalitional alliances' between oppressed subjects (1993: 229). A more abrupt way of putting this is to say that after 1955 Genet became interested in collective practices of revolution.

In spite of Genet's subversive assault on what the queer theorist Michael Warner has called 'regimes of normality' (1993: xxvi), his work of the 1940s and early 1950s shows little interest in dismantling governmental power structures, or in making alliances with other revolutionary

---

1 One of the aims of Derrida's *Glas* was to rescue Genet from the biographical prison that Sartre had supposedly placed him in. For four excellent accounts of Derrida's deconstructionist tactics in *Glas* see Jane Marie Todd, 'Autobiography and the Case of the Signature: Reading Derrida's *Glas*', *Comparative Literature*, 38:1(1986), 1–19; Christina Howells, 'Derrida and Sartre: Hegel's Death Knell', in H. J. Silverman (ed.), *Derrida and Deconstruction* (London: Routledge, 1989), pp. 168–91; Robert Harvey, 'Genet's Open Enemies: Sartre and Derrida', Durham, *Genet*, 103–16; and Simon Critchley, 'Writing the Revolution'. Although I do not adopt his psycho-existential methodology, my reading is, to an extent, similar to Sartre's in the sense in which it concentrates on a single event, which, in my view, lays the foundation for his work to come.

subjects. At this point in his career, mainstream society was largely something to resist, not to overthrow. The drawback with this position, as Pascale Gaitet has pointed out, is that when the State exerts its authority, transgression yields to obedience (2003: 138). In *Our Lady of the Flowers*, for instance, the cross-dressing anti-heroes of the book, lose all too quickly their feminine aliases when interpellated in court:

> They went straight to the bar, where each raised his right hand and replied 'I so swear' to a question no one asked. Our Lady saw Mimosa the II enter. The clerk, however had called out 'René Hirsh'. When he called 'Antoine Berthellot', First Communion appeared; at 'Eugene Marceau', Lady-apple appeared. Thus, in the eyes of Our bewildered Lady, the little faggots, from Pigalle to Place Blanche lost their loveliest adornment, their names, lost their corolla, like the paper flower that the dancer holds at his fingertips and which, when the ballet is over, is a mere wire stem. (2002: 260)

Dazzled by what Eve Kosofsky Sedgwick calls 'the exemplary spectacle' of the State (2004: 140), Genet's gender outlaws, unlike the revolutionaries in *The Balcony*, *The Blacks* and *The Screens*, are rendered powerless. In the ritualised naming ceremony described above, their performative critique of gender and sexuality only goes so far. The political limitations of this position have not gone unnoticed by queer and feminist readers of his work. According to Michael Lucey (1997), James Creech (1997) and Grace Bullaro (1997), Genet's early desire for transgression depends, too often, on existing 'regimes of the normal' remaining squarely in place. And there is even a case for arguing, as Alan Sinfield (1998) and Ivan Jablonka (2004) have done, that there is a dangerously racist and homophobic side to Genet's novels, which is absent from his late theatre and political militancy.

A major reason for Genet's hesitation to endorse revolution in his early writing is undoubtedly due to historical factors. Unlike the politically febrile world of the 1950s and 1960s, there was in the 1940s no revolutionary programme that coincided with Genet's quest for radical inclusivity. Furthermore, there was no such thing as a queer political movement for Genet to commit himself to – the first stirrings of gay liberation in France occurred in May 1968 (White, 1993: 578). When he was asked if he had 'engag[ed] in a politics of homosexuality' in an interview with the BBC *Arena* programme in 1985, Genet responded that how could he, a youth of 13 or 14, 'have decided to make homosexuality a political issue?' (2004: 259). Quite literally, then, Genet's sexual and gender subversion in the 1940s, despite its implicit acknowledgement of equality, had nowhere to go other than inward – it could only be resistant and largely private.[2] The following quote from *Our Lady of the Flowers* encapsulates Genet's position well. Here, the narrator is reluctant to take his queer revolt beyond the prison walls:

> The world of the living is never too remote from me. I remove it as far as I can with all the means at my disposal. The world withdraws until it is only a golden point in so sombre a sky that the abyss between our world and the other is such that the only thing that remains is our grave. So I am beginning here a really dead man's existence. More and more I prune that existence, I trim it of all facts, especially the more pretty ones, those which might readily remind me that the real world is spread out twenty yards away, right at the foot of the walls. (1966: 176)

Genet's insistence on solitude problematises Didier Eribon's utopian interpretation of his prose writing. According to Eribon's study, Genet's homosexuality is inherently communitarian and revolutionary. He illustrates his point by concentrating on the moment in *The Thief's Journal* when Genet describes experiencing a form of solidarity with the Carolinas, the transvestite prostitutes of Barcelona, as they laid a wreath of flowers 'on the site of a demolished street urinal' (Genet, 1965: 52). For Eribon, this fleeting identification with other outcast subjects is fundamental to Genet's politics, which, in his view, are characterised by an attempt to transform abjection into a source of pride: '[Genet] wrote *for* [the Carolinas]. *The Thief's Journal* is a plea in their favour, in the same way that everything he wrote can be considered as an attempt to rehabilitate infamy and infamous beings' (2001: 29; original italics; my translation). Eribon sustains his point by looking forward to Genet's post-1968 political engagement, and by claiming that his experience of sexual shame allowed him to empathise with the struggles of other minorities, such as Blacks and Arabs in the Third World and France: '[t]he "homo", because he has lived through shame and humiliation is well placed to empathize with what other oppressed subjects feel' (*ibid.*: 319–20; my translation).

Eribon's analysis is compelling, and I have much sympathy with it, but ultimately he ignores to his cost one of the major themes of Genet's novels: the narrator's desire to cut himself off from the world in order to achieve a state of saintliness: '[l]ike beauty – and poetry, with which I merge it – saintliness is individual. Its expression is original. However,

---

2 When asked by his friend Juan Goytisolo why he did not ally himself with revolutionary movements prior to the 1960s, Genet replied that 'it was simple. No party or group asked me. Perhaps the image of a thief or homosexual pushed them away from a man like me' (in Neutre, *Genet*, p. 51; my translation). However, Goytisolo recognised that Genet's late plays express the same revolutionary desire as his later militancy (*ibid.*: 329).

it seems to me that its sole basis is renunciation' (Genet, 1965: 174). As a consequence, Eribon downplays Genet's reluctance to join with the Carolinas in their public display of pride. Genet, for instance, tells the reader that he 'belonged to the ironic and indulgent crowd' (*ibid*.: 53). This is very different from Genet's more 'out' behaviour with the Black Panther Party and the Palestinians, with whom he stood in public solidarity. Finally, the emphasis that Eribon places on Genet's desire for community in *The Thief's Journal* means that he overlooks his attraction to the police force and to authority in general. In his eulogy to the misogynist and homophobic Armand, Genet notes, 'his body remained just as bulky, and I loved him for protecting me. Finding such authority in a man devoid of fear – so I wish to believe – I began to feel myself thinking, with a strange, new lightness' (*ibid*.: 156). What these examples prove is that while Genet's early novels certainly can and should be used for revolutionary ends (as indeed Eribon does), the author himself was unable to make the leap from rehabilitation to revolution. The larger political world – effectively the capitalist nation-State – remained untouched by his critique.

Before I consider Leo Bersani's attempt to offer a very different account of Genet's early politics, I want to reflect on why his prose texts, much more indeed than his theatre, have proved so important to queer readers. In the novels *Our Lady of the Flowers, Miracle of the Rose, Funeral Rites, Querelle of Brest* and *The Thief's Journal*, there is no desire, on the narrator's part, to depict himself or his characters as victims of a hierarchical and oppressive society. Nor is there any interest in asking for tolerance or acceptance from mainstream readers. Rather, they offer a brash and unashamed acceptance of gay sexuality, while, at the same time, questioning the normative value system of the reader. The following extract from *The Thief's Journal*, Genet's autobiographical narrative about his life as a criminal, beggar and prostitute, is typical of his queering strategy. Here homosexuality is equated with criminality, and celebrated for that reason:

> Repudiating the virtues of your world, criminals hopelessly agree to an organized forbidden universe. They agree to live in it. The air there is nauseating: they can breathe it. But criminals are remote from you – as in love, they turn away and turn me away from the world and its laws. Theirs smells of sweat, sperm and blood. In short, to my body and my thirsty soul it offers devotion. It was because the world contains these erotic conditions that I was bent on evil. My adventure, never governed by rebellion or a feeling of injustice, will be merely one long mating, burdened and complicated by a heavy and strange erotic ceremonial (figurative ceremonies leading to jail and anticipating it). (1965: 5–6)

In this passage, the confidence of the narrator's voice, along with the hyperbolic theatricality of the language, brings supposedly shameful and forbidden acts into visibility without any apology or desire for assimilation.[3] Hence the ubiquitous use of the pronoun '*vous*' in Genet's prose, which in French establishes a sneering sense of distance between narrator and reader, imagined, here, as straight and bourgeois:

> Talent is courtesy with respect to matter; it consists in giving song to what was numb. My talent will be the love I feel for that which constitutes the world of prisons and penal colonies. Not that I want to transform them or bring them round to your kind of life, or that I look upon them with indulgence or pity: I recognize in thieves, traitors and murderers, in the ruthless and the cunning, a deep beauty – sunken beauty – which I deny you. (*ibid.*: 91)

If Genet's writing is political because he questions, so flagrantly, the assumptions and abjections of heterosexual culture, he is nevertheless careful not to provide his heroes with an essentialised identity. Anticipating the ideas of contemporary queer and feminist theorists, sexuality and gender in Genet's novels and early plays are, as Gaitet demonstrates (2003: 36–47), grounded in a logic of performativity. In *The Thief's Journal*, for instance, the butch male Stilitano acts out his masculinity by wearing a crude, home-made prosthetic penis (1965: 40); the narrator can become 'a young woman' by dressing in an 'an Andalusian petticoat with a bodice' (*ibid.*: 55); and virile men and gangsters are referred to as 'wives', 'girlfriends', 'widows' and 'mothers'. In Genet's novels, sexuality and gender are plastic and constructed: men experiment with 'staged femininities' (Harris, 1999) and butch males are queered.

'Gender trouble', in Genet, is arguably at its height in *Our Lady of the Flowers*, his first novel depicting the death of Divine. Here grammar, the very thing which according to Lacanian psychoanalysis produces sexual identity, is disrupted, as it becomes impossible to differentiate 'he' from 'she': 'I shall speak to you about Divine, mixing masculine and feminine as my mood dictates' (2002: 190). By refusing to represent sexuality and gender as biologically determined essences, Genet prevents the straight

---

3 Stunning, close readings of what we might call the 'camp' or 'feminine' component in Genet's language are provided by Hélène Cixous, 'Le rire de la Méduse', *L'Arc*, 61(1975), 39–54; Jacques Derrida, *Glas*, trans. J. Leavey, Jr and R. Rand (Lincoln: University of Nebraska Press, 1990) and 'Countersignature', Hanrahan, *Genet*, 7–42; Mairéad Hanrahan, *Lire Genet: une poétique de la différence* (Montréal: Presses de l'Université de Montréal, 1997); Nathalie Fredette, 'Jean Genet: les pouvoirs de l'imposture', *Etudes Françaises*, 31:3 (1995), 87-101; and Elizabeth Stephens 'Disseminating Phallic Masculinity: Seminal Fluidity in Genet's Fiction', Hanrahan, *Genet*, 85-97.

patriarchal world from naturalising its own discourse of power through the exclusion of subjects who do not fit the heterosexual norm. For if, as Genet shows, all identity is performative, a matter of trying and failing (always) to match an enforced psychical identification to a pre-existing set of appearances, it is impossible to posit any sense of propriety or authenticity, which, in turn, deconstructs any sense of what it might mean to be 'true' and 'proper' – the very thing which heteronormative interpellation depends upon.

More radically still, Genet's provocative commitment to the evil trinity of betrayal, theft and homosexuality, poses a threat to the heterosexist assumptions inherent in traditional concepts of ontology. Where being, as the influential performance theorist Sue Ellen Case has shown (1991: pp. 3–4), is conventionally represented by patriarchy as the supreme good, a proper state to aspire to, Genet desires what he calls in *The Thief's Journal* 'an impossible nothingness' (1965: 77). Like a perverse saint or martyr, Genet's 'passion' is to transcend the world by identifying himself with everything heterosexual society rejects – criminality, abjection and death:

> The atmosphere of the planet Uranus appears to be so heavy that the ferns there are creepers; the animals drag along, crushed by the weight of the gases. I want to mingle with these humiliated creatures which are always on their bellies [...] Amidst hideous reptiles, I pursue an eternal, miserable death in a darkness where the leaves will be black, the water of the marshes thick and cold. Sleep will be denied me. On the contrary, I recognize with increasing lucidity, the unclean fraternity of the smiling alligators. (*ibid.*: 35)

In opposition to earlier critics such as Sartre (1988) and Georges Bataille (1993) who critiqued the reactionary logic inherent in Genet's desire to be a saint, more contemporary queer readers such as Bersani in the essay 'The Gay Outlaw' have highlighted its political aspects. For the latter, Genet's solidarity with abjection, not only posits the possibility of alternative attitudes towards being, it allows us to rethink the very notion of community:

> Our own thinking about a radical queer community has not, so far, produced much more than demands to let us into the dominant community or, at the most, attempts to reconceptualise that community subversively [...] Genet will make an immense leap in this direction [...] rais[ing] the possibility of breaking the tie, of repudiating the debt, and therefore starting to think over what might be valuably human in the human community. (1995: 151)

As read by Bersani, Genet is not simply interested in rehabilitating abject subjects, as Eribon posits. Rather, he is driven by a desire to negate the straight world altogether: '[h]e [Genet] is basically uninterested in any redeployment or resignification of dominant terms that would address the dominant culture' (*ibid.*). In contrast to Eribon, who dwells on rare moments of fraternity in Genet's prose, Bersani contends that he refuses to 'participate in any sociality whatsoever' (*ibid.*: 12). Provocatively, this 'rejection of relationality' and subsequent demand for 'homoness' is where, Bersani proposes, the utopian thrust of Genet's queer politics resides: 'Genet's homosexuality allowed him to imagine a curative collapsing of social difference into a radical homoness in which, all relations with the other having been abolished, the subject might begin again, differentiating itself from itself and thereby reconstituting social' (*ibid.*: 16).

Although most of Bersani's essay is taken up with *Funeral Rites*, the Ur-novel of Genetian betrayal, he clarifies what is an ostensibly dialectical reading of Genet by looking at the early play, *The Maids*. For Bersani, Clare's suicide is a form of self-sacrifice, the act which finally releases the sisters from the citational and repetitive performance which they are unable to extricate themselves from: 'Madame may attend Solange's trial, but she has nonetheless been killed as that difference from the maids that constituted them as maids' (*ibid.*: 177). In so far as it 'eliminates Madame as a relational term' rather than as an actual person (*ibid.*: 176), Claire's death is, for Bersani, a moment of creative destruction (rather than deconstruction). According to Bersani, this has crucial political consequences. It holds out the promise of an exit from the repetitive scenario in which 'structures of oppression outlive agents of oppression' by simply producing 'new agents to fill the [eternal] slots of master and slave' (*ibid.*: 174).

Bersani's interpretation of Genet's early politics discloses their strengths and weaknesses. In *Funeral Rites* and *The Maids*, Genet's resistance to the straight world is radical and aggressive: he wants to dissolve its structures, to recreate the world differently. But, at the same time he is unable, if we concur with Bersani, to imagine a collective form of revolt that would enable him to achieve this. There is nothing beyond negativity and negation. Although Eribon discloses the beginnings of a communitarian impulse in *The Thief's Journal*, too often this impulse, as Hans Mayer also warns in a well-balanced study of Genet's writing (1982: 225), is compromised by a fascination with solitude and self-abnegation. As such, Bersani is correct, I think, to say that the locus of radical energy in the early work is found in Genet's refusal to participate in normative society by annihilating both self and Other as relational terms (and we ought not to forget, in this context, that in *The Maids*, Claire dies and Solange remains on stage awaiting the arrival of the police). This situation is reversed in Genet's late plays and subsequent political militancy. Here the rejection of the social does not simply gesture towards the potential creation of a new people; the collective is already constituted and impatient, like the actors in *The Blacks* or the Palestinians in *Prisoner of Love*, to bring a new earth into being. Despite queering, at every opportunity, the *faux* naturalness of heteronormative ideology, the politics of Genet's novels are resistant rather than revolutionary. Because he can see no way beyond pre-existing structures of oppression, the most he can do is to subvert them from within, either through a process of rehabilitation, or by negating the self that upholds them.[4] One of the paradoxes – if not the dangers – of this insistence on marginality and transgression is that the straight reader needs to remain securely in place if the resistance is to have any affect or shock value. In an interview in 1964, Genet revealingly claimed that he wanted his books to be read by 'Catholic bankers', ordinary people and 'policemen' (2004: 9). The ideal reader that Genet is searching for means that there is a dubiously conservative element in his prose writing that some of his best readers, such as Eribon and Bersani, in their understandable desire to accredit the entirety of his *œuvre* with revolutionary significance, tend to downplay.[5]

Resistance continued: early theatre, cinema and dance

Irrespective of his move into more collective and public forms of art-making in the late 1940s and 1950s, Genet's early experiments in theatre, cinema and dance share many of the same political and aesthetic concerns as his queer novels – just as importantly they also take place,

4 As I mentioned, this does not mean that queer readers today are prevented from finding revolutionary liberation in Genet's early writing. Eribon, in *Une morale du minoritaire*, for instance, is very perceptive about this aspect of Genet's work (pp. 25–44). Paul Woodward, in his essay with Carl Lavery, provides an autobiographical account of how reading Genet can change queer lives. See 'Jean, Ron, Franko and Me: Genet, Body Art and Abjection', in Finburgh *et al.*, *Performance and Politics*, pp. 117–27.
5 It is of course possible to say that Genet's search for a straight reader is political in so far as the latter's worldview is challenged in the very act of reading. While I do not dispute this possibility, the fact remains that Genet's literature of transgression is always dependent upon existing structures of oppression remaining in place. Hence, my point that there is a strong conservative tendency in his early thought and writing.

at least dramatically, in some of the same hermetically sealed spaces. In *Deathwatch*, three criminals, Green-Eyes, Maurice and Lefranc, are involved in a queer *ménage à trois* that results in Maurice being strangled by Lefranc in their prison cell; in *Splendid's*, a glamorous gang of armed robbers, La Rafale, is trapped inside of a luxury hotel and betrayed by a duplicitous police officer; and in the homoerotic ballet, *'adame Miroir*, set in a palace of bevelled mirrors, a sailor, narcissistically and violently, attempts to coincide with his own image.

The political significance of these works, as Martin Hargreaves (2006) and Elizabeth Stephens (2006) have explained, resides in their 'camp' subversion of phallic masculinity. In these macho domains, male identity is all role, something which is performed and constructed. There is no substance for it. Tellingly, the attempts of characters such as Lefranc and the Police Officer to identify with the image of virile masculinity they are playing ends in failure and disappointment. In both the 1947 and 1988 versions of *Deathwatch*, Lefranc, after murdering Maurice, is abandoned by Green-Eyes, the criminal he desires to become. And in *Splendid's*, the Police Officer's frustrated attempt to convince the members of the gang to sacrifice themselves in a violent showdown causes him, first, to execute Jean, the ex-leader of the gang, who has been forced to dress as a murdered heiress, and, then, to double-cross its members by siding again with the police:

THE POLICE OFFICER: I was with the wrong guys. I forgot the fun; I'm going back to the force. You are my prisoners now.
RITON: Already!
BOB: You wouldn't dare. We were mates.
SCOTT: Well played.
THE POLICE OFFICER: I'm not playing. I've never played. Just now, I was with you. I backed you up. It's your cowardice that disgusted me. Put your hands up. (2002: 244; my translation)

In *Deathwatc*h and *Splendid's*, Genet's interest in performative notions of gender merges with Sartrean notions of existential authenticity. The result of this synthesis is to transform theatre into a critical space where heteronormative notions of gender and sexuality are deconstructed, but where the dream of an authentic mode of existence remains a possibility. To use Creech's terms, the problem of the *homosexual* self is supplemented with the problem of 'the homosexual *self*' (1997: 128; original italics). In Genet's early theatre, to want to become a 'real' man is an impossible and futile passion, a recipe for death, violence and destruction. The implication is that the desire for a fixed gender is akin to *mauvaise foi*. Better then, Genet implies, to abandon it altogether and to exalt the fakery and plasticity of it all. This release from a regime of heteronormative power results in a sense of corporeal and psychic liberation. In her analysis of the dancing body in the queer ballet *'adame Miroir*, Stephens is quick to say that, 'the body that writes itself in Genet's work is not a stable, essential one, secure within its own boundaries, but rather one that is both constituted and opened through the process of self-representation' (2006: 166). This emphasis on iteration leads her to conclude that dance, for Genet, is full of political potential; it provides 'a strategy of resistance, a technique for subverting the sexual and gender discourses imposed by dominant cultures' (*ibid.*: 165).

The same desire to resist heterosexual culture is apparent in the 1950 film *Un chant d'amour*. The plot of the film is centred on the attempts of two prisoners to overcome the sexual misery imposed by incarceration. The activities of the prisoners disturbs and excites the prison guard who, after seeing a garland of flowers swung between the two cells, feverishly runs from cell to cell in the hope of gaining a better view. Frustrated by his distance from the prisoners and angered by his inability to share their fantasy, he finishes by entering the cell and beating the older prisoner with his belt.

In many ways, *Un chant d'amour* offers itself as a Foucauldian parable in reverse. Here the all-seeing gaze of the prison guard no longer functions, as Foucault famously argued in his 1975 text *Discipline and Punish: The Birth of the Prison*, as a Panopticon-like device preventing the prisoners from engaging in transgressive sexual acts. On the contrary, his presence only seems to excite them more. Indeed, their flagrant disregard for heteronormative discipline ends by overwhelming the guard-voyeur, and he is compelled to disclose Panopticonism's dark side through a crude and violent display of power.[6] In *Un chant d'amour*, Genet shows how an identification with the supposed object of shame (in this instance homosexuality) is a technique for resisting the invisible circuits of disciplinary power.[7] However, as with the novels, there is no desire to escape from the prison cell in *Un chant d'amour*. The guard retains his authority, and the social order repeats and

---

6 A detailed analysis of *Un chant d'amour* is provided by Jane Giles in *The Cinema of Jean Genet: Un chant d'amour* (London: BFI, 1991) and *Criminal Desires: Jean Genet and Cinema (The Persistence of Vision)* (London: Creation, 2002).
7 This is reminiscent of the infamous moment (in *The Thief's Journal*, trans. B. Frechtman (London: Penguin, [1949] 1965)) when Genet is arrested in Spain and humiliated by the police officers, who discover a used tube of Vaseline, 'the very sign of abjection', in his belongings (p. 14). Instead of disowning the abject object, he glorifies it.

reproduces itself, despite the former's obvious pleasure and complicity in the transgressive scene.

Although it was written in 1947, three years prior to *Un chant d'amour*, Genet's second play *The Maids* marks an important transformation in his aesthetics and politics. As well as taking place in a site other than the prison, it is the first time, as Kristin Ross reminds us (1997: 14), that Genet pays serious attention to women in his work. The politics of the play are different, too.[8] Unlike the male prisoners in his novels and in the film *Un chant d'amour*, the sisters, Claire and Solange, based on the infamous Papin sisters, are not simply interested in resisting Madame through performance; they actively seek to destroy her and so effect a real change in their situation.[9] Initially, they attempt to do by this by informing on Monsieur, her shadowy lover, and then, when that plan fails, by poisoning her tea with Gardenal. While it lacks the historical specificity characterising *The Balcony*, *The Blacks* and *The Screens*, *The Maids* is the first of Genet's texts to function as an overtly political allegory. Its suggestive plot and complex investigation into the psychology of oppression and revolt means that it can be used to comment upon the difficulties of producing a revolutionary break with any form of established order.[10] The tragedy of *The Maids* transcends its domestic setting and ultimately becomes a revolutionary tragedy, a play that discloses the psychic and existentialist ties preventing revolutionary subjects from accepting their freedom. Like the characters in Sartre's play *No Exit*, and

---

8 In an interview with Rüdiger Wischenbart and Layla Shahid Barrada in 1983, Genet explained that all his plays from *The Maids* to *The Screens* were politically motivated. See *The Declared Enemy*, p. 246. On the surface, this might appear to challenge my claim that Genet's theatre underwent a major aesthetico-political change from *The Balcony* onwards. However, on closer inspection, as I explain in the main text, *The Maids* remains wedded to Genet's work prior to 1955. The 'revolution' in *The Maids* is not collective, as it is in the three late plays, and neither does it engage so obviously with wider issues to do with history and/or the problem of the nation-State that so obsessed Genet in his late theatre and politics. It is confined to Madame's bedroom. The revolution to this extent is mistakenly named; it is best defined as 'individual revolt'.

9 *The Maids* is based on a real event: the murder of Madame Lancelin and her daughters by their live-in domestics, the Papin sisters in Le Mans in 1933. Yet, as with all of Genet's plays, actuality is merely the starting point for theatre, not its *raison d'être*. For two interesting studies of *The Maids* and the Papin sisters, see Ian Magedera, *Les bonnes* (Glasgow: University of Glasgow French and German Publications, 1998); and Rachel Edwards and Keith Reader, *The Papin Sisters* (Oxford: Oxford University Press, 2001).

10 Kristin Ross would concur. She believes that Genet's two early works about women, *The Maids* and the 1966 film *Mademoiselle* (the screenplay was written in 1951), 'are vehicle[s] for Genet to find the dark underlining of [...] Third Republic optimism and pervert it' ('Schoolteachers, Maids and Other Paranoid Histories', Durham, *Genet*, 7–29: 17).

differently from the cast in *The Blacks*, Claire and Solange, despite their revolutionary impulses, remain obsessed with their imaginary desire for an essence, and refuse to see that images are mere simulacra concealing the generative void of freedom. To cite Denis Diderot's famous paradox, they lack the insensitivity of the actor and finish instead by becoming the part. In this respect, it is telling that Claire should die in Madame's bed, dressed in her clothes, while Solange remains waiting for the police to arrest her, content in the knowledge that she has become a famous criminal. This tragic dimension inherent to the play calls into question, as Christopher Lane skilfully points out (1997: 881), the attempts of readers who regard the play, perhaps too quickly, as a positive exercise of sexual and gender deconstruction.[11] For what the play, at least in its original written form, makes so glaringly obvious is that 'iterability' is always threatened by a psycho-existentialist attachment to identity: the sisters want to have an essence.[12] Playing the game and dressing up as Madame, allows them to achieve this. Importantly, this reading also diverges from Bersani's conclusion in the 'Gay Outlaw'. Whereas Bersani, the queer critic, sees Clare's suicide as an act of non-relationality, a technique of erasure, the existentialist argument regards it as another act of bad faith, a method for obtaining an essence. Subjecting Bersani's reading of *The*

11   In this respect, Oreste Pucciani's 1963 study of the work, although a little dated, retains its relevance. It reminds us of the aesthetic and political tension in the play, the sense in which its disruptive theatricality, is contained in, and bound by, a conventional theatrical frame. See 'Tragedy, Genet and *The Maids*', *Tulane Drama Review*, 7:3 (1963), 42–59. In Pucciani's analysis of Genet's dramaturgy, the drive to deconstruct identity is negated by the need for a dramatic resolution to the sisters' predicament. In other words, the audience spies a character behind the role; there is depth beyond the surface. While more recent stagings of the play have tended to circumvent the psychological realism of the original piece, Lane is correct to highlight the problems involved in reading the original play-text as a straightforward example of deconstruction. As I explain in the note below, Genet's script is very different from the experimental *mise-en-scènes* that have followed in its wake. Reading the play, as Bersani does, is very different from seeing it performed live.
12   More experimental productions of the play such as The Living Theatre's 1965 *mise-en-scène* and Víctor García's version in 1969 manage to avoid the sense of existentialist 'bad faith' haunting the original text. They do so by rejecting the play's investment in naturalism and by stressing, instead, its theatricality. The Living Theatre achieved this by casting men rather than women in the three roles; and García transformed the play into a dazzling Artaudian ritual, from which all traces of psychology were expunged. Since the 1970s, *The Maids* has tended to be played in this way, but it needs to be pointed out that these experimental and deconstructionist stagings all consciously depart from the dramaturgical conservatism of the original text either by ignoring stage and casting directions, or by making the denouement deliberately ambivalent. In 1947, Genet had not succeeded in finding the deconstructionist metatheatricality that so problematises 'reality' in *The Balcony* and *The Blacks*. To that extent, *The Maids*, regardless of its subsequent iterations, is best defined as a transitional work. In a recent interview with Carl Lavery, Richard Schechner made a similar point, see Finburgh *et al.*, *Performance and Politics*, pp. 215–17.

Maids to an existentialist critique does not invalidate the political potential that he attributes to negationism; it simply highlights the extent to which the individual needs to emerge transformed from her experience. The recourse to oneness cannot be, as it is in *The Maids*, another excuse for reneging on freedom.

Genet's attempt to abandon the prison as a *topos* of incarceration is also apparent in his 1955 work *Elle*, a one-act play that deals with the papacy. The play's central intrigue focuses on the attempts of a Jewish photographer to capture the image of the Pope. In a discussion that looks forward to the metaphysical musings of the Bishop and Envoy in *The Balcony* (the first version of which was written at the same time as *Elle*), the Papal Clerk says to the Photographer that while he sees the Pope every day, he has never actually seen 'Him':[13]

THE CLERK: Who would dare to say that he has seen Him? Does He exist? Yes, because He shows himself to be there. But where does He exist? If I see Him with my own eyes, then it's not Him. If it's Him, then it's not my eyes? How then could I ever really see Him? (2002: 451; my translation)

The Papal Clerk points out the uselessness of photographing the Pope. For if to be a Pope is to be a symbol, then it is impossible to represent the Pope by photographing the individual who embodies the symbol. Like the Queen in *The Balcony*, the Pope in *Elle* exists everywhere and nowhere – the function gains its prestige from the alchemical powers of performance alone. The Pope is an actor, all image:

THE POPE: Don't speak of Saintliness. I am a mannequin, slightly at odds with itself, the pitiable creature – or rather that's what I hope to be – to whom, to which, you are going to give the form of a Pope. Get started. Lower my arms, raise my foot, shift my neck, hold my left cheek, hold my right cheek, get me to puff out my chest, to pull out my tongue, but transform me into a Pope for fifteen million men. (*ibid*.: 457; my translation)

Like a sort of ultimate commodity, the photograph of the Pope dominates consciousness by veiling, fetishistically, the living reality that produces the image. Hence, the Pope's apoplexy when the Photographer

---

13 There is a major problem with the English translation here. Genet plays on the feminine form of the phrase 'Sa majesté le Pape', which allows him to refer to the Pope as *Elle* or She. Since this does not make sense in English, I have used the masculine pronoun 'he'.

claims to have captured on camera the moment when he supposedly drew near to God:

THE POPE: How did you recognize this [moment]?
THE PHOTOGRAPHER: For a second, your face was covered over by such a sense of solitude, it was bathed in such a soft light.
THE POPE: Idiot! Such solitude! Such soft light! [. . .] Any actor of talent could have found, even quicker than I did, a face as pale, as moving, as eloquent as the one I adopted. Of course, I'm speaking of an actor who is also an atheist – if such a person exists. (*ibid.*: 460; my translation)

The Pope's attempt to disenchant his image, to wreck its power, highlights the political dimension of the play. For what Genet is effectively doing in *Elle* is explaining the logic of 'spectacular domination' – the process whereby reality is first transformed into a theatrical image, and then used by existing power structures to impose their value system on the world. However, while *Elle* certainly lends itself to such a politicised reading, again there is no attempt, surprisingly, to locate his attack on the image within a concrete historical or revolutionary context. To borrow the title of Eve Kosofky Sedgwick's famous study of queer, Genet's politics, unlike his sexuality, remain within the closet; they take place in the sad and lonely corridors of the Vatican, and are an affair for individuals, not groups.[14] The key section of the play, for instance, centres on the five songs that make up 'The Tears of The Pope', a cycle in which the Pope melancholically recounts his failure to reconnect with the simple shepherd boy he once was, drowned, as he now is, in images and symbols, that have alienated him from being itself:

THE POPE: Always I was focused on an image with which I tried to identify: Priest, Vicar, Bishop, Cardinal [. . .] I was elected by the Sacred College and here I am.
    As I was saying: focused on an image: loved by it. Sadly, the more I was seduced, the more I lost all my internal density, and I saw my image dancing outside of myself. (*ibid.*: 461; my translation)

The Pope's melancholy explains why *Elle* is best regarded as a transitional moment in Genet's career, a bridge between the early and late plays. While it focuses, like *Splendid's*, *'adame Miroir*, *Deathwatch* and *The Maids* on an individual performing his identity, Genet's desire to

---

14 The title I am alluding to here is Kosofsky Sedgwick's study *Epistemology of the Closet* (Hemel Hempstead: Harvester Wheatsheaf, 1991).

queer the world is no longer confined to sexuality and gender; it is concerned instead with disrupting the institutions and state apparatuses that dominate everyday life in mainstream society. With *Elle*, Genetian resistance makes its first hesitant steps towards becoming revolution. Or, to put this another way, the revolutionary self starts to 'come out' also.

Late theatre

In *The Balcony*, *The Blacks* and *The Screens*, Genet's attempt to queer reality undergoes a crucial transformation. For the first time in his work, the audience is confronted with groups, 'races' and peoples engaged in collective revolt against oppressive State structures. *The Balcony*, for instance, explores the difficulty of revolutionary action in a capitalist economy manipulated by a spectacular notion of community; *The Blacks* challenges the audience to come to terms with the reality of decolonisation in France itself; and *The Screens*, as David Bradby pointed out (1997), is the only French play of the time to deal with the Algerian War. In his late theatre, as opposed to his early work, Genet became a quintessentially French playwright, interested in, and attuned to, questions of national identity. This, of course, does not mean that he was a nationalist playwright in the conventional sense, or, indeed that he had anything in common with the *théâtre populaire* movement, which, under the direction of Jean Vilar, aimed at democratising the country according to a Republican socialist model.[15] Genet's main aim was to confront the audience with the repressed realities of decolonisation and modernisation, and to explode the contradictions inherent in the spectacular consensus on French identity that emerged in these years. In keeping with the expansive logic of Michael Warner's notion of queer politics (1993: vii–xxxi), Genet's late theatre 'queered' the very notion of Frenchness itself.[16]

In order to represent these epic events, Genet's plays leave the hermetic enclosure of the prison cell behind and are situated in the public

---

15 For a discussion of Genet's relationship with the *théâtre populaire* movement, see Carl Lavery, 'Between Negativity and Resistance, 221–4.
16 According to Warner, queer politics are not exclusively about sexual liberation; they are against *all* regimes of normality. See 'Introduction' in M. Warner (ed.), *Fear of a Queer Planet: Queer Politics and Social Theory* (Minneapolis: University of Minnesota Press, 1993), pp. xxvi–ii.

spaces of cities, countries and continents. His new dramatic interest in geography and history is doubled by a more experimental and ambitious approach to scale, scenography and casting. Instead of just three actors in confined environments (*Deathwatch, The Maids, Elle*), spectators now witness large casts performing in vertiginous and ambivalent spaces (*The Balcony* and *The Blacks*) or on vast stages that transform the theatre into an enormous historical landscape (*The Screens*).

Genet's attempt to extend the spatial and political dimensions of his dramatic universe is mirrored in the structural changes that take place in his late theatre. Due, no doubt, to Sartre's philosophical and aesthetic influence, Genet's use of metatheatre in *Deathwatch, The Maids, Splendid's* and even *Elle* functions as a corrective, and thus essentially conservative device. The audience is set apart from the stage and invited to judge the actions of fictional characters, who, despite their investment in theatricality, are contained within a standard dramatic frame. Starting with *The Balcony*, by contrast, theatricality is no longer compromised by the activity of dramatic characters on a distant stage; rather, it conditions the very structure of the theatrical event, and leaks into the auditorium itself (or, in the case of his plans for the 1966 production of *The Screens*, the social space of the city).[17] In semiotic terms, Genet disturbs the boundaries between 'dramatic' space (the realm of fiction) and 'theatrical' space (the domain of the actor's body). The result of this reconfiguration of theatrical space is to transform theatre into a site of encounter. In his late theatre, Genet no longer wants the reader/spectator to judge characters; he seeks to change her through the performance event itself, to problematise her notion of national identity.

It is notable that this change in Genet's dramaturgy is paralleled by the appearance of theoretical commentaries, prefaces and letters, all of which are focused on exploring the uneasy relationship between theatre and politics. The 'Avertissement' to *The Balcony* for instance, highlights the contradictions involved in conventional theories of committed drama; the 'Preface to *The Blacks*' argues for a negative view of aesthetic politics; and 'Letters to Roger Blin' is adamant that the stage is neither a place for didactics nor verisimilitude. Although Genet is highly critical of established models of engagement in these texts, it would be a great error to assume that they rule out the possibility of political art per se. Rather, as I analyse in greater detail in Chapter 3, these writings are best read as 'oblique attempts' to articulate an alternative *modus operandi* for

---

17 I am referring to the essay 'That Strange Word', a text where Genet describes how he would like to stage the play in a graveyard in the centre of Paris. See *Fragments of the Artwork*, trans. C. Mandell (Stanford: Stanford University Press, 2003), pp. 103–12.

political theatre, in which affect is more important than didacticism, and where aesthetic autonomy, though always problematised, is nevertheless jealously guarded.

Revolutionary history

The aesthetic and political shift that occurred in Genet's theatre in the mid-1950s raises obvious questions about causality. What brought it about? And why should it have resulted in a new interest in collective revolt? As I show in the following pages, these questions can only be addressed by stepping beyond the text and by concentrating on the complex interplay between history and personal experience in Genet's personal life and thought. While such an approach is necessarily speculative, this is a risk, I believe, that needs to be taken.

It is important to bear in mind, as Said has argued (1995: 235–41), that *The Balcony* was written in 1955, one year after the defeat of French forces at the battle of Dien Bien Phu; that *The Blacks* was completed in 1958, two years before France relented to international pressure and granted independence to fifteen countries in Africa in 1960; or that the long gestation period of *The Screens* was roughly coterminous with the duration of the Algerian War. Starting with Mao's seizure of power in China in 1949 and closely followed by Ho Chi Minh's victory in Indochina in 1954, an alternative type of politics came into being in the 1950s, a politics in which old ways of thinking about revolution were challenged by new theories and practices of collective revolt developed in the Third World. In Africa, Asia and South America, home-grown independence movements merged socialism with nationalism in order to revolt against western imperialism, and in the process collapsed many of the shibboleths of Marxist-Leninism, including the primacy accorded to the industrialised proletariat, and the supposed vanguard value of intellectual labour. Ross notes:

> The Chinese revolution presented itself as an alternative both to capitalism and to socialist modernization as represented by Soviet Socialism. Mao's fundamental notion of 'the people' lent primacy to the political by enlarging the political field of 'classes', going beyond their strict economic definition and liberating them from mutual isolation. The project lay in the suppression of the contradictions between manual and intellectual labour, between cities and countryside, and, by extension, the undoing of a

whole bourgeois politics founded on the division between those who have knowledge and those who don't, those who command and those who obey. (2002: 98)

Considered in relation to his theory of political revolution (see Chapter 1, pp. 33–48, in this book), it is easy to understand why this more dynamic concept of revolt would have affected Genet. Unlike the increasingly conservative and patriotic version of revolution offered by Stalinist bureaucrats in the French Communist Party, Third Worldism (which had a particularly strong basis in Paris in the 1950s and 1960s) appealed to him for several reasons: it was committed to overthrowing the idea of empire; engaged in an existential quest to shake off the shame of abjection; and assumed, at least in theory, that one person was the equal of any other, irrespective of an individual's class or skin colour. Just as importantly, it issued a challenge to France's idiosyncratic model of imperialism which strove to civilise the world and to transform the colonised into French subjects.

Yet despite this, Genet is not a Third World playwright in the mould of Aimé Césaire or Kateb Yacine. Plays like *The Balcony*, *The Blacks* and *The Screens* were not addressed to the colonised, and neither did they set out to gain the sympathy of the coloniser.[18] Rather, they were intended to remind French spectators that a new world was on the verge of coming into being, a world where France was no longer central. Genet's late theatre is more accurately described as an early – and devastating – critique of the injustices and hypocrisies of decolonisation. The period, that is, when France was desperate to leave the traumas of Indochina and Algeria behind, and to reinvent itself as a modern capitalist nation-State, committed to a bright technocratic future from which all traces of class and racial conflict had been expunged. Ross's description of what she refers to as the 'promise of evenness' gives a good indication of the logic driving France's desperate quest to modernise:

> Modernization is even because it holds within itself a theory of spatial and temporal convergence: all societies will come to look like us, all will arrive eventually at the same stage or level, all the possibilities of the future are being lived now, at least for the West: there they are, arrayed before us, a changeless world functioning smoothly under the sign of technique. The process of development in the West has been completed; what comes now

18 In this context, it seems important to remember that before Peter Stein's production in 1983, Genet insisted that *The Blacks* could only be played by black actors. This underlines the extent to which the play's politics are located in their dynamic interaction with white European audiences. For an excellent critique of this production, see Bradby, 'Blacking Up'.

is already in existence: the confused syncretism of all styles, futures, and possibilities. Modernization promises a perfect reconciliation of past and future in an endless present, a world where all sedimentation of social experience has been levelled or smoothed away, where poverty has been reabsorbed, and most important, a world where class conflict is a thing of the past, the stains of contradiction washed out in a superhuman hygienic effort, by new levels of abundance and equitable distribution. (1995: 10–11)

In order to trouble this hygienic and abstract model of history, Genet sought to stain the new image of post-imperialist France by dwelling on the defeats of the recent past: '[i]f my theatre stinks, it's because the other kind smells nice' (2003: 107). The specific aim behind this abject theatre, as I show in the next chapter, was to create a sense of affective shock that would encourage French spectators to disidentify with the spectacular image of Frenchness that circulated with such giddiness in magazines and official cultural policy at the time. It is vital to understand, here, that Genet's longstanding hatred of France, although intense, was never absolute. One of the reasons why 1968 appealed to him was because it promised a new France, a 'smiling world liberated from nationalism' and committed to a worldwide rejection of capitalism (Genet, 2004: 28). As such, when Genet talks of hating France, it is a specifically white, bourgeois and nationalist country that he has in mind. This tempers the argument of Neutre who, in the first part of his book, suggests that Genet's anti-Westernism is driven by an erotic and poetic desire to become a man of the global South: '[i]n the South, Genet found his ideal' (2002: 25; my translation). What Neutre overlooks is that Genet's attempt to disidentify with his national and 'racial identity' did not lead him to identify with the oppressed Other per se; rather, it allowed him to identify with the latter's oppression. Genet's anti-Europeanism was conditioned by his capacity to hear the 'call of the Other'. This distinction is politically important: it shows that the quest for non-identity, not essence, is at the core of Genet's commitment. To reinvest in essence, as all Genet's late plays show, is simply to reinvest in oppression.[19]

The emphasis that Genet places on disidentification illuminates the politics involved in his desire to destabilise the theatrical frame and to place the spectator on stage from *The Balcony* onwards. As I show in

---

19 To repeat a point I made in note 5 of the Introduction (p. 3), Jérôme Neutre shows how in the last phase of his career Genet moved away from this essentialist stance.

Part II, decolonisation and modernisation were, primarily, spatial processes, designed to reorder and racially segregate metropolitan France. As such, if theatre were to contest the injustices involved in these strategies of exclusion, it would be necessary to rethink its own mode of spatial production. It is not by accident, in this respect, that *The Blacks* exploits theatre's spatial immediacy in order to stage a real encounter between 'proper' French citizens and real black actors. Or that in *The Balcony*, Irma breaks the theatrical frame and accuses the actual audience of acting like clients in a brothel. In both instances, Genet's late theatre reverses the attempts of the politicians and bureaucrats of the Fourth and Fifth Republics to enforce a strict logic of separation and privatisation whereby different classes and 'races' were spatially incarcerated and disciplined. Contrary to French urbanists at the time who attempted to make the link between identity and place synonymous and easy to decipher, Genet's theatre sought, at all times, to manufacture a sense of spatial 'dis-ease' and discomfort, to blur boundaries and destructure walls. In this way, then, Genet's theatre acts as a spatial corrective; it discloses the injustices and exclusions of French modernisation, while, at the same time, offering a way beyond them. Returning to Lefebvre's terminology, Genet's theatre is a site where the contradictions of 'abstract space' (capitalist space) are directly lived (2004: 352–400). In the process, theatre becomes what it always has the potential to be: a representational space or heterotopia in which difference is not simply represented as a consumable abstraction but experienced, publicly, in the here and now.

Wound as event

While Genet's late theatre is certainly caught up in what a Hegelian might call the *Geist*, or spirit of an époque, historical context alone is not enough to account for the author's new interest in revolutionary politics. The study of history explains *what* movements he was willing to endorse, it does not disclose, however, the catalyst behind such an endorsement, or, for that matter, address itself to the specific form that his late theatre would take. In several of the best accounts of his work, including those of Eribon and Jonathan Dollimore (1995: 351–2), Genet's sympathetic response to Blacks, immigrant workers and the Palestinians is seen as a natural consequence of his outsider status. In this narrative, Genet's queerness, as with that of Federico García Lorca, is supposedly what determines his later political affiliations. The assumption being that his fight to overcome sexual oppression, along with his *bâtardise*, produced identifications with other oppressed subjects. No matter how commonsensical or seductive such an approach might be, it is ultimately too mechanistic. As Bersani points out in the polemical 'Prologue' to *Homos*, not every queer or bastard necessarily becomes a revolutionary, 'we have all known men who lust for other men while otherwise feeling quite comfortable with "regimes of the normal"' (1995: 2).

To explain the new revolutionary orientation that took place in Genet's work in the 1950s, something else needs to be taken into account, something, that is, that would have the transformative force of an 'event'. More to the point, it encourages us to analyse, in detail, Genet's persistent attempts to get to grips with a traumatic experience he recounts undergoing while travelling by train from Salon to Saint-Rambert-d'Albon in the early to mid-1950s. As White correctly insists, this episode, whether true or mythopoetical, marks a major turning point in Genet's career. In its wake, Genet's obsession with crime and eroticism gave way to a more expansive and democratic view of politics. He became interested in overthrowing oppression, not merely resisting it:

> Before this moment [Genet] was a novelist; afterwards a playwright. Before he was a dandy; afterwards, he lost interest in his appearance. Before his mentor was Cocteau, *le prince frivole*, afterwards, Giacometti, the long-suffering, dust-covered sculptor of human solitude [. . .] Before he wrote about himself, the diabolical individualist; afterwards, he became the poet of the dispossessed of the world. (1993: 464)

Looking back on the incident in the 1967 essay 'What Remains of a Rembrandt Torn into Little Squares All the Same Size and Shot Down the Toilet', Genet tells the reader how, at that time in his life, he was suffering from a profound bout of depression which 'was in the process of corrupting [his] entire former vision of the world' (2003: 91).[20] In

---

20 The presidential pardon that Vincent Auriol granted Genet in 1947 removed him from the criminal underworld that he had known so well and left him alienated and alone. He had lost contact with the source of his former creativity. This loss of artistic inspiration was exacerbated by the appearance in 1952 of *Saint Genet: Actor and Martyr*, Jean-Paul Sartre's existential biography, which purported to explain the trajectory of Genet's life by tracing it back to a determining event at the age of 7 when he was accused of being a thief. According to Sartre's invasive reading, Genet's homosexuality, attraction to crime and desire to write were all freely chosen, existential acts through which he attempted, unsuccessfully, to rediscover a lost essence of being that had been stolen from him. Sartre's study had a disastrous impact on Genet's creativity by disclosing the motivation behind his writing and by imprisoning him in a fixed image. In an interview in 1964, he explained to Madeleine Gobeil that

this fragile state, Genet mentions that he suddenly caught the eye of a decrepit old man sitting opposite him in a third-class railway carriage. At this moment, Genet's world disintegrated: '[w]hile looking at the passenger sitting opposite me, I had the revelation that every man *is worth as much as* every other, I did not suspect [. . .] that this knowledge would bring about such a methodical disintegration' (*ibid.*: 91–2; original italics). In 'What Remains of a Rembrandt', Genet's discovery of what he calls 'a sort of universal identity with all men' is characterised by an intense form of dislocation (*ibid.*: 92); he is unhinged, decentred, made fluid. The experience is so intense, so ungraspable, that in his attempts to express it language breaks up:

> What I experienced I could convey only in this form: I flowed out of my body, through my eyes, into the traveller's, *at the same time that the traveller flowed into my own*. Or rather *I had flowed*, for the look was so brief that I can recall it only with the help of this tense of the verb.
>
> [. . .] What was it, then, that had flowed out of my body – I fl. . .– and what part of the traveller flowed out of his body? (*ibid.*: 93; original italics)

Unlike the sense of sexual *jouissance* which was the motor of Genet's novelistic writing – 'my adventure [. . .] will be one long mating' (1965: 5) – here his experience is all negation. As he describes it in 1967, he is disgusted, anxious and plunged into deep sorrow:

> The sadness that had swooped down upon me is what troubled me most. After the moment I had this revelation while gazing at the unknown passenger, it was impossible for me to see the world as I used to. Nothing was certain. The world suddenly floated. I remained for a long time as if sickened by my discovery, but I felt that it wouldn't be long before this was going to force me into serious changes, which would be renunciations. My sadness was an indication. The world was changed. In a third-class carriage between Salon and Saint-Rambert d'Albon, it had just lost its beautiful colours, its charm. (2003: 97–8)

he felt 'a kind of disgust' when Sartre's book appeared because he saw himself 'naked and stripped bare by someone other than himself'. The sense of horror he felt meant that he was unable to write in his former style: 'it took me a while to recover. I was unable to continue writing. I could have continued to develop novels mechanically. I could have tried to write pornographic novels in a kind of automatism. Sartre's book created a void that allowed a sort of psychological deterioration to set in' (*The Declared Enemy*, p. 12). The psychological deterioration that he talks about here was further compounded by the end of a love affair with the young prostitute, Decimo C. and by his awareness that he was ageing and losing his looks and vitality. This combination of miseries provides an accurate description of Genet's state of mind at the time.

Genet's despair and disenchantment are caused by an intuitive awareness that eroticism is no longer possible. If all men are the same, then to desire another is to desire the self. Tellingly, the theatricalised glorification of abjection so characteristic of his novels is missing from this text. Where Genet was able to eroticise Salvador's filthy lice-ridden body in *The Thief's Journal*, in the train carriage his dirty travelling companion disgusts him:

> Eroticism and its furies seemed denied to me, utterly. How to ignore, after the experience on the train, that every attractive form, if it encloses me, is myself? But if I tried to grasp this identity, every form, monstrous or loveable, lost its power over me.
> 'The search for the erotic', I told myself, 'is possible only when one supposes that each being has its individuality, that it is irreducible, and the physical form is aware of it and is aware only of it'. (*ibid.*: 100-1)

The pain inflicted upon Genet as he unwittingly exchanged glances with his travelling companion is well conveyed by his choice of metaphor. Midway through the essay, Genet describes his experience as 'a wound', an image that communicates a sense of primordial violence.[21] To wound someone physically is to rupture the wholeness of the body, to mark the skin. To wound someone existentially, as happened to Genet, is to put a hole in being itself. Read metaphorically, 'the wound' is a trope for a painful blast of emptiness that leaves subjectivity tottering on an abyss. This distinguishes the significance Genet attaches to the wound in the Rembrandt essay from the meaning he accords it in *The Thief's Journal*. In the latter text, the wound is used to describe a sense of shame experienced by other people, often straight males, whose predicament is dissected from a distance (1965: 215–24). In the early novels, the narrator is not affected ontologically by the wound; he remains in a position of control and resists the collapse into voidness. In 'What Remains of a Rembrandt', by contrast, the narrator has been affected profoundly by the wound, and the reader observes him struggling to incorporate his experience.

At first, Genet's 'experience' on the train appears to have much in common with what Bersani calls non-relationality and curative homoness. In both instances, the subject loses the Other as she falls into a space of in-difference, and annihilates her identity. However, as opposed to Bersani's interpretation, the experience here is more dependent on

---

21 For a good reading of the wound in *The Thief's Journal*, see Colin Davis, 'Genet's *Journal du voleur* and the Ethics of Reading', *French Studies*, 68:1 (1994), 64–7.

ontology than sexuality. In other words, the gay subject does not have a privileged relationship to 'curative homoness', as Bersani appears to hint at. Rather, the fall into non-being is aleatory and unpredictable: it can strike anyone at any time. Indeed, it could be argued, especially if we recall Genet's own conclusion to 'What Remains of Rembrandt', that the experience of oneness is the very antithesis to any form of sexuality at all.[22] The loss of a specific object of desire is the very thing that allowed Genet, at least initially, to expand the horizons of consciousness to include all oppressed subjects, and not simply, as was the case previously, prisoners, prostitutes and murders. This would appear to be given further weight by looking at the significance he attaches to the wound in 'Rembrandt's Secret' and 'The Studio of Alberto Giacometti', two essays which he produced when he was working on *The Balcony*, *The Blacks* and *The Screens*.

In 'Rembrandt's Secret', Genet uses the metaphor of the 'wound' to reflect upon the ethical and aesthetic fracturing that took place in Rembrandt's career after the death of his wife Saskia. As theorised by Genet, Saskia's death caused Rembrandt to abandon his narcissism, and to restore, instead, the 'dignity [...] of every being and object that seems to lack it' (2003: 86):

> His reading of the Bible exalts his imagination [...] It is the Old Testament especially that inspires him and his theatricality. He paints. He is famous. He becomes rich. He is proud of his success. Saskia is covered with gold and velvet ... She dies. If nothing remains but the world, and painting to approach it, the world has only – or more precisely is only – one single value. And *this* is nothing more than *that*, and nothing less.
> [...] This process brought about slowly and perhaps obscurely, will teach him that each face has value and that it refers – or leads – to one human identity that is equal to another. (*ibid.*: 86–7; original italics)

The wound's 'strong kindness' performs a similar role in Genet's essay on Alberto Giacometti (*ibid.*: 84). In this text, the wound is now posited as the very source of aesthetics and ethics:

---

[22] While erotics played an important role in Genet's commitment to the Black Panther Party and the Palestinians, it is an exaggeration to say that the erotic forms the core of his revolutionary engagement. In Genet's writings on politics, he emphasises, again and again, that his love for the Palestinians was chaste. The following anecdote from is a good case in point: 'The first two *fedayeen* were so handsome I was surprised at myself for not feeling any desire for them. And it was the same the more Palestinian soldiers I met [...] What for a long time I took to be a kind of limpidity, a total lack of eroticism, might have been due to the fact that each individual was completely autonomous' (*Prisoner of Love*, p. 178).

> Beauty has no other origin than a wound, unique, different for each person, hidden or visible, that everyone keeps in himself, that he preserves and to which he withdraws when he wants to leave the world for a temporary, but profound solitude. There's a big difference between this art and what we call 'sordid realism' [*misérabilisme*]. Giacometti's art seems to me to want to discover that secret wound of every being, and even of every object, so that it can illumine them. (*ibid.*: 42)

In Genet's view, the secret of Giacometti's art is found in its capacity to explore this strange terrain beyond surface appearances, and to express the singularity – that is to say, the wound – of the Other:

> [E]ach being is revealed to me in its newest, most irreplaceable quality – and it's still a wound – thanks to the solitude where this wound places them, about which they know almost nothing, and yet in which their entire being flows. [. . .] Solitude, as I understand it, does not mean a miserable condition, but rather a secret royalty, a profound incommunicability, but a more or less obscure knowledge of an unassailable singularity. (*ibid.*: 50-1)

Like Rembrandt's paintings, Giacometti's sculptures express an impossible truth that everyday language, with its grounding in discrete units of spatio-temporal experience, is unable to articulate. By piercing the surface of things and wounding the viewer, they stun her into a new awareness: '[w]hat a respect for objects. Each one has its beauty because it is "alone" in existing, there is the irreplaceable in it' (*ibid.*: 67). Importantly, Genet is at pains to stress that Giacometti's art of solitude, his sculpting of the wound, does not turn its back on the world. This is social art of an entirely different kind, one which produces alternative forms of togetherness grounded in a sort of irreducible or ontological sociability:

> Giacometti's art is not, then, a social art because it establishes a social link – man and his secretions – between objects; it's rather an art of high-class tramps, so pure that what could unite them might be a recognition of the solitude of every being and every object. 'I am alone', the object seems to say, 'thus caught in a necessity against which you can do nothing. If I am nothing but what I am, I am indestructible. Being what I am, unreservedly, my solitude knows yours'. (*ibid.*: 67-8)

In 'The Secret of Rembrandt' and 'The Studio of Alberto Giacometti', the wound opens what is perhaps best described as a *utopos* in the self from which beauty and equality are able to emerge. Genet underscores the radically democratic potential of the wound when he establishes a connection between his experience on the train and Giacometti's sculptures:

> About four years ago, I was on a train. Opposite me in the compartment, an appalling old man was sitting. Dirty, and obviously, mean, as some of his remarks proved to me [. . .] His gaze crossed, as they say, mine, and, although I no longer know if it was short or drawn-out, I suddenly knew the painful – yes, painful feeling that any man was exactly – sorry but I want to emphasize 'exactly' – 'worth' any other man. 'Anyone at all', I said to myself, 'can be loved beyond his ugliness, his stupidity, his meanness'.
> [. . .] Do not misunderstand: it was not a question of a goodness coming from me, but of a recognition. Giacometti's gaze saw that a long time ago, and he restores it to us. I say what I feel: this connection revealed by his figures seems to be that precious point at which the human being is brought back to the most irreducible part of him: his solitude of being exactly equivalent to every other human being. (*ibid*.: 49)

In this account, the wound, as in Genet's experience in the mountains of Ajloun with the *fedayeen*, combines sameness and difference in the same impossible moment. In keeping with the utopian quality of the aesthetic I discussed in Chapter 1, the wound allows the subject to recognise her equivalence to the Other. As well as provoking pain, this unwanted insight produces respect and, most importantly, love: '"[a]nyone at all can be loved beyond his ugliness, his stupidity, his meanness"'. Love, here, has little in common with the intense eroticism that dominates his novels and early plays. There is no longer any desire to possess an object or incorporate the Other. On the contrary, love is both immanent to being and somehow outside of it. We are subjected to it, mere prisoners to its call. By stating that Giacometti 'restores' this experience to us, Genet advances an alternative notion of aesthetic politics in which the production of heterogeneity, knowledge that wounds, is more important than sterile didacticism: '[i]t's only those kinds of truths, the ones that are not demonstrable and even *"false"*, the ones that one cannot without absurdity lead to their conclusion without coming to the negation of them and of oneself – those are the ones that must be exalted by the work of art' (*ibid*.: 91; original italics). Like the wound, the artwork's ability to negate subjectivity performs a political function. It 'discloses' the immanent values of justice and equality which cannot be spoken or known, but only acted upon.

But a nagging doubt remains. If the wound is, as I describe in greater detail in Chapter 3, the source of politics and aesthetics, then how can we account for Genet's pessimistic reading of the wound in

'What Remains of a Rembrandt'? The important point, here, is not to see the wound as a single experience, as something with a definitive beginning and end; rather, the wound is an event, a heterogeneous moment that ruptures the spatio-temporal framework of the world and resists any attempt to capture it as knowledge. According to Alain Badiou, an event is an interruption which, by dissolving the existing state of the situation, allows for something new to emerge. Crucially, Badiou contends that agency does not reside in the event as such, 'there is no hero of the event' (2007: 207), but rather in the subject's reaction to the event, or in what he calls 'fidelity': '[a] subject is nothing other than an active fidelity to the event' (*ibid.*: xiii). In Badiou's theory, the event negates all concepts. Tellingly, he describes it as a 'void', a nothingness (*ibid.*: 56). Its meaning is only revealed in what it gives birth to; in the way in which the subject is able to force its axiomatic 'truth' into existence: '[i]t will therefore always remain whether there has been an event or not, except to those who intervene, who decide on its belonging' (*ibid.*: 207).

Badiou's insistence on 'forcing' means that the event is always contingent. The subject can be faithful and/or unfaithful to it: '[s]ince it is of the very essence of the event to be a multiple whose belonging to the situation is undecidable, deciding that it belongs to the situation is a wager' (*ibid.*: 201) Interpreted from Badiou's position, Genet's pessimism about the wound in 'What Remains of a Rembrandt' is not a total renunciation of an existing aesthetic and political process. On the contrary, it expresses a moment of doubt, which to return, momentarily, to biographical matters, was in all likelihood coloured by the intense depression he suffered in the mid-1960s after the suicide of Abdallah, his lover and the subject of the essay 'The Tightrope Walker'. The fact that Genet went on to commit himself to the causes of 'wounded' peoples in the USA and the Middle East after the publication of 'What Remains of a Rembrandt' in 1967 would appear to prove, beyond any doubt, that his fidelity to the event, while it might have wavered, was ultimately never abandoned. In Badiou's terminology, the wound – or rather the event of the wound – is what permitted Genet to become a 'militant of truth' (*ibid.*: xiii).

Conclusion

The new significance that Genet attaches to the wound in his writing from the mid-1950s onwards corresponds to a radical schism in his work. The all-pervading sense of loss that it gave rise to disrupted Genet's sense of self and allowed him to intuit a universal identity for all subjects based on transcendent notions of justice and equality that, for him, are immanent to the world. After his experience on the train which supposedly occurred in the early 1950s, Genet's desire to queer reality changed focus. Henceforth, the emphasis was no longer on private acts of resistance or on rehabilitating marginalised subjects; rather it expressed a utopian desire to change the course of history by overthrowing the exclusionary apparatus of the French nation-State. Genet's move from *révolté* to *révolutionnaire* has major repercussions for his practice of *art politique*. It suggests that the political work has little to do with fostering dialogue or with disclosing the secrets that bourgeois ideology allegedly conceals. Rather, as I will explore in greater detail in the next chapter, it should strive to open wounds and to produce disidentification with normative notions of self rooted in class, nationality and 'race'.

3

Aesthetic politics: staging the wound

An art is emancipated and emancipating when it renounces the authority of the imposed message, the target audience, and the univocal mode of emancipating the world, when, in other words, it stops wanting to emancipate us. (Rancière, 2007: 258)

Introduction

One of the great unresolved mysteries of Genet's career is his steadfast refusal to admit that his plays are politically motivated, even though they deal with some of the most inflammatory political material staged in modern theatre. In broad terms, Genet's 'abrasiveness', to borrow a word from Maria Shevtsova (2006: 44), has produced three distinctive, if opposed, attempts to get to grips with the politics of his late work. In the first, and most unhelpful, instance, his pronouncements are taken at face value and used to support the reactionary view that he is a nihilist;[1] in the second, less biased, interpretation, they are cited as proof of his

---

[1] See Christopher Innes, *Avant Garde Theatre*, pp. 108, 117; Roy Stewart and Rob Roy McGregor, *Jean Genet*; and Eric Marty, *Bref séjour*.

credentials as a sacred or absurdist playwright;[2] and, in the final, much more pertinent, case, they are disregarded altogether as critics seek to interpret his theatre 'against the grain' and thus disclose its hidden political significance.[3] In what follows, I intend to offer an alternative – or fourth – way of approaching Genet's theatre by focusing on the aesthetico-political potential that he attributes to the wound.

Against commitment

Looking back on the history of Genet scholarship, it is easy to understand why critical discussions pertaining to the politics of his theatre have so often neglected to concentrate on authorial intent.[4] When asked to 'clarify' the political message of his work in an interview with *Playboy Magazine* in 1964, he gave the following negative reply:

> I don't give a damn about that. I wanted to write plays for the theatre, to crystallize a theatrical and dramatic emotion. If my plays are useful to Blacks, it's not my concern. I don't think they are in any case. I think that action, the direct struggle against colonialism, does more for Blacks than a play does. Likewise I think that a maids' union does more for domestics than a play does. (2004: 13)

2 See Robert Brustein, *The Theatre of Revolt: An Approach to Modern Drama* (Boston: Little, Brown & Company, 1964); Rose Zimbardo, 'Genet's Black Mass', *Modern Drama*, 8:3 (1965), 247–58; Martin Esslin, *Theatre of the Absurd*; Bettina Knapp, *Jean Genet* (New York: St. Martin's Press, 1968); Raymond Federman, 'Jean Genet: The Theater of Hate', in P. Brook and J. Halpern (eds), trans. F. Abetti, *Genet: A Collection of Critical Essays* (New Jersey: Prentice Hall, 1979), pp. 129–45; Jacques and Jean Guicharnaud in Brook and Halpern, *A Collection of Critical Essays*, pp. 98–113; Monique Borie, *Mythe et théâtre aujourd'hui: une quête impossible? Beckett, Genet, Grotowski, Le Living Theatre* (Paris: Nizet, 1981); and Gisèle Bickel, *Jean Genet: criminalité et transcendan*ce.
3 This covers most of the best political readings of Genet's work that have emerged to date. See the references cited at pp. 1–6 of the Introduction to this book for specific examples. Two critics whom I did not mention in that (already) long reference and who are relevant here are Richard Coe, *The Vision of Jean Genet* (London: Peter Owen, 1968); and Philip Thody, *Jean Genet: A Study of His Novels and His Plays* (London: Hamish Hamilton, 1968).
4 Michel Corvin and Albert Dichy, as one might expect, pay detailed attention to Genet's own theory of theatre. In his essay on *The Balcony*, Corvin differentiates between a committed dramaturgy and a political dramaturgy, the distinction being that the latter, unlike the former, offers a sustained reflection on its own economy of signification. For Corvin, Genet's play is about politics without ever being political: it does not, for instance, offer any sort of solution or resolution. While I agree with much of Corvin's argument, he remains curiously reticent to discuss the political effects that Genet attributes to aesthetic experience. See Corvin, in Corvin and Dichy, *Jean Genet*, pp. 1133–44.

Genet returned to this theme in an interview with Michèle Manceaux for *Le Nouvel Observateur* in 1970. Responding to a question posed by Manceaux about the possible direction his writing might take in the light of his political commitment to the Black Panther Party, Genet was quick to distance his theatre from that of Brecht. For Genet, the type of engagement practised by Brecht is beset with a worrying paradox:

> I don't think that Brecht did anything for communism, and the revolution [of 1789] was not set off by Beauchmarchais's *The Marriage of Figaro*. I also think that the closer a work of art is to perfection, the more it is enclosed within itself. Worse than that – it inspires nostalgia. (*ibid.*: 48)

In the lines above, Genet invests in a logic which undermines the very foundation of Brechtian aesthetics. Where Brecht wanted to make art serve a political purpose, Genet declares that the more successful the artwork is aesthetically, the greater harm it does to revolutionary praxis. This is because it evokes what he calls 'nostalgia', a form of imaginative reverie through which the subject rediscovers *le temps perdu* of childhood. To put this otherwise, art encourages us, Genet suggests, to turn our back on the world.[5]

Genet expanded on this rigorously anti-committed concept of art in an interview in 1975 with Hubert Fichte. Positioning himself once again against Brecht, and siding with the Idealist philosophy of Kant, he proposed that the aesthetic encourages a form of disinterested contemplation which is the very antithesis of the type of pragmatic consciousness needed for political praxis. Instead of rooting the spectator in a world of acts, aesthetic experience opens up a contemplative space, where the spectator loses her boundaries and topples into the Other: 'contemplating the artwork] I lose more and more the sense of being "myself", the sense of the "I" and become nothing but the perception of the artwork. Confronted with subversive events [. . .] I am less and less free for [. . .] that sort of contemplation' (*ibid.*: 123).

Genet's hostility towards Brecht, whose thinking dominated French alternative theatre in the 1960s and 1970s, is a persistent theme in his aesthetic theory, and demands further explanation.[6] In the same inter-

---

5 It is interesting to contrast Genet's thinking here with that of the Marxist philosopher Ernst Bloch. For Bloch, the return to childhood in art is the very thing that provokes utopian longings. See *The Principle of Hope*, vol. 1, trans. N. Plaice *et al.* (Oxford: Blackwell, 1986). While Genet would not necessarily disagree with this, he seems to suspect those longings of being somehow imprisoned in, and thus negated by, the spectator's experience of the artwork itself.

6 I am thinking here of his influence on directors like Roger Planchon and Antoine Vitez, and critics like Roland Barthes and Bernard Dort.

view with Fichte, Genet compares Brecht unfavourably to Strindberg. In Genet's amazingly coarse and primitive reading, Brecht's language confirms the status quo. Strindberg's poetry, by contrast, brings a new world into being:[7]

> [W]hat Brecht says is nothing but garbage. *Galileo Galilei* cites the obvious; it tells me things I would have discovered without Brecht. Strindberg, or in any case *Miss Julie*, does not present the obvious. It's very new. I wasn't expecting it. I saw *Miss Julie* after *The Dance of Death* [...]. I liked it very much. Nothing Strindberg says could be said in any other way than poetically, and everything that Brecht says can, and in fact has been said prosaically. (*ibid.*: 122)

Genet's rejection of Brechtian poetics is not limited to language alone. It targets the cornerstone of epic theatre: the cigar-smoking spectator.[8] Responding to Fichte's attempt to defend the beneficiary of Brechtian aesthetics, Genet remarked that:

> In this choice of a gesture, smoking a cigar, there is a casualness with regard to the work of art that is in fact not permitted. It is not permitted by the work of art. I don't know the Rothschilds, but with the Rothschilds, you can probably talk about art while smoking a cigar. You can't go to the Louvre and look at *The Marquise of Solana* with the same movement as with the Rothschilds who talk about art while smoking a cigar [...] [I]t's not simply a question of distancing but a lack of sensibility. (*ibid.*: 122–3)

For Genet, the fatal flaw botching Brecht's theory of political art derives from the latter's desire to place the spectator in a superior position to that of the artwork. Because epic theatre allies itself with thought and rationality, Genet argues that it prevents the spectator from being affected by, and thus changed through, aesthetic experience alone.[9]

---

7 Genet, for instance, makes no reference to the use of song in Brecht's text; and neither is he aware of the ways in which, as Heiner Müller noted, Brecht reinvented dramatic language in the German theatre through his use of slang and everyday expressions. See Elizabeth Wright, *Postmodern Brecht: A Re-presentation* (London: Routledge, 1989), p. 3. Also, Brecht, as Genet implies, was never opposed to sensuality or affect. Walter Benjamin's analysis of the sense of 'shock' and 'astonishment' inherent to epic theatre offers a concise refutation of Genet's point. See *Understanding Brecht*, trans. A. Bostock (London: Verso, 1988), p. 13.
8 According to Benjamin, the spectator of epic theatre figures more as 'a reader of novel(s)' than as a normal theatre-goer, who identifies, passionately, with the on-stage action (*Understanding Brecht*, p. 15).
9 Benjamin goes on to say that in Brechtian aesthetics, theatre becomes a public platform by 'filling-in [...] the orchestra pit' (*Understanding Brecht*, p. 1). This deprives theatre of its 'sacral origins' and rescues the actor from the world of the dead. As we shall see, this non-intoxicating theatre is the very antithesis of Genet's theatre of the wound.

Instead of using the specific qualities of the theatrical medium to unveil new worlds, Brecht, Genet implies, reconciles himself to the world as it is currently configured. In doing so, he perpetuates the Aristotelianism that he sought to escape. According to Genet, what Brecht really wants to do is to police theatre, to purge it of its ineffability and troubling doubleness. This leads Genet to accuse Brecht in a different interview of being a mere pedagogue: '[h]e explains everything because he's didactic. Instead of showing things obliquely, he explains them like a State schoolteacher' (Genet, in Corvin and Dichy, 2002: 969–70; my translation). Genet's reading of Brecht reverses the usual meanings associated with committed art. For Genet, didactic art is a contradiction in terms. In its desire to make art useful, Brechtian theatre, Genet proposes, cannot help but repeat the same structures of domination it sought to overthrow. It leaves what Rancière calls the distribution of the sensible untouched.

Genet's hostility towards Brechtian theatre is well illustrated in *The Screens*. In that work, Brecht's famous line from the end of *The Caucasian Chalk Circle* about the land 'belong[ing] to those who are good for it' is provocatively recontexualised (1976: 237). In Brecht's play, the line is delivered by a singer, who provides a wise commentary on events; in Genet's text, on the other hand, the line is spoken by Monsieur Blankensee, an idiotic European coloniser:

> **MONSIEUR BLANKENSEE**: In a German operetta, I forget which, a character says: 'Things belong to those who've known how to improve them . . .'. Who is it who's improved your orange groves, and my forests and roses? (1987: 74)

Monsieur Blankensee's question is, of course, rhetorical. The implication here is that Brechtian theatre does not interrupt bourgeois oppression; it simply repackages it under a different name.

Whether we agree with it or not, and no one can deny that his reading is wilfully one-dimensional and partisan, we should not be surprised by Genet's attack on Brecht. It simply elaborates, in more straightforward language, an argument he had already proposed in the essay 'That Strange Word', published in the avant-garde journal *Tel Quel* in 1967. Here, Genet is adamant that theatre's function is not to reflect or comment upon the social; its main task is to explore a liminal realm associated with everything that resists knowledge – death, poetry, mystery:

> If I speak of a theatre among the tombs, it's because the word 'death' today is shadowy, and in a world that seems to be going so cheerfully toward the

luminosity of analysis, our transparent eyelids no longer protected, like Mallarmé, I think a little darkness must be added. Science deciphers everything, or wants to, but we've had it! We must take refuge, and nowhere else but in our ingeniously lit entrails. . . .No I'm wrong: not to take refuge, but discover a fresh and scorching shadow, which will be our work. (2003: 110)

Genet's commitment to an opacity or 'darkness' that eludes Enlightenment thinking is a persistent theme in his correspondence with the director Roger Blin during the production of *The Screens*. Aware of Blin's leftist sympathies (Blin had signed the 121 Manifesto against the war in Algeria) and concerned that they might influence the play's *mise-en-scène*, Genet stresses that the point of *The Screens* is to illuminate the world of the dead in an unforgettable moment of dazzling transience:

> Not all the living, nor all the dead, nor the generations yet unborn will be able to see *The Screens* [. . .] In order for this event – the performance or performances – without disturbing the order of the world, to impose thereon a poetic combustion, acting upon a few thousand Parisians, I should like it to be so strong and so dense that it will, by its implications and ramifications, illuminate the world of the dead. (1972: 11)

For many, Genet's strident rejection of commitment is read as a refusal, on his part, to endorse any form of political art whatsoever, which doubtless explains why so many commentators, interested in the politics of his theatre, have wanted to 'save him from himself' (Coe, 1968: 314–15). However, things are not so straightforward. Although Genet could say in 'The Avertissement' to the 1960 edition of *The Balcony*, that poetry which puts itself in the service of a cause 'always destroys its pretext' (1991: xiv), at no point does he ever reject the politics of poetry per se. A more nuanced reading of that text allows us to see why:[10]

10 José Esteban Muñoz's comments about the politics of song in James Baldwin's work are useful in understanding what Genet is getting at: 'The singer is the subject who stands inside – and in the most important ways, outside – of fiction, ideology, 'the real'. He is not its author and never has been [. . .] But something also hears this singer who is not the author of the song. He is heard by something that is a shared impulse, a drive toward justice, retribution, emancipation – which permits him to disidentify with the song [. . .] [U]tmost precision is needed to rework that song, that story, that fiction, that mastering plot. It is needed to make a self – to disidentify despite the ear-splitting hostility that the song first proposed for the singer. Another vibe is cultivated. Thus, we hear and sing disidentification'. (*Disidentifications: Queers of Colour and the Performance of Politics* (Minneapolis: University of Minnepolis Press, 1999), p. 21).

A few poets, these days, go in for a very curious operation: they sing the praises of the People, of Liberty, of the Revolution, etc., which, when sung, are rocketed up into an abstract sky and then stuck there, discomfited and deflated, to figure in deformed constellations. Disembodied, they become untouchable. How can we approach them, love them, live them, if they are dispatched so magnificently away? When written – sometimes sumptuously – they become the constituent signs of a poem, and as poetry is nostalgia and the song destroys its pretext, our poets destroy what they wanted to bring to life. (*ibid.*)

Far from abandoning poetry, Genet's critique in the 'Avertissement' is restricted to a particular sort of eulogistic writing which transforms the fluidity of revolutionary desire into a crystallised abstraction.[11] Why else, for instance, would Genet pose the question in the above paragraph about looking for alternative modes of representation that would avoid expressing equality and freedom as distant signs? It is decisive, too, that in the 1962 and 1968 versions of *The Balcony*, Genet removed the discussion about politics and aesthetics that took place in Scene 6 of the 1960 edition from the main text, and placed it instead in the written 'Avertissement'.[12] The point here was to stop the play from offering any sort of message, even a negative one. For Genet, as I will explain in greater detail below, aesthetics have their own politics, which are to be found in the way that they reconfigure sensible experience. In this optic, the crucial question is not how can theatre be made politically efficacious, but, on the contrary, how can it reorder the world for the sake of what Genet called 'a breathtaking liberation'? (2003: 104).

Aesthetic politics

That Genet was interested in developing an alternative notion of aesthetic politics is evident by taking into account the historical events upon which his late theatre is based, and which everywhere pervade it. Without contradicting his investment in autonomy, Genet was able to claim that the catalyst for *The Balcony* was the Spanish Civil War (White, 1993: 446–7); that *The Blacks* was an attempt 'to give voice to

---

11 Genet is surely referring here to the Marxist poet Louis Aragon's celebratory socialism of the 1940s and 1950s. For a good analysis of Aragon's commitment, see Maxwell Adereth, *Commitment in Modern French Literature: A Brief Study of Littérature Engagé in the works of Péguy, Aragon and Sartre* (New York: Gollancz, 1967).
12 See Genet in Corvin and Dichy, *Jean Genet*, p. 435.

something profound that neither Blacks nor any other alienated people could make heard' (2004: 13); and that *The Screens* was 'nothing but a long meditation on the Algerian War' (*ibid.*: 28). More pertinently, in two separate interviews with Rüdiger Wischenbart and Nigel Williams, both of which were given towards the end of his life, he stated that from *The Maids* onwards he had set out to develop an alternative form of committed theatre, which he defines in terms of obliqueness:

> [A]ll of my plays, from *The Maids* to *The Screens*, are, after all, in a certain way – at least I'd like to think so – somewhat political, in the sense that they address politics obliquely. They are not politically neutral. I was drawn to plots that were not political but that took place within a purely revolutionary movement. (*ibid.*: 246)

Genet's reference to obliqueness leaves little doubt that his theatre, though having nothing in common with orthodox schemas of engaged art, was nevertheless purposively politicised: '[a]ll of [my] plays [seek to] address [. . .] political issues. Not politics as such, as it's practiced by politicians, but to address social situations that would provoke a politics' (*ibid.*: 247).[13] The phrase 'provoke a politics' is central here. But what exactly does it mean? And how it does it tally with obliqueness?

At its simplest, Genet's practice of obliqueness suggests that theatre is at its most political when it avoids dealing with contemporary reality in a straightforward or frontal manner. That is to say, when it 'crosses through society', and 'grasps the world from an angle' (*ibid.*: 262). A more complex way of understanding Genet's *oblique* notion of engagement is to see it as a form of theatre which, while firmly grounded in historical actuality, points beyond itself to a place or void that is radically atemporal. Obliqueness, then, is a method for puncturing the realm of appearances; its objective is to reveal emptiness, and, through that revelation, to instigate a new political sequence. In the context of the themes and figures of Genet's late theatre, this calls out for a fundamental transformation in our attitudes towards those subjects who embody what Rancière calls 'the part with no part' (1999: 11) – revolutionaries, Blacks and Arabs. Significantly, this disclosure is dependent upon shattering the ontological foundations of the spectator, not in encouraging

---

13 Some indication of what Genet means by aesthetic politics was demonstrated in the televised interview recorded in 1985 for the BBC's *Arena* series when he subverted the traditional *mise-en-scène* of the interview format by asking the camera-man questions and encouraging him to discuss his opinions on air. See *The Declared Enemy*, p. 263.

her to make choices about the world through a clear exposition of political themes and dilemmas.

According to Marie-Claude Hubert, in her excellent study *L'esthétique de Jean Genet*, one of the ways in which Genet 'provokes a politics' is by reflecting on the relationship between images and power: '[i]n *Elle*, as in *The Balcony*, Genet [. . .] meditates on how, at the very heart of any social group, power manipulates the image in order to achieve its ends' (1996: 7; my translation). For Hubert, Genet's late theatre contests this manipulation, by drawing attention to its own mechanisms and by showing the audience that it is 'nothing but an art of imposture' (*ibid.*: 105). What makes Hubert's reading so compellingly correct is her refusal to separate politics from aesthetics. Implicit to her argument is the idea that politics are always already aestheticised in so far as they are always already theatricalised. Or as Genet puts it: 'What is a theatre? First of all what is power? It seems to me that power can never do without theatricality. Never. Sometimes the theatricality is simplified, sometimes modified, but there is always theatricality' (2004: 131).

As interpreted by Hubert, Genet's aesthetic of obliqueness has, perversely, clear parallels with postmodernist revisions of Brecht's epic theatre made by critics such as Elizabeth Wright (1988) and Fredric Jameson (1998). Yet while Genet and Brecht certainly have more in common than the former would like to think, there is a key distinction that needs to be insisted upon.[14] Whereas Brecht seeks to express political knowledge through the aesthetic, Genet believes that the aesthetic is a source of politics in itself. For him, the work's political charge resides in its ability to reorder sensible experience so as to communicate an essentially ineffable or impossible notion of equality and justice.[15] A more philosophical way of putting this is to say that unlike Brecht who is concerned with epistemology, Genet is fascinated with ontology; or, more accurately, with the void that troubles being.

Further light is shed on this politics of obliqueness by looking at two of Genet's more obscure texts from the 1970s.[16] In the essay 'The Palestinians' published in the *Journal of Palestine Studies* in 1973,

---

14 For an essay that highlights the similarities between Genet and Brecht, see Carl Lavery, 'Alienation Effects in Jean Genet's *Les nègres*', in C. Smith (ed.), *Norwich Papers: Essays in Memory of Janine Deakins and Michael Parkinson*, 4 (1997), 313–19.
15 In a perceptive article, Allen Francovich argues that Genet has 'an organic view of politics' which is embedded 'in the structure of the work'. See 'Genet's Theatre of Possession', *The Drama Review*, 14:1 (1969), 25–45: 29.
16 One critic who does cite them is Jérôme Neutre. See *Genet*, pp. 238–51. Although I disagree with certain aspects of his study, he nevertheless provides one of most interesting readings of Genet's politics to date, primarily because he is interested in taking the latter's own writings on politics and aesthetics seriously.

Genet distinguishes between two types of revolutionary art. On the one hand, he says, 'there is the work which serves the revolution; this is constructive in the sense that it destroys bourgeois values'. On the other hand, and opposed to this conventional version of political art, Genet describes a form of artistic work that is 'essentially violent and inflammatory, in the sense that it refuses to submit to any value or to any authority. It disputes even the existence of man. This was the kind I meant when I said that artistic work cannot serve the revolution, I insist that it rejects all values and all authority' (1973b: 32). In spite of saying that 'there must be no question of preference' between these two forms of art, it is evident that Genet's sympathy resides with the latter; its negation of the world provides the reader or spectator with the freedom to recreate herself:

> As for the revolution and its demands, they are always practical orders, and when I say that artistic work is inflammatory I mean that in the long run it upsets all established order [...] [I]t is the duty of the revolution to encourage its adversaries: works of art. This is because artistic work, which is the product of the struggle in isolation, tends to contemplation, which, in the long run, may turn into the destruction of all values, bourgeois or otherwise, and their replacement by something that will more and more come to resemble what we call freedom. (*ibid.*)

In many ways, Genet's argument here reiterates the same point he made to Fichte about the artwork's capacity for provoking disinterested contemplation or nostalgia. Only on this occasion, Genet is no longer contrasting political acts with aesthetic acts; he is pointing to the fact that the aesthetic articulates its own politics by allowing the subject to transcend her alienated condition. Through her confrontation with the artwork, the subject experiences the creative and egalitarian playfulness of the Schillerian *Spieltrieb*. To that extent, aesthetic politics are, for Genet, linked to, but necessarily different from, what I termed in Chapter 1, political aesthetics. Contrary to the revolution which is compelled to realise the aesthetic in life itself, the task of the artist, conversely, is to produce an autonomous work that allows the political promise, the dream of a non-alienated life, to be heard. In this respect, art's obliqueness does more than merely show contradictions; it offers a tantalising and immediate glimpse into the utopian *promesse du bonheur*.

According to Genet, the objective of political revolution (and here again we see his proximity to Schiller) is not to create new systems, but to encourage more imaginative and poetic ways of being in the world. The subject is to make herself into a work of art. So while revolutionary poetry and written poetry are separate entities in Genet's thought, they both ought to work, in their different ways, for the same goal: equality and freedom – the end of reification. Genet made a similar point in a letter he wrote to the political militant Patrick Prado in 1970. In that text, he argues that artists are at their most radical when they refuse to compromise the autonomy of their vision. For him, the Catholic poet Paul Claudel 'betrays his religion', in so far as 'poetry refuses to serve any ideology' and 'sticks in the throat' of any system (1970: my translation). Towards the end of the letter, he applies the same logic to Rimbaud's writing. For Genet, Rimbaud's political importance has less to do with putting his poetry in the service of the Paris Commune than it does with his attempt in *Les Illuminations*, his final work, to create a poetic experience that transforms subjectivity through language alone: 'Rimbaud? It is in *Les Illuminations* where he goes beyond his anger against provincialism and Cavaignac. What comes before *Les Illuminations* is quite weak. "Change life" is a banal phrase. "Change life" (he must have got that from Marx). That's just politics' (*ibid.*: my translation).

Genet's rationale for his unorthodox reading of Rimbaud (and dismissal of Marx) is evinced in the following sentence: '[p]oetry goes farther than politics, but politics (of a certain kind) prepares for poetry; for what happens then is that there is a communication between all men. I say this to you because I *know* I'm right' (*ibid.*; my translation). Here Genet repeats his longstanding claim – based on an intuition – that poetry is more radical than revolutionary politics. Where revolutions aim to produce equality, poetry, Genet implies, already possesses it through its capacity for a transcendent form of 'communication'. In other words, aesthetic experience takes the subject beyond herself and reveals an impossible community, where individuals belong to the totality without being subsumed by it. To labour the point somewhat: Genet is, once again, refusing to conflate politics with poetry in his analysis of Rimbaud's writing. Rather, he makes it clear that they exist in a sort of friendly rivalry, in which each is dependent upon the other for its own realisation.

Staging the wound

Genet's oblique theory of aesthetics demands a new approach to the politics of his late theatre. What is needed is not another theoretical model that imposes ideas on his work from the outside, but a mode of interpretation that tries to piece together his practice of aesthetic politics, internally, from his own scattered writings. As I demonstrate below, this unfashionable 'return to the author' leads us back once again to the wound, which, in Genet's thought in the 1950s and 1960s, exists as shorthand for aesthetic experience in general.

In the same way that Genet's 'event' on the train gave birth to a more politically expansive theatre from the perspective of content, it also transformed his thinking about the type of experience that theatre should provoke. In 'Letter to Jean-Jacques Pauvert', published in 1954, and written prior to the 'event of wounding', Genet's thinking about theatre is wracked with frustration. He complains in Pascalian language about how 'modern theatre is a diversion', and castigates it for lacking the 'power of a poem, that is to say, of a crime'. His enthusiasm for envisioning what theatre might be like 'with the Mau-Mau', is immediately thwarted by his awareness that in the 'western world, more and more affected by death, and turned towards it' theatre has lost its impact, being nothing other than the '"reflection" of a comedy of a comedy'. Mired in this dreary state, modern theatre, Genet suggests, in a phrase with strong Platonic overtones, can only be 'a theatre of shadows' (2003: 39).

Four years later, however, and in response to his experience of wounding, Genet's approach to theatre has changed. The sense of depression clinging to the Pauvert text has been replaced by something more energetic and pressing. In the 1958 essay 'The Tightrope Walker' Genet's language is charged, pointed and interrogative:[17]

> *And your wound, where is it?*
> *I wonder where it resides, where the secret wound is hidden where every man runs to take refuge if his pride is hurt, when he is wounded? This wound – which becomes the innermost core – it is this wound he will inflate, fill. Every man knows how to reach it, to the point of becoming this wound itself, a sort of painful heart.*
> *[. . .] It is into this wound – incurable, since it is himself – and into this solitude that he must throw himself, it is there he will be able to discover the strength, the audacity and the skill necessary to his art. (ibid.: 72; original italics)*

According to Genet, the task of the performer is to disrupt everyday language and to allow a new reality to emerge. This is best achieved, contends Genet, when the performer abandons the security of the ego and

---

17 Although it is focused on the circus, the theory of performance advanced by Genet in 'The Tightrope Walker' holds good for his theatre, too. The same themes are repeated in his instructions to performers in 'Letters to Roger Blin'.

journeys in and through the solitary recesses of self that skirt the wound. By becoming the wound, the performer, Genet proposes, leaves her previous identity behind and discovers the powers of metamorphosis. She becomes a monster, neither female nor male, human nor animal:

> Your make-up? Excessive. Extravagant. Make it elongate your eyes all the way to your hair. Your nails will be painted [. . .] Man or Woman? Definitely a monster. [. . .] During the first of your turns on the wire, they'll understand that this monster with mauve eyelids could dance nowhere but there. No doubt, they will tell themselves, it is this peculiarity that puts him on the wire, it is that elongated eye, those painted cheeks, those golden nails that force him to be there, where we – thank God! – will never go. (*ibid.*: 74–5)

Like Tadeusz Kantor and Heiner Müller, Genet proposes that the performer who embodies the wound startles us because she has gone over, seemingly, to the realm of the dead. She has renounced the world of acts for a world of pointless gesture. On Genet's wounded stage, the actor exists as a block of absence, a solid void. She 'fills in' and 'make[s] perceptible' a 'nothingness' which 'she draws from' (*ibid.*: 75):

> People flee from him. He is alone [. . .] He moves in an element that is like death, like the desert. His speech awakens no echo. Since it must utter what is addressed to no one and no longer has to be understood by anything that is living, it is a necessity that is not required by life, but by the death that commands him. (*ibid.*)

By divesting herself of self, and embodying an impossible doubleness, the performer discloses, in and through her physical presence alone, what the audience fears. She 'illuminates' the tomb:

> *If we go to the theatre, it is to penetrate into the hall, into the precarious anteroom of that precarious death that sleep will be. For it is a Celebration that will take place at the close of day, the most serious one, the last one, something very close to our funeral.*
> *[. . .] Your brief tomb illuminates us. You are enclosed within it while at the same time your image keeps escaping from it.* (*ibid.*: 81–3; original italics)

As well as drawing from the wound, the performer needs to be able, argues Genet, to communicate it, to make it visible as an absent presence, and in this way to affect the audience physically. The actor must be prepared to inflict violence – ontological violence – on the spectator: '[t]

he audience – which allows you to exist, without it you would never have the solitude I spoke about – the audience is the animal you will finally stab. Your perfection, as well as your boldness, will, during the time you appear, annihilate it' (*ibid.*: 82). As I will discuss later in this chapter, theatre's capacity for lacerating or stabbing the audience transcends any surface nihilism it might seem to have. As with the art of Rembrandt and Giacometti, the hole in being that theatre 'shows' produces new, unspeakable allegiances of equality, which leave all essentialised notions of identity behind.

From a theatrical perspective, it is telling that the impact of the wound in 'What Remains of a Rembrandt' should be so powerfully spatial. As I showed in the previous chapter (see pp. 69–77), in his struggle to articulate his experience aboard the train, Genet draws attention to the way in which the distance separating subject from object collapsed, and left him floundering in a sort of *terra infirma*: 'His gaze was not that of another person: it was my own I met in a mirror, *by accident and in solitude and forgetting myself*' (*ibid.*: 93; original italics). Significantly, he describes undergoing a similar process of dislocation when looking at the paintings and sculptures of Giacometti. For Genet, Giacometti's art estranges our perception of the world. Distinguishing between a face experienced in everyday life, and one represented by Giacometti on a canvas or in sculpted form, Genet notes:

> A living face does not give itself over so easily, but the effort to discover its significance is not too great. I think – I venture – I think it is important to isolate it.
> [. . .] To examine a painting, a greater effort and a more complex operation are necessary. It is in fact the painter – or sculptor – who has carried out for us the operation described above. It is thus the solitude of the person or object represented that is restored to us, and we, who look, in order to perceive it and be touched by it must have an experience of space – not of its continuity but its discontinuity.
> Each object creates its own infinite space. (*ibid.*: 47)

Genet is concerned to show here how Giacometti's ability to isolate an object produces an alternative experience of space. By giving us the opportunity to look, the artwork pulls us into its orbit and unsettles the boundaries between self and Other. In his analysis of Giacometti's statues, Genet describes how they strove endlessly to escape their inert state: '[t]heir beauty – Giacometti's sculptures – seems to me to stem from the incessant, uninterrupted to-and-fro movement from the most extreme distance to the closest familiarity: this to-and-fro doesn't end, and that's how you can tell they are in movement' (*ibid.*: 51).

For Genet, Giacometti's sculptures are inherently theatrical. In common with the actor-marionettes so beloved of Edward Gordon Craig, they are endowed with a physical presentness that affects viewers by disrupting their sense of place and time. To gaze at a Giacometti sculpture, Genet suggests, is to abolish the solidity of self:

> This capacity to isolate an object and make its own, its unique significations flow into it is possible only through the historical abolition of the one who is looking. He must make an exceptional effort to divest himself of all history, so that he becomes not a sort of eternal present, but rather a vertiginous and uninterrupted passage from a past to a future, an oscillation of one extreme to another, preventing rest. (*ibid.*: 55)

The disturbing dynamic that Genet discerns in Giacometti's art illuminates the aesthetics of his own performance practice. It suggests that 'the theatre of the wound' will be a theatre that exploits the spatio-temporal immediacy of the theatrical event in order to reverse conventional spatial and temporal positions and so disorientate its audience. In this context, it is inevitable that Genet should compare theatre to architecture:[18]

> But drama itself? With the author, it has its dazzling beginning, so it is up to him to capture this lightning and organize, starting from the illumination that shows the void, a verbal architecture – that's to say grammatical and ceremonial – cunningly showing that from this void an appearance that shows the void rips itself free. (*ibid.*: 107)

Similar to Georges Bataille's notion of anti-architecture which works to break apart the 'dams' of 'social stability' (1997: 21), the function of Genet's theatre is not to domesticate reality or to keep the troubling presence of the real at bay. On the contrary, it is to make the 'house' feel unhomely by revealing the void upon which it stands.

While theatre's potential for dislocating space and time can be achieved in many different ways, through, for instance, *mise-en-scène*, or by altering the 'environment', it is important to keep a more basic, ontological factor in mind: namely, that theatre concerns real bodies on an actual stage. With a typically elegant turn of phrase, the theatre phenomenologist, Bert O. States remarks:

> There is a sense in which signs, or certain kinds of signs, or signs in a certain stage of their life cycle, achieve their vitality – and in turn the vitality of

---

18 Matthew Melia offers telling insights into Genet's concept of architecture. See 'Architecture and Cruelty in the Writings of Antonin Artaud, Jean Genet and Samuel Becket' (Ph.D. dissertation, Kingston University, 2007).

theatre – not simply by signifying the world but by being *of* it [...] [We tend generally to undervalue the elementary fact that theatre – unlike fiction, painting, sculpture and film– is really a language whose words consists to an unusual degree of things that *are* what they seem to be. In theatre, image and object, pretence and pretender, sign-vehicle and content, draw unusually close. (1985: 20; original emphasis)

The 'closeness' referred to by States prevents the spectator from losing herself completely in the theatrical image. She is always aware of the presentness of the actor, that the person playing the role is not the role. In *The Balcony* and *The Blacks*, in particular, the gap separating actor from character, theatre from drama, is confused to the extent that a palpable sense of what Chaudhuri calls 're-realisation' occurs (1986: 88). In this confusion between being and appearing, what we are left with on stage is the dense reality of a body that is very definitely there but resistant to all attempts to transform it into a sign.

To express this in a way that will have important political ramifications in Part II of this book, Genet's exploitation of theatre's presentness makes the actor homeless, and turns the stage into a *utopos*, a simultaneous everywhere and nowhere. Just as Giacometti's sculptures, endlessly shuttle back and forth between 'extreme distance' and the 'closest familiarity', Genet's actors are impossible to pin down or stabilise.[19] Through their vacillation, the solidity of what they represent (and even who they are) starts to unravel. In the process, space becomes unsettling and vertiginous. The effect of this disorientation is to reveal the void or emptiness that accompanies the experience of being wounded.

The politics of the wound

The wound's ability to disrupt the ontological foundations of subjectivity, described in the essays on Rembrandt and Giacometti, is politicised in the 'Preface to *The Blacks*' and in the 'Avertissement' to *The Balcony*, two texts which were written in 1956 and 1960 respectively. In the 'Avertissement', the wound, although never mentioned by name, is

---

19 For a more detailed analysis of the relationship between theatre and art in Genet's work, see Robert Nugent, 'Sculpture into Drama: Giacometti's Influence on Genet', *Drama Survey*, 3:3 (1964), 378–85; Clare Finburgh, 'Facets of Artifice: Rhythms in the Theatre of Jean Genet, and the Painting, Drawing and Sculpture of Alberto Giacometti', *French Forum*, 27:3 (2002), 73–98; and Mara de Gennaro, 'What Remains of Jean Genet?', *Yale Journal of Criticism*,16:1 (2003), 190–209.

present through analogy and association. In the same way that Genet exhorted the performer to 'stab' the audience in 'Tightrope Walker', so in the 'Avertissement' he claims that theatre 'should explode, should show us naked, and leave us distraught, if possible, and having no recourse other than ourselves' (1991: xiv). The explosive theatre that Genet mentions in the 'Avertissement' is designed to inflict maximum pain and suffering; its purpose is to disorient the audience emotionally, ontologically and spatially. For Genet, this can only be achieved by abandoning conventional models of political drama:

> The imaginary representation of an action or an experience usually relieves us of the obligation of attempting to perform or undergo them ourselves, and in reality.
>
> When the problem of a certain disorder – or evil – has been solved on stage, this shows that it has in fact been abolished, since, according to the conventions of our times, a theatrical representation can only be the representation of a fact. We can then turn our minds to something else, and allow our hearts to swell with pride, seeing that we took the side of the hero who aimed – successfully – at finding the solution. (*ibid.*)

While the 'Avertissement' makes no direct reference to Sartre, the entire argument of the text is opposed to his aesthetics. For Sartre, political theatre is ostensibly a theatre of situations, that is, a theatre where spectators are encouraged to identify with, and learn from, the actions of characters confronted with a specific limit-situation. In the manifesto 'For a Theatre of Situations', Sartre states that the situation in question will be universal – by which he means that it will correspond to the great political dilemmas of the age: 'situations must be found which are so general that they are common to all. Immerse men in these universal and extreme situations which leave them only a couple of ways out, arrange things so that in choosing the way they choose themselves, and you've won – the play is good' (1976: 4–5).

Sartre's theatre of situations is aesthetically conservative. Little attempt is made to reinvent the theatrical form; crucial questions of representation are not posed; and the spectator is engaged through traditional techniques of identification and empathy.[20] By insisting on imaginary empathy, putting oneself in the same position of the Other, Sartre transforms theatrical experience into judicial experience. The audience is encouraged to judge the actions of characters and then to

---

20 The conservatism of the Sartrean stage is apparent in the statement in which he claimed that his theatre 'derive[s] from the Corneillean tradition' (*Sartre on Theater*, p. 36).

use that judgement on itself. Supposedly, the result of this existential witnessing is to effect a real change in the world outside the theatre. Art is a spur to action, a type of praxis: 'I want the audience to see our century from outside, as something alien, as a witness. And at the same time to participate in it, since it is in fact making this century. There is one feature particular to our age: the fact that we know we shall be judged' (*ibid.*: 76).

From the standpoint of the 'Avertissement', Sartre's view of theatre is seriously mistaken. Differently from Sartre, Genet does not believe that empathy with characters placed in dramatic situations provides access to the real. On the contrary, it erodes the real by replacing actual experience with imaginary experience.[21] Strangely, Sartre, the great exponent of concrete philosophy, has forgotten that theatre is fiction, not fact. By doing so, he falls into the same trap as playwrights who invest in socialist realism – he offers imaginary solutions to real-life problems. As Genet notes: '[n]o problem that has been exposed [on the stage] ought to be solved in the imagination, especially when the dramatist has made every effort to show the concrete reality of a social order' (1991: xiv).[22]

In order to avoid such a contradictory scenario, Genet states in the 'Avertissement' that the aesthetic assumptions of theatre need to change drastically. Instead of representing the world naturalistically and offering formal resolutions to thorny problems, theatre ought to distance itself from reality and exist as 'an active explosion', which overwhelms the spectator with 'evil' (*ibid.*). Significantly, evil here is not to be understood according to its usual theological usage; rather, it stands for everything that disturbs the contours of self and the subject's sense of propriety. In Genet's hands, theatre is negative and negating, a disorienting *sensorium* where the wound of being is made palpable and the world uncanny and strange.

Genet's desire to make the world unrecognisable explains why he studiously banishes everything real and naturalistic from the stage. In

---

21 The relationship between fiction and reality troubled Genet throughout his career. On the opening page of *Prisoner of Love*, he warns the reader that his book is not reality: 'So did I fail to understand the Palestinian revolution? Yes, completely? [...] [B]ecause the occupied territories were only a play acted out second by second, by occupied and occupier. The reality lay in involvement, fertile in hate and love, in people's daily lives; in silence' (p. 3).

22 It is interesting to compare Genet's critique of Sartrean methods with Jerzy Grotowski's rejection of empathy. Grotowski rejects empathy for its ineffectiveness: '[t]he audience – all Creons – may well side with Antigone throughout the performance, but this does not prevent each of them from behaving like Creon once out of the theatre' (*Towards a Poor Theatre*, E. Barba (ed.), trans. J. Andersen and J. Barba (London: Methuen, 1995), p. 29).

The Balcony, *The Blacks* and *The Screens*, time is mashed up and fractured; space vacillates and moves; and actors are compelled to walk backwards, to lose themselves in costumes and masks, and to become objects: dogs, cheese-graters, the wind, and so on. Genet's landscape is a landscape of evil, a world in which all hopes are dashed, and all optimism crushed. In it, revolutions, like human relationships, invariably fail. The worst is always certain. However, just as the autonomy of the artwork is never fully capable of transcending reality, so the negativity of Genet's theatre is provisional. In keeping with the logic of the wound, it demands that reality be changed. As he puts in the 'Avertissement': '[i]f the "good" is to appear in a work of art it does so through the divine aid of the powers of song, whose strength alone is enough to magnify the evil that has been exposed' (*ibid.*).

The political meaning attached by Genet to a theatre that opens wounds is developed more explicitly in his 'Preface to *The Blacks*'. In this text, he confesses that he accepted the commission to write the play because it afforded him the opportunity to 'wound the Whites, and through this wound, to introduce doubt' (see the Appendix, in this book, p. 230). By producing doubt, Genet marks 'whiteness'. As the theatre theorist, Adrian Kear explains, such an operation is inherently affective; it provokes a 'phenomenological shudder' by compelling the spectator to disidentify with the very thing she takes for granted: the body:

> Whilst 'white' may 'operate as its own other' to the extent that the colonial 'black' mirrors its typography and mimics its perspicacity, the disruptive effect of disturbing its field of vision might be characterised more properly as the disjunctive resituating of white as other, producing the disorientating experience of 'whiteness' as 'otherness'. (2001: 195)

The 'evil' driving Genet's theatre of the wound is ultimately dialectical; its negation of accepted images and tropes, along with its commitment to the void, is intended to produce positive results. What Genet is seeking to do in his theatre is to transform the spectator into stranger, a subject who no longer knows where she is. Through this loss of bearings, the spectator, like Genet on the train, is encouraged to catch a glimpse into a different world, in which he recognises the suffering of the Other. In a key passage from 'Preface to *The Blacks*', he explains:

> Theatrical expression is not a speech. It does not address a human's rational faculties. It is a poetic act that seeks to affirm itself as a categorical imperative, in front of which reason puts itself on hold, without, however, surrendering. I believe it is possible to find the unique expression that would be understood by all humans. But instead of leading societies towards

ever increasing mutual understanding, transformations in History harden around them a crust of singularity, to the point where our primary preoccupation will be to crack this crust, under which a human being is longing to be free. (Appendix: 228)

Locating the politics of Genet's theatre

Although Genet's notion of political theatre has little in common with existing models of commitment, his insistence on autonomy and negativity is close to that of Theodor Adorno.[23] According to Adorno, art is at its most political when it refuses to serve the world; when, in other words, it insists on its own uselessness. This is because, for Adorno, the artwork's autonomy offers a 'schema' for an alternative notion of 'social praxis':

> Much more importantly art becomes social by its opposition to society, and it occupies this position only as autonomous art. By crystallizing in itself as something unique to itself rather than complying with existing social norms and qualifying as 'socially useful', it criticizes society by merely existing, for which all puritans of all stripes condemn it [. . .] Art's asociality is the determinate negation of a determinate society. (2004: 296)

Adorno's thinking here is based on a dialectical interpretation of Kant's notion of disinterestedness.[24] In his view, art's 'free appearance' absolves it from an administered and reified world where every object is compelled to have a value and a price. By insisting on its own lack of purpose, art resists the logic of exchange value. This is why, Adorno claims, the autonomous work is inherently and authentically social: its rejection of utility is a living reminder that life can and should be different:

> Even in the most sublimated work of art there is a hidden 'it should be otherwise'. When a work is merely itself and no other thing [. . .] it becomes bad art – literally pre-artistic. The moment of true volition, however, is mediated through nothing other than the form of the work itself, whose crystallization becomes an analogy of that other condition which should be. As eminently constructed and produced objects, works of art, including

---

23 The only other critic who sees a possible connection between Adorno and Genet is Edward Said. See 'On Genet's Late Work', in J. Ellen Gainor (ed.), *Imperialism and Theatre* (London: Routledge, 1995), pp. 230–42: 239–40.
24 See Adorno, *Aesthetic Theory*, G. Adorno and R. Tiedeman (eds), trans. R. Hullot-Kentor (London: Continuum, 2004), pp. 1–18.

literary ones, point to a practice from which they abstain: the creation of a just life. (2007: 194)

In 'a world which', as Adorno says, 'permanently puts a pistol to men's heads' (*ibid.*: 180), the artist is compelled to prevent the audience from gaining any pleasure or satisfaction from the artwork. Rather, she should look to communicate, through form alone, the horror of contemporary existence: '[f]or the sake of reconciliation authentic works must blot out every trace of reconciliation' (2004: 306). For Adorno, contemporary art's refusal to reconcile itself to happiness, allows for a return of the historical repressed. Its negativity unfolds the alienation that capitalism's culture industry tries so hard to deny. As a result of this extreme negationism, a dialectic inversion takes place: the dream of a better life emerges from the fact that it is so tragically absent:

> Art is no more able than theory to concretize utopia, not even negatively. A cryptogram of the new is the image of collapse; only by virtue of the absolute negativity of the collapse does art enunciate the unspeakable: utopia [. . .] Through the irreconcilable renunciation of the semblance of reconciliation, art holds fast to the promise of reconciliation in the midst of the unreconciled [. . .]. (*ibid.*: 41)

In Adorno's view, art has no need to step beyond itself to be political, for it is always already implicated in social and economic structures. Art's autonomy, stresses Adorno, is never complete; it is stained with heteronomy, that is to say, with history: '[a]rt is related to its other as is a magnet to iron fillings [. . .] The artwork is related to the world by the principle that contrasts it with the world, and that is the same principle by which spirit organized the world' (*ibid.*: 9).

There is much in Adorno's thought which chimes with Genet's notion of aesthetic politics. Like Adorno, Genet has no interest in art which offers itself as a message or tries to make itself the equivalent of a real act. Rather, the artwork should function according to its own self-sufficient logic and exist as an unhealed scar. For Genet, as for Adorno, the artwork's necessary attachment to suffering and negativity is the thing that allows the promise of happiness to be heard. In this way, both thinkers remain committed to the utopianism of Idealist aesthetics: they see the artwork as a vehicle for disclosing the presence of a more egalitarian form of society that resides in what Badiou in his book on Beckett calls 'the other life [that] radiates beneath the insult' (2003: 69–70).

If the discussion were to end here, it would be possible to claim Genet as a resistant playwright in the vein of Adorno, an artist who posits the aesthetic as an autonomous site where society can be rebuked and the world remade.[25] However, despite these similarities, Genet's notion of aesthetic politics, as I noted earlier, is ultimately more grounded in contemporary reality than Adorno's. Reading Adorno, one sometimes has the impression that the aesthetic is enough by itself to resist the tragic way of the world. As such, there appears, in his thought, no need to realise the artwork's promise in life itself. To experience art is to be granted immediate release from reification, to discover an alternative, more humane space. In this way, as Rancière cautions, Adorno betrays the doubleness of the Schillerian promise. Diverging from Schiller who envisaged aesthetics as both a separate sphere for art-making *and* as a technique for transforming life, Adorno insists, too much, on the artwork's autonomy. He is content to make life into art, not art into life. For Rancière, Adorno's attempt to 'refuse any form of reconciliation' with the world has a 'heavy consequence' (Rancière, 2004: 59; my translation): it reintroduces a hierarchy or inequality into the very notion of the aesthetic, and finishes by policing what should have remained a non-coercive experience.

In *The Balcony*, and particularly in *The Blacks*, Genet disrupts the fetish character of art, its grounding in semblance, by introducing into the artwork the very thing that, according to Adorno, it should expunge: pure unmediated life. In both of these plays, the 'free appearance' of the artwork is interrupted, as the actors stray dangerously close to the real itself. In *The Balcony* and *The Blacks*, it *seems*, at times, that actual experience has replaced aesthetic experience. However, in drawing attention to this confusion between the symbolic and real, Genet is not interested in renouncing the aesthetic politics that he practises. He simply wants to highlight the limitations of theatre: to show that the aesthetic promise needs to be realised in life itself. In this way, Genet's late theatre, while always insisting on the specificity of its own redistribution of the sensible, points beyond itself to the type of political aesthetics that characterised his revolutionary commitments in the 1960s and 1970s.

In the extent to which it merges autonomous aesthetics with what we might call anti-aesthetics, Genet's theatre is best defined as an ambivalent theatre, a theatre where the aesthetic frame is stretched to breaking point, without being eradicated completely. Intriguingly, the effect of this doubleness is to heighten the political potential of the artwork. For if aesthetic politics are predicated upon an interplay between autonomy and heteronomy, which I understand here in terms of sign and body, symbol and thing, then to introduce heteronomy into autonomy, in the

---

25 Adorno refers to art as a 'wound' in the opening chapter of *Aesthetic Theory*, p. 2.

way that Genet does, is to highlight the extent to which the aesthetic, in its guise as a separate sphere of/for art-making, is both escape route and prison. By showing this, Genet gives flesh, so to speak, to the revolutionary promise that the artwork harbours, while always underscoring its virtuality. There is then a distinct melancholy about Genet's late theatre.[26] For what he discloses so well is the unhappy paradox that haunts aesthetic politics: that they are both real *and* not real, gestures not acts. They need a political revolution to consolidate their utopian insights. Insisting on this pragmatic point allows Genet to avoid the *aporia* that blinds Adorno. Unlike the latter, he recognises that aesthetic politics lack self-sufficiency.

Genet's interest in drawing attention to the melancholy of aesthetic politics offers an intriguing insight into his attraction to theatre. Of all the arts, theatre is the one that deliberately plays on the ambivalence between autonomy and heteronomy, gesture and act. As Samuel Weber (2004) and Hans-Thies Lehmann (2006) have both argued, theatre is a virtual art, an art composed of bodies that are both real and signs. As such, theatre is always haunted, at every moment of its existence, by heteronomy, by the audience's awareness that the dramatic is dependent upon the theatrical, that the character is an actor, and that each gesture is a real gesture. Theatre's fleshy heteronomy means that the political promise contained in aesthetic politics is simultaneously stronger and weaker than in other art forms. Stronger because the audience is actually presented with bodies that have become other than self; weaker because those same bodies are trapped within the space of theatre itself. Theatre prevents us from losing ourselves, as the novel and cinema do, in the disembodied signs of language or in the weightlessness of the celluloid image. Rather, theatre's thereness, what Michal Kobialka refers to as its spatial 'ontology' (2003: 560), brings the promissory element of the aesthetic down to earth, and demands its realisation by showing us, in the most immediate manner possible, that the heteronomous subject is caught in an imaginary prison from which she needs to escape. To pre-empt the terminology which will dominate Part II of this book, Genet's negative and wounding theatre floods the heterotopic space of the auditorium with utopic possibilities, which insist upon realisation in the world beyond the artwork.

26 Andrew Gibson says the same thing about Rancière's notion of aesthetic politics and Badiou's inaesthetics. See 'The Unfinished Song: Intermittency and Melancholy in Rancière', in M. Robson (ed.), *Jacques Rancière: Aesthetics, Politics and Philosophy* (Edinburgh: Edinburgh University Press, 2005), pp. 61–76; and *Beckett and Badiou: The Pathos of Intermittency* (Oxford: Oxford University Press, 2006), pp. 162–71.

Conclusion

In this chapter, I have been concerned to unpack Genet's theory and practice of political theatre. I have done so by concentrating on his own writings and by explaining how his metaphor of the wound discloses an oblique notion of aesthetic politics that evades accepted models of *art politique*. Towards the end of the chapter, I suggested that Genet's blend of negative aesthetics and anti-aesthetics creates a doubly political theatre which disorients spectators. The aim is to make them feel *unheimlich*, not at home. This reference to the *unheimlich* is far from gratuitous. In the second part of this book, I intend to examine how Genet's wounding theatre contests, directly, the disciplinary spatial practices of the French nation-State in an age of modernisation and decolonisation. As I have been arguing in Part I, the rationale was to create a space where spectators could disidentify with consensual notions of Frenchness and glimpse, instead, the possibility of a different, more expansive world.

PART II: Spatial politics in the late plays

4

Exploding the bordello in *The Balcony*: spectacle, allegory and the wound of theatre

> The historical materialist leaves it to others to be drained by the whore called 'Once upon a time' in historicism's bordello. He remains in control of his powers, man enough to blast open the continuum of history. (Benjamin, 1969: 262)

Introduction

Published in 1956, and revised on three occasions in 1960, 1962 and 1968, *The Balcony* is the first of Genet's plays to take contemporary historical and political reality as its major theme. Whereas his early work, most notably the novel *Funeral Rites*, dealt with history indirectly, without being interested in affecting its outcome, *The Balcony* addresses what was, arguably, the most pressing political problem facing *gauchiste* militants and progressive artists in the 1950s and 1960s. What could be done, politically and aesthetically, to provoke a revolutionary consciousness in an age of modernisation and spectacle?[1] For reasons outlined

---

1 Scott Durham offers an alternative reading of *Funeral Rites* as a historical novel. See 'The Divided Event: The Aesthetics and Politics of Virtuality in *Funeral Rites*', in Hanrahan, *Genet*, 59–76: 59: 62. In his reading, the text expresses the spirit of the

in the previous chapter, *The Balcony* has little interest in exploring this question naturalistically or in offering pedagogical solutions to it. Genet wants to wound, not to convince. In what follows, I argue that he does this by fashioning a purposefully ambivalent theatre which situates itself somewhere in the impossible gap between sign and experience, and autonomy and heteronomy. Because the two productions which are historically germane to my argument in this chapter – Peter Zadek's at the Arts Club in London in 1957 and Peter Brook's at the Théâtre du Gymnase in Paris in 1960 – failed to highlight this aspect of the work, I have decided to focus on the political potential inherent in Genet's text.[2] By exploring how Genet's dramaturgy stretches theatrical experience to breaking point, I aim to show how the politics of *The Balcony* are bound up with the major technological and economic upheavals occurring in France at the time. To be more explicit, the political significance of the play, in my view, is found in the way it contests, thematically and formally, what one might call, with a glance at Guy Debord, spectacular space.

Historical focus

Irrespective of its publication date in 1966, the sociologist Lucien Goldmann's article 'The Theatre of Genet: A Sociological Study' remains one of the key essays of Genet scholarship. In it, Goldmann contends that Genet is the most historically aware of all contemporary French playwrights, the one whose late plays 'assign a central place to the problems of history as a whole, thereby making them the key to understanding his work's unity' (1979: 34). Basing his methodology on the collective categories of structural sociology, Goldmann proposes that Genet's theatre expresses the agonistic *Weltanschauung* of the radical

---

époque as opposed to representing it in a straightforward manner. It is also possible to say, as Didier Eribon does, that Genet's novels exist as ethnographic documents of gay life in Paris between the wars. See *Une morale du minoritaire*, pp. 229–30.

2 Although Genet did not criticise these contemporary stagings of *The Balcony* on political grounds specifically, he was nevertheless extremely disappointed by them. He was forcibly removed from the dress rehearsal of Zadek's production in London in 1957 for voicing his complaints so vociferously. See White, *Genet*, pp. 480–2. Equally, in a letter to Bernard Frechtman in 1960, Genet explained how Brook had misunderstood, fundamentally, the function of satire in the play. See Corvin and Dichy, *Jean Genet*, p. 936. His short 1962 article 'How to Perform *The Balcony*' details his dissatisfaction with all existing productions of the play to date. See *The Balcony*, pp. xi–xiii.

left in Europe of the 1950s and 1960s. Differently from Eugène Ionesco, whose petty bourgeois everyman Bérenger succumbs in the end to alienation, Genet's plays articulate the ideas of a more militant class:

> [A]longside this widespread 'Bérenger phenomenon', there are – particularly in France and Italy – strong socialist and anarchist unionist traditions. These comprise a small number of workers and creative intellectuals and a fairly large number of educated people who refuse to accede to modern capitalism. They are concerned with the problem of establishing a human order that will effectively guarantee individual liberties. The frustrated hope for a Socialist revolution in the West and the development of Stalinism in the East constituted a set of difficult problems for this group. It now finds itself maintaining a genuinely negative attitude toward capitalism [. . .] while knowing that this rejection brings with it intellectual and practical difficulties which are incomparably serious and decisive. (*ibid.*: 33)

In tandem with the totalising practices of structuralism, Goldmann is happy to posit Genet's theatre as 'the literary transposition of this latter group's world vision' (*ibid.*), but less willing to accord it political or historical intentionality. In Goldmann's reading, Genet's identity as a thief and outcast somehow allowed him to stumble, magically, upon this radical consciousness. This point of view, whereby Genet's historical acuity is a matter of accident rather than design, informs, specifically, Goldmann's reading of *The Balcony*:

> *The Balcony* poses a very important problem to the sociologist. The play represents a transposition of the decisive historical events of the first half of the twentieth century in a manner that is very likely non-conscious and involuntary. The theme of *The Balcony* is how awareness of the importance of the executive function develops in a society which has long been dominated by property-owners but in which people still imagine power to be in the hands of the long outdated fixtures: the Bishop, the Judge and the General. And Genet is telling us that this awareness is created by the threat of revolution and its subsequent defeat: a fairly accurate reflection of western European history between 1917 and 1923. (*ibid.*: 39)

Goldmann's assessment of *The Balcony* is perceptive but problematic. As opposed to contemporary reviewers and critics who often viewed the work through the lens of Sartrean existentialism, Goldmann recognises, correctly, that the work discloses important political contradictions and historical anxieties.[3] However, his desire to downplay authorial

---

3 See for instance the existentialist reading of Benjamin Nelson, '*The Balcony* and Parisian Existentialism', *Tulane Drama Review*, 7: 3 (1963), 60–79.

intent, along with his subsequent and strange silence about the form of the work, means that his reading of the play is simultaneously specific and not specific enough.[4] In many ways, Goldmann is hoisted by own historical petard. Ironically, his attempt to posit Genet as a historical playwright prevents him from grasping the historical specificity of the latter's critique. As I demonstrate below, the play's contemporary relevance does not reside, as Goldmann believes, in its analysis of Fascism between the wars, but rather in its sensitivity to new, more intense techniques of alienation that came into being in the late 1940s and 1950s.[5] That Genet was very much aware of addressing these concerns is apparent in his insistence that *The Balcony* was not just 'the portrait of any world, but of the western world' (2004: 242), a remark which, as Maria Shevtsova explains (1987: 45), highlights the extent to which the play is a purposeful attack on late capitalism in general.

Modernisation in context

According to numerous historians and sociologists, the modernisation of France was an intense, breathless affair. Before modernisation, there were food shortages and rationing; after it, France was flooded, in the wake of the Marshall Plan, with commodities and luxury items such as washing machines, cars and refrigerators. The appearance of new commodities in France from the late 1940s onwards was synonymous with the reordering of social time and space. In Henri Lefebvre's view, the state-led modernisation of the country under the direction of Jean Monnet, the Planning Commissioner, deliberately dismantled old

---

4 Maria Shevtsova criticises Goldmann's reading from a different angle. From her perspective, Goldmann's collective notion of world-view is not 'operational' when it comes to understanding Genet, primarily because he did not belong to any social group. See 'The Theatre of Genet in Sociological Perspective' in Finburgh et al., *Performance and Politics*, pp. 44–53.
5 My critique of Goldmann's interpretation is the opposite of Bernard Dort's. See in Brook and Halpern, *Genet*, p. 117. According to Dort, Goldmann fails to account for Genet's interest in metatheatricality, which, in his opinion, removes the play from history. The problem with Dort's rejection of history in Genet's theatre is that it neglects the fact that the aesthetic, in so far as it is autonomous and heteronomous at the same time, is always already historical. This heteronomy of the aesthetic is particularly important when it comes to understanding the politics of allegory, which Benjamin famously described as confronting the observer 'with the *facies hippocratica* of history as a petrified, primordial landscape' (*The Origin of German Tragic Drama*, trans. J. Osborne (London: Verso, 2003), p. 166).

customs and styles of living and replaced them with a new bureaucratic society in which capitalist discourse infiltrated every area of life:

> During the period under consideration (1946–61), daily life changed – not in the sense of displaying its latent wealth, but in the opposite direction: impoverishment, manipulation, passivity. Capitalism was in the process of conquering new sectors in these years [...] In great detail, and with many convincing arguments, people were having it explained to them how they should live in order to 'live well' and make the best of things; what they should choose and why; how they would use their time and space. The features marked society while wrecking the social. (2005: 26)

For Lefebvre, the point of this new discourse was to resolve class tensions, and to produce a new type of classless person for a new type of modernised nation-State:

> After the Liberation, the 'people' still had a meaning in France. Peasants, artisans, workers – in short, all those who did not belong to the 'dominant' and 'propertied' classes – still had numerous links, not only in workplaces but also in houses, streets, districts and regions. Over the next fifteen years, this unity began to break up not into clearly differentiated and opposed classes, but into layers and strata. (*ibid*.: 28)

Unsurprisingly for a dialectician such as Lefebvre, the colonisation of everyday life in France was not without its anxieties. As existing patterns of individual and collective identity were dismantled, the world was increasingly experienced as unreal and plastic. The French no longer knew who they were and felt invaded by American goods and values. In his review of the 'deep malaise' that accompanied the 'undeniable satisfaction' offered by the commodity, Lefebvre explains that 'what transpired was a threatening and increasing expropriation [of individual existence] by the outside' (*ibid*.: 26). People, in other words, were uneasy about the intensified commodification of life. This accounts, first, for the popularity of the deeply conservative Poujadist movement in France in the mid-1950s, and, then, in the subsequent decade, Charles de Gaulle, who mythologised himself as the living embodiment of Frenchness.[6] In both cases, the return to conservative values was an attempt to keep an increasing sense of social angst at bay. Drowned in the 'quantitative

---

6   Poujadisme derives its name from the leader of the movement Pierre Poujade who offered a patriotic version of Frenchness based on the conservative values of *la France profonde*. In an age of spectacle and doubt, Poujadisme promised a way out of anxiety by promising a return to the known. The party won fifty-three seats in the elections of 1956.

and repetitive' rhythms of consumption and assailed 'by disembodied images and alien voices', reality itself, argues Lefebvre, was perceived, more and more, as spectacle. Lefebvre's argument is substantiated by looking at French cultural output in these years. Whether it was in the films of Jacques Tati, the novels of the *nouveaux romanciers*, the plays of Ionesco or Arthur Adamov, or in the newspaper columns of Roland Barthes, France had entered '*l'ère du soupçon*'. Reality itself had become sign, surface and myth, and authentic experience was increasingly mistrusted. Ross explains how 'at the dawning of image culture', people were 'terrified of their own fictiveness [. . .] and thereby of being an abstraction' (1995: 147).

In Lefebvre's estimation two strategies were developed by the technocrats of modernisation to assuage this growing sense of social disquiet. On the one hand, a spectacular myth of Frenchness was manufactured to veil the perceived loss of a cohesive national identity, 'Frenchness [was] obsolete, antiquated; yet it [was] exalted on television and in the press' (2005: 59). And, on the other hand, there was a new importance – an existential importance – placed on private space. In order to deal with the bewildering reality of everyday life, the French retreated into their homes:

> The more threatening the outside world becomes, the greater the importance and continuity of the interior – that which surrounds or protects subjective interiority. Disdained during the years of protest, things become 'goods' once again; the environment forms an integral and integrated part of the 'person', of their identity. (*ibid.*: 60–1)

Lefebvre's consideration of what sociologists at the time such as Edgar Morin, Cornelius Castoriadis and Jean Baudrillard called 'privatisation' highlights the extent to which the modernisation of France was an inherently spatial phenomenon. In the 1950s, the home became synonymous with self, a narcissistic haven where the subject strove to protect herself from the uncanniness of the outside world:

> State and society, as they are, create anxiety, and compensate for it – that is to say, a demand for security that is closely bound up with the need for identity and continuity. The owner of a house is there for life, especially if he has earned it by the sweat of his brow. He has his place in space. He dwells in the Same, and 'the other' cannot assail him or drag him out. He is installed in the identical, the repetitive, the equivalent. The permanence of property symbolizes, and at the same time realizes, the continuity of an ego. (*ibid.*: 60)

Predictably, however, this dream of sheltering the self was undone at the very moment it began. By confining people to purpose-built housing complexes in new towns such as Sarcelles in the northern suburbs of Paris, and by bombarding them with images, distinctions between public and private space were rendered meaningless. This led, inexorably, to a further intensification of spectacular capital. The house (and, in particular, the living room and kitchen) was the perfect stage for the commodity to advertise itself as a 'good', either on the radio or in the glossy pages of new lifestyle magazines. The French homeowner was held captive in her own domestic interior, trapped by the reflective surfaces of the fridges and washing machines that surrounded her. As such, privatisation not only transformed space into a product in its own right (the fantasy of home ownership took hold in France in the 1950s and 1960s); it was able to exploit the domestic as a stage to sell other products.[7] As a result of privatisation, the existential doubts experienced by the French masses during the managed modernisation of the country were calmed. On the one hand, they were seduced by the fulfilment promised by the commodity; and, on the other hand, they were buoyed by a new myth of technocratic and aspirational Frenchness which was, in essence, nothing but spectacle and simulation.

Lefebvre's dialectically complex reading of modernisation provides the specific context that is missing in Goldmann's interpretation of *The Balcony*. It allows us to see how Genet's deconstruction of the 'theatre house' is not simply an attack on capitalism in general, but a concerted attempt to draw attention to, and subvert, its new spectacular forms. Where the managers of the spectacle sought to supply fulfilment, Genet, by contrast, aimed to blast the spectators with uncanniness. Yet Genet was under no illusions about the task at hand. He realised that the spectacle, like the brothel in *The Balcony*, was resistant to simplistic notions of aesthetic critique. Accordingly, alternative strategies were required to prevent the utopian hopefulness of the artwork, its *promesse du bonheur*, from being consumed as just another cultural product.

The function of allegory

In 'The Avertissement' to the 1960 edition of *The Balcony*, Genet contends that while political art should make every 'effort to show the concrete reality of a social order' (1991: xiv), it ought to avoid imitating the

---

7 See Kristin Ross, *Fast Cars, Clean Bodies: Decolonization and the Reordering of French Culture* (Cambridge, MA MIT Press, 1995), pp. 213–14.

world it represents. Naturalistic notions of mimesis, according to Genet, compromise the political charge of the work by encouraging the spectator to identify with the action or *ethos* of the play, which, he contends, disperses and corrodes the historical truth of the situation at hand. In an argument which resonates with Freud's psycho-economic interpretation of tragedy as a form of imaginary 'compensation' or surplus expenditure (spending without cost) (Freud, 1990a: 123), Genet claims that to have seen an action represented on stage is to have committed it. Theatre's grounding in simulation, in other words, removes the need for praxis: '[w]hen the problem of a certain disorder – or evil – has been solved on stage, this shows in fact that it has been abolished' (Genet: 1991: xiv).

Although Genet's short text neglects to explain his prejudice against reflective mimesis in any *detailed* philosophical sense, it is evidently bound up with a rejection of Aristotelian poetics. Differently from Plato who distrusted theatre because of its potential for epistemic anarchy, Aristotle conceived of theatre as a method of instruction, a form of pedagogy through play:

> The instinct for imitation is inherent in man from his earliest days: he differs from other animals in that he is the most imitative of creatures, and he learns his earliest lessons by imitation. Also inborn in all of us is the instinct to enjoy works of imitation. What happens in actual experience is evidence of this; for we enjoy looking at the most accurate representations of things which in themselves we find painful to see, such as the lowest forms of animals and of corpses. (1967: 35)

Aristotle's pedagogic theory of aesthetics is based on a double idea, which ultimately deconstructs the conservative notion of mimesis that he purports to advance.[8] By proposing that we learn by imitating Others, and that art allows the spectator to confront (and reject) experiences that she would normally find unbearable, Aristotle is able to posit art as a form of production, a method for purging antisocial energies and impulses. In *The Poetics*, Aristotle suggests that we experience catharsis in tragedy because we recognise the artifice involved in theatre. The recognition of illusion is what encourages us to drop our defences and to invest, imaginatively, in the events of the on-stage world. Imagining, for Aristotle, is the very opposite of doing: play prevents praxis. In this respect, catharsis is dependent upon a delicate balancing act. We must

---

8 Two detailed accounts of the paradox involved in Aristotle's account of mimesis can be found in Philip Lacoue-Labarthe, *Typography: Mimesis, Politics, Philosophy* (Stanford: Stanford University Press, 1998); and Adrian Kear, 'Troublesome Amateurs: Theatre, Ethics and the Labour of Mimesis', *Performance Research*, 10:1 (2005), 26–44.

believe *and* not believe in what we are seeing at the same time. This clarifies the importance that Aristotle places on likeness or adequate representation: '[t]o have the habit of feeling pleasure (or pain) in things that are like to reality is very near to having the same disposition towards reality' (1969: 309).

The above line merits further reflection, for it suggests that mimesis, in Aristotle's thinking, does not, as it seemingly purports to do, reflect a timeless or substantial truth that exists beyond the walls of the auditorium. Rather, mimesis manufactures 'truth'. Perversely, then, Aristotelian theatre can be regarded as an early example of spectacularisation. We learn about the world not by imitating real acts, but by identifying with actors simulating false ones. As such, knowledge, in Aristotle's theatre, is the product of a spectacle that both draws attention to, and conceals its own investment in, illusion.

If theatre is to change the status quo, it would appear, as Genet suggests in the 'Avertissement', that mimesis must be avoided. Instead of representing a world *like* the one we take for real, the point is to fashion a form of representation that is deliberately theatricalised and estranging. For once the notion of likeness is rejected, the connection established by Aristotle between representation, catharsis and knowledge is severed. What remains in its place is the authentically unreal, a spectacle that highlights its own spectacularity.

In *The Balcony*, Genet departs from the Aristotelian schema that he implicitly rails against in the 'Avertissement' by investing in allegory. In keeping with allegory's ability to say 'X' but mean 'Y', Genet constructs a performance which speaks otherwise, a theatre in which sign and referent are no longer identical. (Etymologically, allegory derives from the Greeks *allos* (other) and *goria* (speaking).) This technique, of course, jams the Aristotelian circuit. The performance no longer purports to reflect reality; rather, it highlights its own theatricality by insisting on its necessary dependence upon a pre-existing text. *The Balcony* is a play that compels spectators to read it, to engage in a process of interpretation. By doing so, Genet discloses what Aristotelian theatre, like the society of the spectacle, always wants to hide: that reality is a product of signs, not a thing in itself.[9]

In order to understand the complexity of Genet's allegorical vision in *The Balcony*, it is important to start at the beginning and to read naïvely. Shorn of its troubling formal ambiguity, and read as a dramatic fiction, *The Balcony* is a play that narrates the shattering defeat of a

---

9 For an excellent explanation of how allegorical fragments belong simultaneously to (at least) two different contexts, see Erika Fischer-Lichte, *The Show and the Gaze of Theatre: A European Perspective*, trans. Jo Riley (Iowa City: University of Iowa Press, 1997), pp. 275–89.

populist revolution by the repressive forces of the status quo. In keeping with allegory's taste for the fantastic, the fate of the revolution is sealed in 'Le Grand Balcon', a high-class bordello, managed by Madame Irma, the lover of George, the Chief of Police. The defining period of the play, politically speaking, occurs between Scenes Eight and Eleven, when the Court Envoy, an *escapé* from the Royal Place (which, we are told, has been blown up by the rebels), exhorts Irma to put her studios and costumes in the service of the existing regime. Anxious to protect her 'studios' and careful to 'save her skin', Irma agrees to dress up as the dead Queen and to appear, with three of her 'clients' playing the roles of Bishop, Judge and General, on the balcony of the brothel. Opposed by these prestigious images, Chantal, the former prostitute and now the voice of the revolution, is defeated on the balcony when a beggar calls out 'Long Live the Queen!' (1991: 74). Immediately afterwards Chantal is shot from a bullet that allegedly comes from somewhere offstage. Her image is swiftly appropriated by the Church, and the 'Bishop' cynically transforms her into a saint: 'I had the presence of mind to turn her into one of our saints . . . I had her image emblazoned on our flag' (ibid.: 77).

Chantal's murder does more than mark the defeat of revolutionary hope; it establishes a more repressive, totalitarian regime. On learning of her death, Roger, her lover, enters the brothel in a last desperate attempt to save the revolution by dressing up as the Chief of Police and mutilating his rival. The great irony or tragi-comedy of *The Balcony* stems from the fact that Roger is unable to read allegorically: he confuses signifier and signified, spectacle and reality. Instead of castrating the Chief of Police, Roger ends by castrating himself, and exits the play dripping 'blood', or so it seems, on Irma's expensive carpets. The Chief of Police, on the other hand, experiences a very different trajectory. Roger's identification confers his image with a physical reality that until that moment it had lacked. At the end of the play, he descends to his 'tomb' secure in the knowledge that he has transcended the flesh and become a simulacrum: 'I've arrived! My image! I belong to the nomenclature. I've got my simulacrum. Goal!' (ibid.: 94).

Interpreted thematically, *The Balcony* would appear to illustrate Goldmann's thesis that the play is an allegory about ideology, a work that allows us to understand how corporate capital, by unleashing the forces of Fascism in the 1920s, managed to maintain its hegemony in a period of economic and social crisis. The problem here is that any attempt to offer an allegorical reading of *The Balcony*, as Goldmann does, by concentrating on the dramatic axis alone is immediately undercut by the play's denouement (or rather its *renouement*).

At the very end of the play, Irma clears the stage of the dramatis personae, turns off the house lights, and tells the actual audience that it needs to go home so that she can prepare her salons for a new performance, which will presumably repeat the same scenarios it has just witnessed. Despite the delicious confusion caused by the burst of gunfire that follows her speech, the connotation is that the brothel, like Genet's play itself, stages history as simulacrum. This complicates, necessarily, the play's allegorical meaning. It suggests that *The Balcony* is not simply a historical allegory as such, but an allegory about allegory, a play that warns us of the dangers that we run when we confuse the signifier, as Roger does, with the signified.

This loss of what the literary critic Theresa M. Kelly calls the 'secure transcendental referent' of conventional allegory establishes an important connection between Genet's signifying practice in *The Balcony* and the modernist concept of allegory advanced by Walter Benjamin in his book *The Origin of Tragic Drama* (Kelly, 1997: 9).[10] For Benjamin, the contemporary impulse to allegory in modernist work has its origin in the *Trauerspiel*, or play of mourning that emerged in Germany from the political and theological debris of the Reformation and Counter-Reformation in the sixteenth and seventeenth centuries. Unlike tragic theatre which, Benjamin proposes, is committed to the expression of interiority in the mythical instant (the idea that the suffering of a dramatic character called King Lear is somehow eternally valid), the allegorical play shifts its attention to the exterior world of natural history, a saturnine landscape of petrified objects that God has forsaken:

> Thus, one might say, nature remained the great teacher for the writers of this period. However nature was not seen by them in bud and bloom, but in the over ripeness and decay of her creations. In nature they saw eternal transience, and here alone did the saturnine vision of this generation recognize history [. . .] In the process of decay, and in it alone, the events of history shrivel up and become absorbed in the setting. (2003: 179)

10 There is a good argument for considering *The Balcony* as a baroque allegory in itself on account of its metatheatricality; use of language; episodic structure; and obsession with death. And it is not surprising, in this respect, that critics have often been tempted to compare the play to Pedro Calderón's *Life is a Dream*. The difficulty here, though, is that Genet's metatheatricality has little in common with Calderón's investment in *theatrum mundi*. Where Calderón's theatricality is intended to reveal the presence of God, Genet's reveals nothingness. See Lionel Abel, *Metatheatre: A View of Dramatic Form* (New York: Hill & Wang, 1963); and Albert Bermel, 'The Society as Brothel: Genet's Satire in *The Balcony*', *Modern Drama*, 19:3 (1976), 146–55. For an excellent discussion of the role of the baroque in Genet's novels, see Nathalie Fredette, *Figures baroques de Jean Genet* (XYZ: Montreal, 2001). In a related context, two readings that distinguish between Genet's use of metatheatre and Pirandello's are Edith Melcher, 'The Pirandellism of Jean Genet', *French Review* 36:1 (1962), 32–6; and Bernard Dort, 'Genet et Pirandello ou d'un théâtre de la représentation', *Lendemains*, 19 (1980), 73–83.

According to Benjamin's melancholic account, allegory's signifying economy is fragmentary and emblematic; it appropriates figures and images from other texts, and stitches them together in new ad hoc constellations: 'the profound vision of allegory transforms things and works into stirring writing' (ibid.: 176). In this way, baroque allegories, argues Benjamin, cannot be decoded according to a single (often) moral key that holds the meaning of the work in place. Rather, they represent history as a catalogue of failure and error whose tragic course can only be redeemed by a messianic 'miracle' that pieces together the shattered fragments and ruins of stereotypical archetypes into a reconstituted and redemptive whole:

> That which lies here in ruins, the highly significant fragment, the remnant, is, in fact, the finest material in baroque creation. For it is common practice in the literature of the baroque to pile up fragments ceaselessly, without any strict idea of a goal, and in the unremitting expectation of a miracle, to take the repetition of stereotypes for a process of intensification. (ibid.: 178)

Benjamin's ideas help us to understand the allegorical economy of *The Balcony*. Like the *Trauerspiel*, *The Balcony* is a play that deals in historical wreckage and revolutionary ruin. Distinct historical referents in the play are certainly recognisable, but it is impossible to establish a single time period or consistent locale for them. We are in the realm of fragmentation and catastrophe. History, here, is suspended, caught in the hellish time of endless repetition. The crucifix that hangs in the brothel, along with the names of the characters and the architectural kitsch of the Chief of Police's monument, bring to mind the Spanish Civil War and Franco's Valle de los Caídos;[11] Chantal's raucous singing recalls the *pétroleuses* who raged during the Paris Commune; the tragic fate of Chantal and Roger is reminiscent of the murders of Rosa Luxemburg and Karl Liebknecht during the Spartacist Revolution in Germany in 1919; the explosion of the Royal Palace resonates with the events that followed the French Revolution of 1789; and the Chief of Police's arrival in power, after successfully defeating a socialist revolution, is entirely in keeping with a Marxist reading of Fascism and Nazism in Italy and Germany between the wars.

Importantly, though, the historical pessimism of *The Balcony* – what Genet refers to as 'evil' in the 'Avertissement' – is not relegated

---

11 The Chief of Police's tomb is a direct reference to Franco's *Valle de los Caídos* (Valley of the Fallen), a monument built by Republican prisoners in the mountains to the north of Madrid to honour the Nationalists who died during the Civil War. The original title for the play was *España*.

to the past. As Richard Schechner's environmental production of the play highlighted in New York in 1979–80, history in *The Balcony* is not dramatic history, history we can believe in. It is history, replayed and re-encoded for immediate consumption by the audience.[12] In Schechner's production, the revolution was literally reduced to sound effects, as Irma played by the late Ron Vawter, was able to evoke it by simply spinning a record on a turntable.

The spectator who goes to *The Balcony* hoping to see a conventional historical play is mistaken. And it is no coincidence in this respect that all of the action, with the exception of Scene 6 in the 1960 version, takes place in what the French critic Michèle Piemme calls 'scenic space', the space that 'one sees on stage'. By problematising the reality of 'dramaturgic space', the space of fiction and hearsay, Genet disturbs the solidity of the theatrical frame (1979: 156). He makes us doubt the ontological and epistemological status of the action. We are never quite sure if what we are seeing is true, or simply an elaborate fantasy for a client whose identity remains ambiguous until the closing moments. In this way, Genet (and he does this to even greater effect in *The Blacks*) allows the audience to know that what is being represented is all artifice, a mere game. He shows that history is inherently performative, something that is always being constructed in the present.

One of the peculiar effects of Genet's theatricalisation of allegory in *The Balcony* is to delimit the play's signifying potential. In contrast, say, to Beckett's 1957 work *Endgame*, the allegorical structure of *The Balcony* prevents us from engaging in a plethora of different interpretations. We always know, more or less, that it is an allegory about history, politics and representation. This is underscored by Genet's comments in the 'Avertissement' when he talks about wanting to portray, accurately, 'the concrete reality of a social order', while at same time making that representation non-consumable. Here Genet establishes an important clash between what the play *says* thematically and what it *does* formally. Self-negating art like this immediately raises historical questions; it prompts us to think about the larger factors that caused him to invest in such a suspicious mode of performance. To understand Genet's signifying tactics in *The Balcony*, a double move is required. We need to read the dramatic content of the play allegorically, and then to juxtapose that reading with what the work is doing formally. In this way, we can better

---

12 This version is the very opposite of Giorgio Strehler's interpretation of the play. When Strehler staged the play at the Piccolo Theatre in Milan in 1976 he attempted to highlight the play's historical actuality by stressing its affinities with Italian Fascism and contemporary military regimes in Chile and Greece. See *Un théâtre pour la vie* (Paris: Fayard, 1980), p. 343.

grasp the play's relationship to, and subversion of, the new spatial practices that paved the way for the expansion of the society of the spectacle into all corners of French life in the 1950s. In keeping with what I mentioned in Chapter 3, this approach necessitates an attentiveness towards the work's deliberate cultivation of internal contradiction and paradox. As Genet's prefaces and letters argue, the aim of political art is to question reality and to disturb the spectator's sense of being in the world. Or, as Rancière puts it:

> The dream of a suitable political work is in fact the dream of disrupting the relationship between the visible, the sayable and the thinkable without having the term of a message as a vehicle. It is the dream of an art that would transmit meanings in the form of a rupture with the very logic of meaningful situations. [...] Suitable political art would ensure, at one and the same time, the production of a double effect: the readability of a political signification and a sensible or perceptual shock caused, conversely, by the uncanny, by that which resists signification. In fact, this ideal effect is always the object of a negotiation between opposites, between the readability of the message that threatens to destroy the sensible form of art and the radical uncanniness that threatens to destroy all political meaning. (2006: 63)

Allegorising the spectacle

In *Society of the Spectacle*, written roughly a decade after the first version of *The Balcony*, Guy Debord borrowed and updated Georg Lukács' theory of reification to show how life in mediatised, consumerist France of 1967 had lost its reality: '[i]n societies where modern conditions of production prevail, all of life presents itself as an immense accumulation of spectacles. Everything that was directly lived has moved away into a representation' (1983: 1).[13] For Debord, the spectacle is not limited to individuals voyeuristically consuming images on a screen; it is grounded in how they experience daily life: '[t]he spectacle is not a collection of images, but a social relation among people, mediated by images [...] It is a world vision which has become objectified' (*ibid.*: 4–5).

In accordance with his dependence on Marx's theory of the commodity, Debord is quick to root the spectacle in economics. As he sees it, the spectacle is born from a developed mode of capitalist production,

---

13 The references to Debord are not to page numbers but to the maxims he offers. There are no page numbers in the 1983 translation of the text.

in which exchange value triumphs over use value. The act of consuming an image, argues Debord, robs the individual of her active participation in the world and transforms her into a spectator:

> [T]he more he contemplates the less he lives; the more he accepts recognizing himself in the dominant images of need, the less he understands his own existence and his own desires. The externality of the spectacle in relation to the active man appears in the fact that his own gestures are no longer his but those of another who represents them to him. (*ibid.*: 30)

According to Debord, the spectacle renders party politics superfluous. In his view, 'the spectacle aims at nothing other than itself' (*ibid.*: 14), which is why, he claims, it has no ideological agenda: '[j]ust as it presents pseudo-goods to be coveted, if offers false models of revolution to local revolutionaries' (*ibid.*: 57). As long as the spectacle is supported by the existing regime, it matters little whether that regime is Marxist, Liberal or Fascist. What the spectacle really aims at is a total occupation of the social, in which the spatial and temporal coordinates of everyday life are rendered homogeneous: '[t]he spectator feels at home nowhere, because the spectacle is everywhere' (*ibid.*: 30).

In Genet's play, the brothel, fittingly defined as a 'house of illusions', simultaneously reflects and produces falsification (1991: 28). In Irma's studios, clients identify with pre-existing social types and ideological images, all of which are based, conspicuously, on relationships of domination. In doing so, they provide those images with a living reality or substance:

BISHOP: To become a bishop, to rise in the hierarchy – whether by virtue or vice – would have meant my becoming further and further removed from the ultimate dignity of being a bishop. (*ibid.*: 5)

As well as being a place where fetishistic activities are staged, the brothel is a fetishistic site in and by itself. Its devotion to Aristotelian notions of mimesis, in reflecting, that is, a supposedly timeless social reality, conceals the fact that social relations are historically produced.

The threat (real or not) posed by the revolution affects a crucial shift in the destiny of the clients and reveals a new *modus operandi* for the brothel. With the arrival of the Envoy, who exists as a kind of emissary for the spectacle, Le Grand Balcon is called upon to be more active in its production of the unreal, and the clients are ordered to play their roles in public. Intriguingly, after they have defeated Chantal on the balcony, the clients want to assume power, to carry out actual tasks:

BISHOP: It's within our power to change the meaning of this masquerade. (*Authoritatively*) I am already the symbolic head of the Church in this country, and I intend to become its actual head. Instead of blessing and blessing and blessing *ad nauseum*, I'm going to sign decrees, appoint priests, and build a basilica. (*ibid.*: 79)

At first glance, the clients' new taste for action over contemplation appears to contradict the logic of the spectacle. Unwittingly, they seem to have stumbled upon a mode of praxis through its opposite: the simulacrum looks as if it might lead to the real. Yet despite the potential for subversion implied in this process of what a Derridean would refer to as iterability (difference through repetition), the clients have no desire to change the world; they are merely performing a predetermined social script, in which everything has been worked out in advance.[14] Their desire to act in the real then is a contradiction in terms: it simply affirms what is already in existence. Depressingly, all it does is to complete the tautological rationale of the spectacle, the sense in which it is 'the existing order's uninterrupted discourse about itself, its laudatory monologue' (Debord, 1983: 24).[15]

This is not to say, however, that *The Balcony* merely reflects the social; it can produce new images of domination, too. The generative power of the brothel is most evident in the destiny of the Chief of Police. Like the clients, the Chief of Police desires to be an image. But, where the clients can base their identifications on pre-existing models – '[w]e've been waiting two thousand years to perfect our roles' (1991: 79; original italics) – he has the more arduous task of bringing a new prototype into existence: '[i]t's harder for me. I have to try and bring into being a new type, a new illustration. But oh, the trials and tribulations' (*ibid.*: 84). For all his buffoonery, the Chief of Police is aware that the brothel is the sole place where he can undergo a reverse process of transubstantiation and so penetrate the collective consciousness as a disembodied simulacrum. Note his delight, for example, when Roger enters the brothel, dresses

---

14 Clare Finburgh uses Derrida's notion of iteration to propose an alternative way of negating the brothel. For Finburgh, to perform a role is to change that role in so far as repetition always produces difference. See 'Speech Without Acts: Politics and Speech Act Theory in Genet's *The Balcony*'; Hanrahan, *Genet*, 113–29: 120–6.
15 Genet's critique of the Symbolic Order distances my view of the play from Jacques Lacan's conservative reading. According to Lacan, *The Balcony* demonstrates the need for the Symbolic, without which desire itself is threatened. On the contrary, I would suggest that desire is trapped in the Symbolic. To free desire, the Symbolic needs to be suspended and overthrown in the name of the new. Where Lacan sees the real as inherently traumatic for subjectivity, I contend that the encounter with nothingness is what allows us to find a different form of commonality. See Lacan, 'Sur *Le balcon* de Genet', *Magazine Littéraire*, 313 (September 1993), 51–7.

up as the Chief of Police, and demands to play the role of the Hero: '[d]id you see me? Did you see me? There? Just now? Larger than large, stronger than strong, deader than dead?' (*ibid.*: 94). At this moment, the Chief of Police's ascent to power is complete; he is both image and reality, the new star of the spectacle.

The Chief of Police's relationship with Irma is central to the allegorical significance of the play. Although the brothel works to produce a totalitarian order based on discipline and repression, it is ultimately Irma who controls the mechanisms of representation. Irma has little interest in the kind of image that she disseminates; her primary motivation is to falsify reality and, by doing so, to intensify the erotic need for spectacle, '[t]he more killing there is in the suburbs, the more men I get in my studios [. . .] They're attracted by my unchanging mirrors and chandeliers' (*ibid.*: 33).

Irma's role as a kind of Mata Hari of capital is established from the outset. One of her first lines is to demand 'twenty quid' from the client playing the Bishop (*ibid.*: 2); and throughout the play she is obsessed with her accounts and safeguarding her assets: 'I've got to protect my jewellery, my studios and my girls' (*ibid.*: 36). Just as importantly, Irma is concerned to police the scenarios played out in her salons, which she does through a system of strategically placed surveillance cameras:

> IRMA: No, I don't like the way they're looking at each other – it's much too clear-eyed. You see the dangers of being over-conscientious. It'd be a catastrophe if my clients started exchanging friendly smiles with the girls. It'd be an even greater catastrophe than if they fell in love with one another. (*ibid.*: 27)

Mirroring the historical process whereby the spectacle manufactured a false image of consensus in post-war France by dissolving the tensions and contradictions of social life, Irma strives to distance her clients from her 'girls' in order to establish an economy based on individualism and privatisation. Friendliness is perceived by Irma to be catastrophic because of the way it replaces separation with intimacy and monologue with dialogue. Relational acts like these threaten the value system of the brothel, since they treat people as ends, and not as mere commodities. Irma knows that the brothel feeds off alienation and counterfeit needs. In her conversation with Carmen in Scene Five, she explains that the brothel supplies a sense of enjoyment which everyday life is unable to compete with:

> CARMEN: When they're with their wives – do they still carry with them [. . .] the joys they find in the brothel. . .?

[. . .] IRMA: Possibly. They must do, I suppose. Yes. Like a fairy light left over from last year's carnival waiting for the next – or perhaps, like an imperceptible glimmer at the imperceptible window of an imperceptible castle which they can turn into a blaze of light at the flick of a switch whenever they want to go there, to rest. (*ibid.*: 28)

What Irma judiciously neglects to say here is that the satisfaction offered by the brothel is pure simulation. The prostitutes, like the ultimate commodities they are, belong to the realm of the dead. They have been reified to such an extent that all life, as the Chief of Police realises, has being drained out of them: '[o]ut there the revolution's tragic and joyous – not like this house where everybody's dying by inches' (*ibid.*: 40).

The brothel's ability to combine economics and politics in a condensed power-base anticipates, all too clearly, Debord's thinking in his 1967 text. For Debord, the society of the spectacle comes into being when 'the commodity has attained the *total occupation* of social life' (1983: 42; original italics). When this process is complete, history is stopped, and the only thing that remains is the endless circulation of the same old images and scenarios: '[b]ecause history itself haunts modern society like a spectre, pseudo-histories are constructed at every level of consumption of life in order to preserve the threatened equilibrium of present *frozen time*' (*ibid.*: 200; original italics).

Debord's analysis explains why the walls of Irma's salons are lined with mirrors. Like the contemporary French consumer mesmerised by the shininess of domestic appliances that I referred to earlier, her clients have abandoned all hope of making history, preferring rather to watch themselves perform fake acts in isolated rooms that are hermetically sealed off from the revolution occurring beyond its soundproofed walls. In common with the prostitutes who work in the brothel, the clients have lost their taste for the new. In the bordello, the negativity that, for Hegel, produces history has been suspended: '[t]here's no possibility of doing evil here. Because you live in evil' (1991: 4).

The Balcony's allegorical critique of spectacle poses difficult questions about the possibility of revolutionary action, both in terms of political praxis and aesthetics. Traditional economic readings of Marxism, grounded as they are in crisis and shortage, are unable to deal with the insidious workings of spectacle. Like Roger, Marxists who cling to nineteenth-century ideas of political economy are restricted by a blind commitment to materialism, trusting only what they can see. This leaves them vulnerable to the spectacle's capacity for manipulating reality. They are powerless to understand why a spectacular society is immune to real acts and authentic truth, even when that society is on the verge of a revolutionary seizure of power, as it is in *The Balcony*. So while Roger comprehends that political struggle is 'a Combat of Allegories' (*ibid.*: 72), he fails to understand how the status quo can be subverted. His metaphysical attachment to truth rather than representation means that instead of castrating the Chief of Police, he merely castrates himself. Echoing all too closely the historical problems faced by western Marxism in the 1950s and 1960s, Roger is unable to grasp that mimesis does not reflect truth: it produces it.

The same criticism applies to Chantal, albeit for different reasons. In the passage below, she believes that she can subvert the spectacle by competing on its own terrain:

CHANTAL: [. . .] [I]'m different. The brothel has taught me the art of acting many roles. I've played so many parts, I know them all [. . .] And such clever, such crafty, such eloquent ones, that my knowledge, my craft are incomparable. I can talk on equal terms with the Queen, the Hero, the Bishop, the Judge, the General, the Heroic Troops. . . and fool them all. (*ibid.*: 73)

Chantal's faith in the productive power of the image does little to disturb the signifying economy of the spectacle. Her willingness to present (and fix) herself as a positive image of revolution – 'Chantal's image is circulating in the streets' (*ibid.*: 66) – means that she invests in the same logic as the brothel. What Chantal is unable to see is that the positivity of her message, the fact that it is presented as a representation of reality, encourages the masses, in a postmodern variant on Aristotelian mimesis, to take the sign for the thing. Instead of acting in the real, the masses remain stuck in the imaginary. They identify with Chantal's image in the same way that they will later identify with the image of Queen, granting it a reality which it does not have. In this flawed version of revolutionary art, the society of the spectacle has neither been placed in question nor deconstructed. Tragically, it has been confirmed by the very presence of Chantal's image alone. By entering the bordello Chantal has tacitly acknowledged its power, and, in the process, allows her own message to be consumed as just another (bogus) meaning. The distribution of the sensible, in other words, remains immune from attack. As Debord cautions: '[t]he spectacle presents itself as something enormously positive, indisputable and inaccessible. It says nothing more than 'that which appears is a good, that which is good appears''' (1983: 12). The Chief of Police highlights the naïvety of Chantal's practice of aesthetic politics in his laconic reaction to the Revolution's decision to name its cells after constellations:

CHIEF OF POLICE: Andromeda? Bravo. The revolution is giving itself airs, it's getting above itself. If it calls its sectors after the constellations, it'll soon evaporate and be metamorphosed into song. Let's hope they're nice songs.
IRMA: Suppose their songs give the revolutionaries courage? Suppose they're prepared to die for them?
CHIEF OF POLICE: The sweetness of their songs will make them go soft. Unfortunately, they haven't got to the point of softness or sweetness yet. (1991: 48)

Chantal's fate highlights, in reverse, the extent to which *The Balcony* provides its own answers to the questions posed in the 'Avertissement'. Genet realises that if political art is to serve any purpose, it needs to distance itself from reality and negate any positive meaning it might want to offer. Allegory allows him to do this by separating the signifier from the signified and by highlighting the plasticity of the sign. In the process, the spectator is prevented from identifying with the work positively; she always realises that there is a gap between the image and object. Two things happen here. First, theatre becomes a machine for unmaking reality rather than reflecting it; and second, the spectator is encouraged to read the on-stage signs as opposed to identifying with them. The 'coldness' or mechanical nature of this procedure produces, in turn, two very different experiences of allegorical negativity, one of which is dialectical, the other deconstructive.

Viewed dialectically, *The Balcony*'s refusal of mimesis has clear parallels with Adorno's version of negative aesthetics (see Chapter 3, pp. 97–9, in this book). The play's commitment to theatricality allows it to disclose the horrors of the age obliquely, through that which it is not. So while the audience in *The Balcony* can certainly recognise the work as a critique of spectacle, it is unable to consume the performance as real. It realises, at all times, that what it is experiencing is plastic, a matter of convention. Consequently, the homogeneity which the spectacle manufactures implodes. The world appears other than what it allegedly is.

In Adorno's terms, Genet's refusal to supply the audience with naturalistic images of reconciliation opens up a different, non-conceptual form of knowledge. '[T]he primacy of the aesthetic object as pure refiguration does not smuggle consumption, and thus false harmony, in again through the back door [. . .] [T]he principle that governs autonomous works of art is not the totality of their effects. They are knowledge as non-conceptual objects' (2007: 193). As Adorno intimates, *The Balcony*'s negativity is where its revolutionary charge resides. By challenging existing models of spectacular knowledge, it keeps the emancipatory promise of the aesthetic alive. To cite Adorno, *The Balcony*'s self-confessed commitment to evil, 'points to a practice from which [it] abstains: the creation of a just life' (*ibid*.: 194).

If the dialectical moment in allegory posits negativity as *une promesse du bonheur*, the deconstructionist moment sees it in terms of pure *différance*. For the deconstructionist – and I am thinking in particular of Paul de Man's work – allegory transforms the world into writing; it shows that reality is nothing but a play of signs which, by implication, prevents any recourse to metaphysical truth.[16] While this reading of allegory obviously departs from Adorno's notion of negative aesthetics as the guardian of 'truth content', it also destabilises the Aristotelianism upon which the spectacle depends.[17] For where the spectacle attempts to conceal its investment in artifice, deconstructionist philosophy reveals the world to be nothing but a mass of endlessly postponed signifiers. From a deconstructionist perspective, meaning in *The Balcony* cannot be stabilised. There is no position outside the text from which to read it. This changes the political focus of the play. Henceforth there is no need to stop the endless proliferation of signs by tying the play down to a specific critique of spectacularity. The more effective move is to show how the political meaning of *The Balcony* resides in its resistance to all signification, in its consumption of what Maria Shevtsova has called 'empty signs' (1987: 42).[18]

Ultimately, however, there is no obligation in *The Balcony* to separate these two forms of allegorical negation.[19] Irma's accusation at the end of the play brings them together in a productive unity. In the final speech of the work, Irma addresses the audience directly and says: 'You

16 Explaining his rationale, de Man says that: '*Allegories of Reading* started out as a historical study and ended up as a theory of reading. I began to read Rousseau seriously in preparation for a historical reflection on Romanticism and found myself unable to progress beyond local difficulties of interpretation. In trying to cope with this, I had to shift from historical definition to the problematic of readings' (*Allegories of Reading: Figural Language in Rousseau, Nietzsche and Proust* (New Haven, MA: Yale University Press, 1979), p. ix).
17 While I am fully aware that my reading of *The Balcony* ties the play down to a specific meaning which, in de Man's view, would limit its potential for proliferation, to invest in the sense of infinite postponement inherent in his theory of allegory is to run the grave risk – a risk I was not willing to take – of avoiding history altogether.
18 Shevtsova offers a convincing reading of the allegorical doubleness that characterises *The Balcony*. Although I share her opinion that the play is politically 'devastating' in its attack on contemporary capitalist society, I do not consider it to be without utopian possibilities founded in the negation of the current distribution of the sensible. See 'The Consumption of Empty Signs: Jean Genet's *The Balcony*', *Modern Drama*, 30:1 (1987), 35–45: 42.
19 For an excellent discussion of allegory's capacity to combine deconstruction with dialectics, see Gail Day, 'Between Deconstruction and Dialectics', *Oxford Art Journal*, 22:1 (1999), 105–16.

must go home, now – and you can be quite sure that nothing there will be any more real than it is here. You must go. . .You go out on the right, down the alleyway. . .It's morning. . . (*Puts out the last light.*)' (1991: 96). Irma's comments are akin to 'the miracle' that, for Benjamin, ends the *Trauerspiel* (2003: 234). They explode both history and theatre as sources of transcendent knowledge by transforming them into a shower of signs. In this moment of pure dissemination, Genet wounds the audience. Instead of assuaging anxieties about the loss of the real he intensifies them. Contrary to de Man who is content to let this textual unravelling unfold *ad infinitum*, Genet, as we know from the 'Avertissement,' sees the negative as the matrix of the new. Just as the 'second part of the wide arc' of the *Trauerspiel*, according to Benjamin, returns 'to redeem' the world through its negation of the real (*ibid.*: 232), Genet's dissolution of the social in *The Balcony* is an attempt to force a disidentification with rigid notions of self in the hope of reconstructing a different body politic. To use the language of the 'Avertissement', this is the 'good' that comes from a theatre of 'evil'.

Irma's comments at the end of *The Balcony* illustrate, in microcosm, how form works against content in Genet's play. The self-conscious theatricality of her address to the audience – her reminder that this is all just a performance – throws the allegorical meaning it had initially seemed to offer into doubt. *The Balcony* is a work that disavows itself. Yet, such a disavowal does not put an end to the play's allegorical aspects – it merely displaces and complicates them. Read theatrically as opposed to dramatically, *The Balcony* is best defined as an allegory about the work of art in an age of spectacle. It is a play that attempts to evade appropriation by the dominant order, while, at the same, taking a stand against that order. In *The Balcony*, Genet carries out this double agenda by writing a play about spectacle, and then, in the next move, putting the meaning of the work *sous rature*. In this self-cancellation, theatre is no longer simply a tool for speaking about the world; it becomes a mechanism for negating it.[20] Below, I intend to analyse how the play's commitment to negation allows it to function as a political performative in its own right.[21]

20 This reverse reading of Althusser's notion of interpellation is significantly different from David H. Walker's excellent account of the play, 'Revolution and Revisions in Genet's *Le balcon*', *Modern Language Review*, 79:4 (1984), 817–30. According to Walker, the revolution fails because the appearance of the Queen on the balcony acts as a moment of ideological hailing, which brings the masses back to reality. While Walker's interpretation is correct dramatically, like Goldmann's reading, it tells us little about how *The Balcony* functions theatrically. The move from text to performance discloses an alternative notion of interpellation, which, as I have suggested, is full of subversive potential.
21 This is a different approach to the play's politics. Most of the scholars who have written about theatricality in *The Balcony* have tended to concentrate on its deconstructionist potentiality, its ability to transform the stage into a galaxy of signs.

Against spectacular space

From the outset *The Balcony* is a play that raises suspicions about the 'truthfulness' of the representation on offer. In the opening scene, for instance, the audience, after listening to the dialogue between Irma and the client playing the Bishop, initially appears to understand what is at stake in the play, and to know where the dramatic action is located. The sound of gunfire coming from somewhere off-stage, along with the gestural quality of the language, alerts us to the fact that the fantasies of the brothel's clients are threatened by a revolution raging in the streets outside. Nevertheless, in the exchanges between Irma and the 'Bishop' incongruous shifts and different vocal intonations make the audience doubt the authenticity of the dramatic message:

BISHOP: (*After a heavy sigh*) They say that this place is going to be surrounded. The rebels have already crossed the river.

IRMA: (*Worried*) There's blood everywhere. . .I should keep to the wall past the Archbishop's palace, if I were you. And then go through the fish market.
(*A sudden scream of pain from a woman offstage*)
(*Irritated*) I told them to keep quiet. Thank God I had the window padded. (*Suddenly friendly and insidious*). And what did we manage this evening? A benediction? A prayer? A Mass? A perpetual adoration? (1991: 2)

As the stage directions intimate, Irma and the 'Bishop' are not unduly troubled by the revolution, at least not in any naturalistic sense. There is something unhinged about their reactions; the anxiety they purport to express seems manufactured. The theatricality of this exchange – the fact that it just might be a fake performance rather than a real one

See Una Chaudhuri, *No Man's Stage*; Laura Oswald, *Jean Genet and the Semiotics of Performance* (Indiana: Indiana University Press, 1989); and Marie Redonnet, *Jean Genet: le poète travesti* (Paris: Grasset & Fasquelle, 2000). Other critics such as Jeanette Savona, *Jean Genet* (London: Macmillan, 1983) have paid more attention to its Foucauldian dimension. However, they, too, have neglected to focus on affect. The largely post-structuralist-inspired readings mentioned in the 1960s and 1970s differ, radically, from the existentialist, absurdist and ritualistic readings made by critics like Martin Esslin, *Theatre of the Absurd*; Bettina Knapp, *Jean Genet*; Lewis T. Cetta, *Profane Play, Ritual and Jean Genet: A Study of His Drama* (Alabama: University of Alabama Press, 1974), Jerry Curtis, 'The World Is a Stage: Sartre Versus Genet', *Modern Drama*, 17:1 (1974), 33–41; and Robert Abirached, *La crise du personnage dans le théâtre moderne* (Paris: Grasset, 1978), pp. 419–20.

is compounded by the scream that follows Irma's line about the fish market. Although Irma is quick to fix the location of the scream, to tie it down dramatically, the audience is unable to determine if it comes from inside or outside the brothel. If it really is, in other words, the phony 'scream' of a whore or the authentic scream of an individual caught in the whirl of revolutionary praxis.

The ambivalence that surrounds the play is further demonstrated by Irma's conversation with the pimp Arthur, in which she tells him that he will play the role of a corpse in a special scenario later that night:

IRMA: [. . .] And don't be long. You've got a session this evening. Remember?
ARTHUR: (*who was on the way to the door*) This evening? Another one? What is it?
IRMA: I thought I'd told you: a corpse.
ARTHUR: Charming! What am I supposed to do with it?
IRMA: Nothing. You will stay still and get buried. You'll be able to have a rest.
ARTHUR: Ah, because I'm the. . .Great! And who's the customer? A new one?
IRMA: (*Mysteriously*) A VIP, and don't ask any more questions. Go! (*ibid.*: 37)

When Arthur dies from a stray bullet at the end of Scene Six, the audience remembers this conversation and is reluctant to accept his death as 'real': it simply appears as the histrionic conclusion to a theatrical scenario that has already been plotted out.

As one might expect from the discussion in Chapter 3, Genet's anti-theatrical strategy is very different from Brecht's. In Brechtian epic theatre, the *gestus* is designed to make theatrical communication as transparent as possible, to show what theatre hides. In *The Balcony*, by contrast, Genet seeks to evoke, as the directors Georges Lavaudant and Lluís Pasqual attempted to highlight in their productions in 1985 and 1991 respectively, a sense of doubt in the auditorium.[22] Nothing in the play is stable. No word or gesture can be completely pinned down or assigned a definitive meaning. In this way (and this is exactly what Víctor García grasped in his staging of *The Maids/Las criadas*) Genet disrupts the spectacle's need for certitude, for images that represent

---

22 For descriptions of these productions see Corvin and Dichy, *Jean Genet*, pp. 1154–6. Maria Delgado also offers an excellent account of Lluís Pasqual's productions of *The Balcony* at the Teatre Lliure in 1980 and the Odéon-Théâtre de l'Europe in Paris in 1991. See *'Other' Spanish Stages*, pp. 192–4.

'real' objects and thus give the illusion of truth.[23] Genet's attempt to destabilise the theatrical frame means that there is always a sense of the performance deconstructing itself. People and things are perpetually out of place, fleeing towards an invisible and unknowable elsewhere that is located beyond the panoptic eye of the spectator. In the play, everything seems to be as fake as the spectacle itself; the stage exists as scenery.

In the 1962 text 'How to Perform *The Balcony*', in which Genet criticises, openly, the productions of Zadek and Brook (as well as those of Hans Lietzau and José Quintero in Berlin and New York), he proposes that from Scene Four onwards the ambiguity, which has been in existence from the opening scene, ought to be deliberately intensified: 'the thing is to discover a narrative tone that is *always* equivocal, always shifting' (ibid.: xi). Because the play constantly shifts between dramatic and theatrical registers, the spectators should be unable, from this point on, to determine, with any certainty what the action represents and/or to whom it is addressed. Is it, for instance, intended for a 'real' chief of police; a client playing the Chief of Police, or, indeed, as Víctor García's celebrated environmental production in São Paulo in the early 1970s implied so brilliantly, the audience itself?[24] Irma's accusation at the end of play goes some way to resolving the ambiguity. By using exactly the same language to guide the audience out of the theatre as she uses to direct her clients out of the brothel ('You go out on the right, down the alleyway'), Irma completes the analogy between theatre-going and brothel-going that has been a constant allusion throughout the play.[25]

23 It is important to acknowledge the influence that García's production has had on subsequent stagings of Genet's work. García was the first director to theatricalise Genet and to mine the original dramaturgy for its Artaudian's elements. I would like to thank Maria Delgado for pointing this out.
24 Ilka Marinho Zanotto provides a useful documentary account of this production – see 'An Audience-Structure for *The Balcony*'.
25 At all times in the play much is made of the parallels existing between brothel-going and theatre-going. When she explains the function of the whorehouse to Carmen, for instance, Irma's thinking has more in common with a theatre director or performance theorist than with a brothel Madame: 'They all want everything to be as real as possible...Minus an indefinable something, so that it's not really real...It was I who decided to christen my establishment a House of Illusions, Carmen, but I'm only its director, and everyone, when he rings my bell, comes in with his own carefully worked out, ready-made script. All I have to do is rent the hall and provide props, actors and actresses' (1991, p. 30). If Irma's brothel is, to all extent and purposes, a drama studio, then her clients and staff are actors, constrained to perform on what Artaud would reject as a 'theological stage', a stage dominated by an author-God and condemned, in advance, to repetition. Irma's clients show little interest in improvising or in moving off script, demanding at all times to play their characters according to the same fetishistic logic that predominates in western theatre. Nothing is allowed to detract from the suspension of disbelief that procures their enjoyment and protects them from jumping into reality.

This alters, fundamentally, the political dynamic: it suggests that it is not the characters who are obsessed with voyeurism, but rather the actual audience. This transferral from dramatic text to theatrical space changes both the meaning and function of allegory, too. Allegory in *The Balcony* is not simply a network of signs that is unpacked at a safe distance; it engulfs the spectator physically, calling her to attention and engaging her in the heterotopic space of theatre itself. The point of this engulfment is to shift things, to undo the assignation that ties certain experiences to specific places, and which invariably works to discipline bodies. As Roland Barthes noted in a scathing review, this is exactly what Peter Brook's production at the Théâtre du Gymnase failed to do. Where Genet's politics are dependent upon 'disorientating' and unsettling the audience through the production of 'anxiety', Brook, claims Barthes, reduced the play to a melodrama, a play about 'Vice' (2002: 270–1; my translation).[26]

In the same way that minimalist sculptors in the 1960s such as Carl Andre and Robert Morris used stacks of bricks and white cubes to disclose the hidden ideology of the gallery, Irma's words are designed to force the audience to take stock of where it is. As the art critic Michael Fried proposed (albeit critically) in his famous 1967 essay 'Art and Objecthood', the theatricalisation caused by minimalist objects encourages the spectator to question not only the values that she attaches to a work, but everything that is 'perceived to be part of that situation' (1980: 221). The meaning of minimalist sculpture then transcends the confines or interiority of the artwork, and is located in the viewer's attempts to make sense of her experience in the here and now.[27] As a result, minimalism points beyond the timelessness of the work and engages the spectator in history – the very stuff which, as we know for Debord, the spectacle is concerned to reduce to stasis.[28]

---

26 In this context, it is interesting to note Joseph McMahon's account of the experience undergone by audiences in José Quintero's off-Broadway production of the play in 1960. He describes Irma's speech as having the effect of 'an icy hand' which 'reached[ed] into the audience to turn their complicity in being there at all either to guilt or... self-recognition'. (*The Imagination of Jean Genet* (New Haven, MA: Yale University Press, 1963), p. 176.)
27 This focus on exteriorisation explains why minimalism is regarded as a form of allegorical art. See Craig Owens, 'The Allegorical Impulse: Towards a Theory of Postmodernism' (published in two parts), *October*, 12 (1980), 67–86, and *October*, 13 (1980), 59–80; and Benjamin H. D. Buchloh, 'Allegorical Procedures: Appropriation and Montage in Contemporary Art', *Artforum*, 21:1 (1982), 43–56.
28 This distinguishes the theatricality of the minimalist work from the 'presentness and instantaneousness' that Fried associates, favourably, with modernist painting and sculpture ('Art and Objecthood', in M. Philipson and P. J. Gudel (eds), *Aesthetics Today*, revised edn (New York: New American Library, 1980), pp. 214–39: 233). Importantly, the notion of presentness which I am interested in developing is very

In *The Balcony*, this emphasis on history is geographically and temporally specific; it highlights what the society of the spectacle in France of the 1950s attempted to obfuscate: that society no longer exists. In opposition to the spectacle which sought to heal this wound by manufacturing images of national consensus and by encouraging a retreat into private space, *The Balcony* makes this 'lack' palpable in the public space of the auditorium. Irma's comments at the end of the play reveal the void at the heart of sensible experience: she shows that behind the surface spectacle, there is nothing but emptiness. In this respect, Irma's interpellation can be regarded as an attempt to re-realise experience, to develop what Hans-Thies Lehmann has called 'a politics of perception':

> The basic structure of perception mediated by media is such that there is no experience of a connection among the individual images received but above all no connection between the receiving and sending of signs; there is no experience of a relation between address and answer. Theatre can respond to this only with a *politics of perception*, which could at the same time be called an *aesthetic of responsibility (or response-ability)*. (2006: 185; original italics)

For Lehmann, the presentness of theatre has a greater ethico-political force than either television or cinema. This is because, Lehmann claims, theatre's thereness re-establishes the connection that the spectacle severs: the link between 'the receiving and sending of signs'. According to Lehmann, electronic and televisual media radically separate the processes of representation from the people and things being represented. This leads to a *décalage* between the image and the 'reception of the image', which, he argues, drains our capacity for sympathising with the Other. The spectator consumes the world as a televisual form as opposed to a living actuality. She feels no responsibility for its fate or for those in it.

In contradistinction to the bloodless anaesthetic of the spectacle, *The Balcony* re-establishes, through its insistence on live bodies, the lost link between affect and politics. When Irma accuses the audience of abandoning the revolution, the spectator is called to attention and made responsible for her presence at the performance. The gap between politics and perception, in other words, has been sutured. Importantly, though, this act of suturing does not result in an act of identification or empathy. On the contrary, it reveals the void by overwhelming the

different from Fried's modernist version. My notion of presentness, as I explain in the main text, has much in common with the loneliness and endlessness attributed by Fried to the minimalist object (*ibid.*: 231–2).

spectator with loss. Surrounded by other spectators, and confronted with a stage that speaks back, the individual audience member feels, as Genet mentions in the 'Avertissement', isolated and alone; her distance from the Other is made tangible, given actual shape. In this sudden rush of solitude, the theatre house is no longer a 'home' but a site of uncertainty and undoing.

The body of the performer is critical to this operation. After speaking her lines, Genet's script implies that the actress playing Irma, while remaining on stage, withdraws from the communal world of theatre into her own solitary space. Her conscious refusal to communicate, to make dramatic sense, negates the *raison d'être* of the conventional theatrical contract, which is based on the premise that the actor will share her labour with the audience and provoke a communion of sorts. In *The Balcony*, communion, if we can still call it that, works in reverse. The presentness of the actor's body, her simple being-there in space, discloses the wound in community that the spectacle attempts to hide. In the extent to which she embodies the wound, the actor functions in the same way as the abject old man whom Genet encountered in the train carriage. She is not there to allow the spectator to know the Other. Rather, her presence works to produce difference by making communion impossible. She exists to disclose the void.[29] Once again, Lehmann's reading of performance is useful here. According to Lehmann, there is an opaqueness about the live body, which theatre, more than any other art form, with the exception of sculpture, is best able to expose. Contrasting the opacity of theatre to the ethereality of the electronic image, Lehmann notes:

> The electronic image is an idol (not simply an icon). The body or face in video is enough – for itself and for us. By contrast an air of (productive) disappointment always surrounds the presence of real bodies. It is reminiscent of the air of mourning that, according to Hegel, surrounds the ancient Greek sculptures of gods; their all too complete and perfect presence allows for no transcendence of materiality to a more spiritual interiority. Similarly, one can say of the theatre: after the body there is nothing else. We have arrived. Nothing can be or become more present. Within any fascination with the live body there remains this invariably only desired 'rest' that we cannot get access to, a beyond the frame, a background. (*ibid.*: 171)

29 The audience was literally confronted with the void in Víctor García's environmental production of the play. The set was 'a gigantic, eighty-eight foot steel cone', which spiralled from the floor of the theatre to the roof (Zanotto, 'An Audience-Structure for *The Balcony*', p. 60). All of the action took place within the cone, and the actors moved through the structure on harnesses, which allowed them to hang in the air. The audience watched the action occurring, below and above them, from platforms that ringed the cone. As Zanotto describes it, the spectators felt a sense of 'physical dizziness' as they stared into the void beneath them (*ibid.*: 64).

For Lehmann, the live body does not represent; it presents. But critically what it presents is not in any way synonymous with reactionary notions of metaphysical presence. The presentness of the live body shatters the logos. Thought cannot think it. What we are confronted with in the theatre, Lehmann suggests, is the presence of death, radical finitude:

> Theatre [. . .] is a kind of 'intimation of mortality' – in the sense implied by Heiner Müller's remarks that 'the potentially dying person' is what is special about theatre. In media communication technology the hiatus of mathematization separates the subjects from each other, so that their proximity and distance become irrelevant. The theatre, however, consisting of a shared time-space of mortality, articulates as a performative act the necessity of engaging with death, i.e. with the aliveness of life. (*ibid.*: 167)

Lehmann's definition holds good for Genet's strategy in *The Balcony*, and indeed, as we shall see in the forthcoming chapters, for his theatre in general. By withdrawing from us, yet remaining present as a live body, Irma, or rather the actor playing the role, brings absence into presence and negativity into representation. She stresses the fact that time has passed, and that we have shared in that passing. In this way, she shatters the spectacular images of eternal Frenchness that were fabricated by magazines and politicians to temper the anxieties provoked by modernisation. By allowing history to rediscover its lost negativity, she points the way to a different form of community based on the impossible communication of wounded subjects. As Jean-Luc Nancy remarks in *The Inoperative Community*:

> A community is not a project or fusion, or in some general way a productive or operative project – nor is it a *project* at all [. . .] A community is the presentation to its members of their mortal truth [. . .] It is the presentation of the finitude and irredeemable excess that make up finite being: its death, but also its birth, and only the community can present me my birth, and along with it the impossibility of my reliving it, as well as the impossibility of my crossing over into my death. (1991: 15)

Like the empty universality, which, for Genet, allows the wound to disclose the 'truth' of justice and equality, Nancy's inoperable community is founded on 'an originary or ontological "sociality"' (*ibid.*: 28) that establishes a primordial relation without relation, a social world existing beyond the violence of spectacular identity. The emptiness that *The Balcony* leaves us with is an invitation to experience that inoperability, to encounter a different mode of being together. Through the negation of theatre, Genet's play discloses the tear at the heart of the sensible in order to open up the possibility for a new world, a world where the ersatz consensus of the spectacle is replaced by a more existentially and temporally precarious notion of community.

Returning to my point in the Introduction to this book, Genet's exploitation of the spatial immediacy of the theatrical event transforms the site of theatre itself into what Lefebvre calls a 'representational space', a space, that is, where dominant (and dominating) modes of spatial production are disclosed and subverted. In the extent to which social space is always, for Lefebvre, produced through a dynamic interplay between representational spaces and spatial representations, *The Balcony* offers more than a merely symbolic attack on the spectacle. By contesting the privatisation of social space provoked by the modernisation of France in the 1950s, it creates, in and by itself, a differential space, a heterotopia where revolutionary subjectivity might be activated through the wound. Recalling Lefebvre's dictum that every society secretes its own space, it is possible to suggest that Genet's focus on theatre's heterotopic spatiality is an attempt to produce a new type of politically efficacious theatre. As he was careful to explain in the 'Avertissement', this can only be achieved through the cultivation of negativity and absence. For what absence is synonymous with here is the wound – that painful experience of nothingness which, by disturbing the subject's sense of self, allows for the possibility of equality to emerge.

Conclusion

In *The Balcony*, Genet shows that the 'theatre house' does not have to exist as a site where national myths are confirmed or manufactured; rather, if skilfully reconfigured, it has the potential to become a heterotopia where subjectivity is opened to a groundless Otherness, which it is unable to master or control. For this reason, it is perhaps best to consider the experience provoked by *The Balcony* in terms of radical uncanniness, a word, which in German, as Sigmund Freud famously pointed out, has etymological associations with homelessness (the *unheimlich*).[30] In France of the 1950s, the uncanniness discussed by Freud was more sociological than psychoanalytical, triggered, as it was, by the sudden influx of new commodities and alternative styles of living. By refusing

---

30 See Freud, 'The Uncanny', in A. Dickinson (ed.), trans. J. Strachey et al., *Art and Literature*, vol. 14 (London: Penguin, 1990), pp. 335–76: 341–7.

to supply the audience with false images of national unity, Genet denied it all sense of existential consolation. Indeed, by aiming to intensify its feelings of homelessness through the collapse of the fictional walls of the 'theatre house', he sought to explode the spectacular, domesticated world to which many in France in the 1950s had started to retreat.[31] Reading *The Balcony* in conjunction with Genet's 1967 essay 'That Strange Word' underlines the politics involved in the play's attack on domestication. If, as that essay suggests, one of the functions of theatre is 'give birth to a multitude of calendars', then it seems reasonable to claim that *The Balcony*'s attack on conventional notions of time and space was motivated by a desire to see history rediscover its negative flow (2003: 105). As I argued in this chapter, this was the very thing that the society of the spectacle, like Irma's brothel, was concerned to congeal.

---

31 This might also explain why Genet's dramaturgy is so radically opposed, formally and thematically, to the existentialist theatres of Jean-Paul Sartre and Albert Camus. Where they wanted in the late 1940s to use the stage as a forum to create a new, authentic sense of French identity in the wake of the Nazi Occupation of the country, Genet, writing in the mid-to-late 1950s, attempted, instead, to put the very notion of 'Frenchness' in question.

5

Détournement, abjection and disidentification in *The Blacks*

The black body is the object of a strange ambivalence. As soon as it ventures beyond its accepted perimeters – sports stadia or concert arenas – the black body never fails to shock or indeed to disturb. (Condé, in Lionnet, 2001: 6; my translation)[1]

Introduction

In my reading of *The Balcony*, I showed how Genet disclosed the wound inflicted upon French society in the 1950s by the increasing spectacularisation of everyday life. In this chapter, I look at how his 1958 play *The Blacks* opened other hidden wounds of the period, namely those related to insecurities about France's 'racial identity' on the eve of decolonisation – a moment when the country was faced with the prospect of increased numbers of immigrant workers entering the *métropole* from the ex-colonies. I do this by arguing that *The Blacks* uses the heterotopic aspects of theatre to contest the exclusionary tactics adopted by

---

1 It is interesting to note that Condé's husband, Amadou Condé, played Archibald in Roger Blin's 1959 production of *The Blacks*.

the French State in its perverse and impossible attempt to keep France white. In keeping with the utopianism that Genet accords the artwork, I explain how the wound inflicted upon whiteness by *The Blacks* offers the possibility for a new type of collective politics based on what Jacques Rancière calls the 'wrong', a demand for recognition on the part of those who are denied visibility in and by the dominant culture, and who exist as representatives of the 'part who have no part' (1999: 9).[2]

Filth and marginality

In the mid-to-late 1950s, 'race' relations in France underwent a seismic shift, the consequences of which are still felt today in the depressing *cités*, or housing estates located beyond the Boulevard Périphérique that separates central Paris from the *banlieus*. Where Paris had been regarded in the 1920s as a capital of negrophilia, by the 1950s, it had become, in spite of the large numbers of prominent black philosophers and writers installed there, a space of negrophobia – a city where the presence of the black body produced anxiety and fear once it ventured beyond its accepted boundaries.[3] One has only to read Frantz Fanon's 1951

---

2 In Rancière's thought, no single community can ever exist as the 'part without a part' primarily because 'the part with no part' covers all those who are denied representation in and by a given social order. In a recent talk at the Moscow Biennale in 2008, Rancière explains that '"the part of those who have no part" [...] was sometimes misinterpreted as the power of the excluded. But what it truly means is the power of anybody, no matter who, the qualification of those who have no specific qualification' (electronic resource: accessed December 2008). See 'Misadventures of Universality'. However, despite the democratic universality inherent in the concept of the 'part with no part', there are always specific groups or people who exist as representatives of/ for it. See 'Literature, Politics, Aesthetics: Approaches to Democratic Disagreement. Jacques Rancière interviewed by Solange Guénon and James H. Kavanagh', *Substance: A Review of Theory and Literary Criticism*, 92 (2000), 3–24: 5.
3 For two good accounts of how negrophilia transformed into negrophobia in France, see Petrine Archer Shaw, *Negrophila: Avant-garde Paris and Black Culture in the 1920s* (New York: Thames & Hudson, 2000); and Brett A. Berliner, *Ambivalent Desire: The Exotic Black Other in Jazz Age France* (Amherst: University of Massachusetts Press, 2002). To understand the immense contribution made by black writers to Parisian cultural and political life, see Michael Fabre, Black *American Writers in France 1840–1980: From Harlem to Paris* (Urbana: University of Illinois Press, 1991); Tyler Stovall, *Paris Noir: African Americans in the City of Light* (Boston, MA: Houghton Mifflin, 1996); Pascal Blanchard et al., *Le Paris Noir* (Paris: Hazan, 2001); and Philippe Dewitte, 'L'immigration: l'émergence en métropole d'une élite africaine', in P. Blanchard and S. Lemaire (eds), *Culture impériale: les colonies au cœur de la République, 1931–1961* (Autrement: Paris, 2004), pp. 201–11. It is also germane to note, in this context, that the famous incident of epidermalisation referred to by

publication *Black Skins, White Masks*, or Bernard Dadié's 1959 novel *Un nègre à Paris* to understand the racist underside to France's supposedly liberal attitude towards Blacks (this 'myth' was especially prevalent among African-American artists). In these books, as Maryse Condé's epigraph to this chapter underlines, the black body troubled the indigenous white population in France's cities, and was subjected to aggressive looks and disabling stereotypes. Like the infantilised Senegalese infantryman displayed in the advertisements for the popular drink Banania, Africans and West Indians were thought of as jovial but essentially childlike subjects. To depart from this cliché, as many black intellectuals and students at the time were struggling to do, was to find oneself trapped in other roles: sexual athlete, dirty 'nigger', rapist, prostitute and cannibal.

Although it would be erroneous to claim that France was somehow colour-blind before the 1950s, the decolonisation of the French empire between 1954 and 1962, along with the increasing number of students attending metropolitan universities after the Second World War, affected a major change in the way that most ordinary French people felt about 'race'. Instead of settlers or *colons* heading overseas, immigrants from the empire started to settle in France, attracted by higher wages and a better standard of living. Regardless of the fact that many of them had been invited into the country to help lay the foundations for the economic boom of *les trente glorieuses* (this ran roughly between 1945 and 1975), their presence in the hexagon coincided with the appearance of new forms of racist discourse designed to code French national identity in terms of colour rather than class or citizenship.[4] Ross's comments show how racialisation and modernisation form part of the same capitalist process:

> If the consolidation of a broad middle class more or less transpires during these years, it was also during these years that France distances itself from its (former) colonies, both within and without: this is the moment of the great cordoning off of the immigrants, their removal to the suburbs in a massive reworking of the social boundaries of Paris and other large French cities. On the national level France retreats within the hexagon, withdraws from empire, retrenches with its borders at the same time that those boundaries are becoming newly permeable [...] [F]rom this point on national subjectivity begins to take the place of class [...] Class conflict after all implies some degree of negotiability; once modernization has run

---

Fanon in *Black Skins, White Masks*, took place on a train, that is to say, in public space. See *Black Skins, White Masks*, trans. C. L. Markmann (London: Paladin, 1970), p. 79.

4 Although migratory patterns had been changing since the 1930s, these were intensified in the 1950s and 1960s.

its course, then one is, quite simply either French or not, modern or not: exclusion becomes racial or national in nature. (1995: 11–12)

Ross's analysis highlights the tensions and paradoxes involved in France's attempt to decolonise and modernise simultaneously. On the one hand, she stresses how, after decolonisation, the French were encouraged to define themselves racially in terms of an essentialised white identity; and, yet, on the other hand, she illustrates how this was immediately challenged by the arrival in the hexagon of large numbers of immigrants.[5] Instead of existing in the modernised white nation-State promoted by the politicians of the Fifth Republic, both nationally and internationally, the French were confronted with burgeoning numbers of black and Arab bodies in their streets.

Unsurprisingly this contradiction intensified pre-existing forms of racism that had underpinned France's quest to 'civilise' the world from the 1830s onward, and which the Fascist movement Action Française and the Vichy government had tried to 'prove' scientifically in the 1930s and 1940s. In order to resolve the racial discontents caused by modernisation, two interrelated techniques emerged. In the first instance, a new premium was placed on personal hygiene; and second, urban planners engaged in a massive reordering of metropolitan space.

According to Ross, the discourse of cleanliness that swept through French society in the mid-to-late 1950s was designed to act as an agent of separation, a way of differentiating proper French households from the inferior households of the ex-colonised.[6] The target of this discourse was the French housewife:[7]

---

5 Until the late 1970s, the largest immigrant population in France was Portuguese. Before the 1950s, France mostly imported its industrial workforce from Southern and Eastern Europe. However, with the arrival of immigrants from the ex-colonies in the 1960s and the right of workers from the European Community to full employment in Member States, the immigration problem became associated with West Africans and, especially, North Africans. For more in-depth studies into the political vicissitudes of immigration in France, see Maxim Silverman, *Deconstructing the Nation*; Alec Hargreaves, *Immigration, 'Race' and Ethnicity*; and Neil MacMaster, *Colonial Migrants and Racism: Algerians in Paris 1900–62* (New York: Macmillan, 1997).

6 The other effect, of course, was to do with the Occupation. In the period immediately after the Second World War, France underwent a savage process of *épuration*, or cleansing, in which those who had collaborated with the Nazis were rooted out and punished. On the psychological plane, the *épuration* continued into the 1950s and 1960s, as France struggled to come to terms with the Vichy years. In Ross's view, the national obsession with cleanliness reflects the nation's desire to wash itself clean of the stain of Occupation. See *Fast Cars, Clean Bodies*, pp. 71–4.

7 It is interesting to compare and contrast this policy in relation to Frantz Fanon's argument in his essay about how the coloniser is always concerned to target 'native' women by bringing them out of the home. See 'Algeria Unveiled', trans. H. Chevalier, in a *Dying Colonialism* (London: Readers and Writers, 1980), pp. 13–42.

> If the woman is clean, the family is clean, the nation is clean. If the French woman is dirty, then France is dirty and backward. But France can't be dirty and backward, because that is the role played by the colonies. But there are no more colonies. If Algeria is becoming an independent nation, then France must become a *modern* nation: some distinction between the two must prevail. France must, so to speak, clean house: reinventing the home is reinventing the nation. (*ibid*.: 78; original italics)

In Ross's argument, the disappearance of the colonies and subsequent arrival of immigrant workers in mainland France heightened the need for indigenous French families to be clean. Engaging in state-sponsored surveys into the use of soap; entering competitions for 'the best-kept home'; and gazing at advertisements for cleaning products in the pages of *Elle* and *Marie Claire*, convinced the French housewife that she was a 'proper' citizen, ready to reap the rewards of capitalist modernisation. To keep a clean house was a sign that one belonged to what de Gaulle in his speech about the decolonisation of Algeria in 1962 referred to as the 'tide of history'.[8] In this quest for modernity or whiteness, hygiene was associated with moral and national propriety, whereas dirt, by contrast, was a metaphor for backwardness.[9] According to the logic of what Ross terms 'the filth complex', the dirty person did not – or rather could not – belong to a developed nation-State such as France; rather she was mired in the past, unable to partake in the advances of European modernity. Conveniently (and predictably), the 'dark skin' of Arab and African immigrants branded them, in the paranoid era of decolonisation, as biologically and culturally unclean, abject subjects who were not, nor ever could become, properly French.

Importantly, the discourse of hygiene did not stay within the private space of the domestic; it was used as an excuse to reorder France's cities. Once again, Ross's insights into the politics of metaphor are compelling:

---

8   By referring to the 'tide of history', de Gaulle, somewhat ironically, reconfigured himself as a neo-Hegelian. The purpose behind the speech was to show that the collective experiment of imperialism was over, and that France, as a consequence, had to reinvent itself as a modernised capitalist State. As Todd Shepard has pointed out, de Gaulle's speech allowed France to explain imperialism as a necessary stage in history, and decolonisation as the inevitable outcome of a predetermined process. This meant that there was no sense of guilt attached to France's imperialist past and neither was there any need to make ethical and/or financial reparation. See *The Invention of Decolonization: The Algerian War and the Remaking of France* (Ithaca, NY: Cornell University Press, 2006), pp. 6–11.

9   Ross borrows her theory of the filth complex from the sociologist Edgar Morin. In his 1967 study *Commune en France: la métamorphose de Plodémet*, Morin argued that the fear of dirt is what allowed the French peasant to break free from old ties and embrace the culture of modernisation. See *Fast Cars, Clean Bodies*, p. 91.

The history of mid-twentieth-century renovations shows the city to be the logical outcome of capitalist modernization's adroit manipulation of the discourse of hygiene [...] The areas within the city targeted for demolition, the so-called *ilots insalubres*, were densely populated city blocks that had received their name in the 1930s by virtue of their high mortality rate. In 1954 [...] tuberculosis was no longer a problem. (*ibid.*: 154)

Irrespective of the rhetoric of better sanitation, the impulse behind this drive to demolish slum housing was, as Ross shows, fuelled by a segregationist desire. France wanted to separate people on racial grounds: '[it is in the new social geography of the city [...] that we begin to see the political effects of the yoking together of modernisation and hygiene. Over the second half of the twentieth century these effects would become increasingly racial in nature in the form of a kind of "purification" of the social urban body' (*ibid.*: 150).

Under the alibi of better hygiene, Paris was, in the years leading up to, and immediately after, decolonisation, racially purified and whitened. According to Ross, between 1954 and 1970, 44 per cent of workers and immigrants were 'dispersed to the outlying suburbs while the number of *cadres supérieurs* [in Paris *intra muros*] increased by 51 per cent' (*ibid.*: 151). Like old imperialist cities such as Algiers or Dakar, the newly modernised and sandblasted French capital was divided into two separate spaces: the clean, white centre, and the dirty, black outside. Confirming what the postcolonial critic Homi K. Bhabha has referred to as the essentially 'agonistic' psyche of the coloniser, the motivation behind this new production of urban space was typically perverse (1985: 152). Impossibly, France set out to deny the obvious presence of the large immigrant population in the hexagon by banishing it from sight. Urbanism and the discourse on personal hygiene allowed it to do this by either ghettoising Blacks and Arabs in Parisian neighbourhoods such as Belleville and Barbès Rochechouaurt or by ejecting them to the *banlieus*. At the very moment when France was supposedly inventing itself as a post-imperial nation-State, an alternative form of neo-colonialism was born within the *métropole* itself (see Chapter 1, pp. 31–9, in this book).

I have provided this description of the racial and spatial practices operating in France during the early years of the Fifth Republic, since I believe that it allows for a very different interpretation of *The Blacks*, a play which, as I will show, posed serious questions about the significance of colour as the country was on the verge of decolonising and modernising. For many critics and directors who have responded to the work positively, the play is generally seen to offer either an abstract attack on racism, or a celebration of anti-colonial revolution in Africa.[10] What is forgotten in these interpretations, however, is that the play was written to be performed by black actors living in Paris. Contextualising the play historically, sociologically and spatially encourages us to read it as an early attempt to deal with the presence of immigrants workers in metropolitan France.[11] By putting thirteen black bodies on-stage in a French theatre for the first time, and by deconstructing the widely held view that there was such a thing as a 'black essence', *The Blacks* contests, in the most concrete of ways, the exclusionary and racialised agenda that has continued to characterise French urban policy from the 1950s onwards. Its express intent was not to propose a new identity for Blacks in Africa or elsewhere, but to wound, as Genet explained quite blatantly in the 'Preface to *The Blacks*', white French spectators. To that extent, the play is best approached in terms of decolonisation rather than colonisation. Theatre's spatiality, what the critic Bert O. States calls its 'closeness', allowed blackness to take a place and to show itself in metropolitan France.

Against whiteness

Like each of Genet's late plays, *The Blacks* has provoked much dissension and debate, even from those communities whose struggles it appears to support. In both France and the USA, African and African-American reviewers attacked the productions of Roger Blin and Gene Frankel for being politically conservative and for distorting the truth of black experience.[12] Commenting on Blin's 1959 show at the Théâtre de Lutèce, Andrée Clair in *Présence africaine* commented that the play was of no

10 See Allen Francovich, 'Genet's Theatre of Possession'; Anthony Graham-White, 'Jean Genet and the Psychology of Colonialism', *Comparative Drama*, 4:3 (1970), 208–16; Graham Dunstan Martin, 'Racism in Genet's *Les nègres*', *Modern Language Review*, 70:3 (1975), 517–25; and Keith A. Warner, '*Les nègres*: A Look at Genet's Excursion into Black Consciousness', *CLA Journal*, 26:4 (1983), 397–414.
11 From the late 1950s to the present, *The Blacks* has been read in terms of racism and colonialism but no one to my knowledge, with the exception of Bernard Dort in a retrospective essay, has thought to contextualise it geographically and historically. See 'Une extraordinaire jubilation', in Moraly, *Les nègres au Port de la Lune*, pp. 103–9. As a result of this tendency towards abstraction, it becomes impossible to hold specific countries and regimes responsible for their imperialist past and racist present. It is noticeable, for instance, that in the critical reaction to Roger Blin's production of the play in 1959, no reviewer thought to mention that the play was specifically about French imperialism.
12 For a good account of the racial and cultural politics involved in the response to Gene Frankel's staging of the play at St Mark's Playhouse in New York, see John Warrick,

'assistance to Africans in their long and continuing struggle to have those who don't want to, recognize their claim to human and social dignity' (in Webb, 1992: 57). While criticism of this sort has been countered in recent years by contemporary black scholars steeped in the discourses of poststructuralism and cultural studies, much of the confusion surrounding the politics of the play would doubtless have been tempered if Genet had agreed to publish the 1956 text 'Preface to *The Blacks*'.[13]

In that important piece of writing, Genet states, explicitly, that '[t]his play is written not *for* Blacks, but *against* Whites' (see the Appendix, in this book, p. 234; original italics).[14] Responding in advance to the criticisms of the US playwright Lorraine Hansberry, who accused him of degrading black people to fulfil his own aesthetic agenda (June, 1961), the 1956 preface shows Genet to be acutely aware of the dangers involved in conflating his personal experience of humiliation with those of an entire community or 'race':

> For a long time, my situation was that of one humiliated. Do not be surprised that now that my humiliation is ended – ultimately a victory in itself – I show what becomes of the humiliated. I know the danger. Will I not colour with my own particular despair the state of an entire race that knows a different kind of despair, that lives a different kind of despair, of a different order? (Appendix: 233)

Genet realises that to write a play *for* Blacks is to commit the ultimate act of bad faith. Not only does it deprive blacks of their right to speak, but it soothes the guilty conscience of the white liberal writer:

> Wanting to write for the Blacks would derive from that moral abjection that involves taking interest magnanimously, with understanding, in the weak; absolving one's conscience; abstaining from any effective action. It means claiming morality and worthy sentiment for oneself, while the people whom one supports must struggle in abject poverty, up to their necks in it, in dishonest compromise. (*ibid.*: 230)

'*The Blacks* and its Impact on African-American Theatre in the United States', in Finburgh et al., *Performance and Politics*, pp. 131–42.
13 See Sylvie Chalaye, *Du noir au nègre: l'image du noir au théâtre de Marguerite de Navarre à Jean Genet* (1550–1960) (Paris: L'Harmattan, 1998); Hedi Khélil, *Figures de l'altérité dans le théâtre de Jean Genet. Lecture des Nègres et des Paravents* (Paris: L'Harmattan, 2001); and Bénédicte Boisseron and Frieda Ekotto, 'Genet's The Blacks: "And Why Does One Laugh at a Negro?"', Hanrahan, *Genet*, 98–112.
14 The publication of the 1956 preface to the play confirms what Roger Blin had suggested about the politics of the play in two interviews in *The Drama Review* in 1963 and 1967 respectively. See Betinna Knapp, 'Interview with Roger Blin', *Tulane Drama Review*, 7:3 (1963), 111–25 and 'Interview with Roger Blin', *The Drama Review*, 11:4 (1967), 109–10.

If the black population in Europe, Africa or the USA is to express itself, then it must do so, contends Genet, on its own terms: it needs to find its own writers, artists and intellectuals. For Genet, the task facing white writers who want to tackle racism is of a very different kind; their mission is to betray their own 'race', but from the inside, as it were:

> Minorities have to attain their freedoms themselves. We [white writers] must be wary of our enthusiasm for magnanimous causes, since it quickly makes us appear complacent [...] I do not say that we must systematically refuse to give aid to the oppressed, but that it would be vain if, at the same time, we did not exert ourselves against the dominating power we serve, from which we profit, in which we participate; in other words, against ourselves. (*ibid.*)

An important method by which the white European writer can betray his 'race', suggests Genet, is to refuse the *négrophile* aesthetic, which purports to respect black identity as long as it remains subservient to white desire, and refrains from expressing the misery of black experience. Contradicting his earlier claim about black artists needing to find their own voice, Genet is particularly scathing about the African-American choreographer Katherine Dunham's all-black ballet troupe which toured European cities to great acclaim in the early 1950s:

> We still remember her ballets. Were they irreproachable from the point of view of the aesthetics of music hall? It is possible. They were danced by Blacks alone, but what did these Blacks show? Where were they from? What were they ambassadors of? Of which sovereign empire? Pale, faded, they issued from a world without earthly power, without roots, without pain, without tears, a world that does not even want these things; a world of basic life forms that refuses to try to realise itself. Through them, we never got to know the ordeal of a negro world which is realising itself less and less. Not its rage, nor its abject poverty, its anger, nor its fear [...] Not only did their show never insult us, but their misery and despair never featured in it. Instead, everything sang of what we call *joie de vivre*, and reassured us basely of everything we know about life and about the entire black population, by telling us that nothing could wound them profoundly, because their joy was so fresh. (*ibid.*: 228)

For Genet, Dunham's ballets serve no political or ethical purpose. Instead of expressing the anger and humiliation of Blacks, they seek to 'seduce' a 'hostile' or 'indifferent' white public by displaying the 'good taste, skill and genius' of the black performers (*ibid.*: 229). In this way, Genet claims that Dunham's ballets, by trading in negrophilia, offer blackness as a spectacle for consumption.

Genet's response to Dunham's 'betrayal' is to call for a racialised theatre which, 'relies on the reality from which it has derived, and bears witness to it' (*ibid.*). Like Fanon in *Black Skins, White Masks*, Genet is all too aware that Blacks in western cities are compelled to exist as actors. Using a theatrical analogy which will have, as we shall see, profound consequences for the practice of theatre itself, Genet compares Blacks to valets and servants. Their function, he proposes, is to 'charm us' (*ibid.*: 232). However, as with Fanon's existentialist analysis of racism, Genet's statement about black theatricality is not based on essentialised categories; he realises that this propensity for performance is socially and culturally determined:

> I have not said that Blacks are actors by nature, but quite the opposite: that in our own minds they become actors as soon as they are looked at by Whites. And they are always actors because as soon as we see them, before we even see them, we imagine them by using the categories I indicated earlier. Since we refuse to see them in their reality, as people who revolt – otherwise, our attitude towards them would be different – we must presumably perceive them as playing. (*ibid.*)

Genet's comments highlight the extent to which racism in France (as elsewhere) is a spectacle, a theatricalised relationship predicated upon an unequal distribution of space and labour. Where Blacks in French society are obliged to perform their identity according to a rigid script, proper French citizens are positioned as spectators who are able to consume, from a distance, the spectacle on offer. Because all the power resides with the French spectator in this relationship, the black subject is unable to improvise her identity; rather, she is obliged to perform a repertoire of roles that has been fixed in advance. Consequently, as Genet points out in the play, blackness becomes a signifier of incarceration, a trope that designates a body to a specific place and makes it appear in a certain way. Faced with the rigidity of this scenario, the sense in which structure predetermines identity and meaning, there is little point in using the theatrical medium to offer affirmative images of blackness. The more effective strategy is to attack the basis of the theatrical image itself:

> Even if he does not revel in it, the oppressor does not disassociate himself easily from the image of an oppressed person reduced to servility. What purpose, then, would oppression [otherwise] serve, other than to give him an idea of his own strength through the weakness of those who recognise and revere this strength? This image simultaneously reassures and charms him. It is only an image, and it is this image that the oppressed will attempt

to transform. What if this image, which is essentially in the oppressor's head, suddenly worried him? (*ibid.*: 230)

In *The Blacks*, Genet makes the oppressor (the white spectator) anxious in two ways. First, he *détourns* a specific genre of performance, then he proceeds to deconstruct the theatrical frame itself. Genet's decision to locate his critique of racism at the level of theatrical form and medium, or what I have been calling aesthetic politics, is the very thing that makes it so pertinent. For as the black theatre historian Sylvie Chalaye has pointed out, theatre is always more than *divertissement*; it is a mode of political production, which needs to 'recognize its [historical] responsibility in manufacturing a myth as spectacular as that of the nigger' (1998: 13; my translation).

Chalaye's argument reminds us that theatre is an ideological practice in its own right, a machine for constructing identity. When it comes to blackness, moreover, the theatre machine is inherently excessive. In addition to producing a spectacle of blackness, it posits the black subject as a theatrical performer, a kind of natural 'song and dance man'. In a racist society, theatre is a site of incarceration, a performative prison where black identity is fabricated and corralled at the same time. To break this prison house open and thus to contest the image of blackness it sustains, black actors, Genet says, ought to reflect not reality, but the reflection of reality: '[w]e'll play at being reflected in it, and we'll see ourselves [. . .] slowly disappearing in its waters' (1973a: 31). In this infinite regression of appearance, theatre is *abîmé*, shot full of holes.

As well as problematising white society's view of Blacks, Genet's attack on essence also troubles the affirmative concept of blackness promoted at the time by négritude philosophers and poets such as Aimée Césaire, Léon Damas and Léopold Senghor. For all the resonances of négritude poetry in Felicity's great speech in the middle of the play – 'Dahomey! Dahomey! To my rescue, Negroes, all of you! Gentlemen of Timbuktu, come in, under your white parasols! Stand over there. Tribes covered with hold and mud, rise up from my body, emerge' (*ibid.*: 59) – Genet is not interested in defining blackness; he wants to make it unknowable, to erase it as a concept. This explains the difficulty that some of Roger Blin's cast, Les Griots, had with the language and ideas of the play in rehearsal. As Blin explained to Jean Duvignaud in an interview in 1958, some of the actors were shocked and offended by Genet's text – they did not recognise themselves in it, or always understand the irony involved in his deliberately false representation of black identity (October 1958). Like the actors in the 2007 production of the play at the Theatre Royal Stratford East, London, they felt it was too bleak and negative, and, for those reasons, failed to communicate the totality of black experience (see the interviews with Ultz and Excalibah, in Chapters 10 and 11, in this book). Yet, as I explain below, this was exactly Genet's point. For him, the play and its politics were located in negation, not affirmation.

Détournement

The practice of *détournement*, or 'diversion' was originally used by the Situationist International as a tool for subverting all manner of cultural phenomena, including films, comic strips, advertisements and even cities. In *The Blacks*, however, the object of *détournement* is more limited, since it is focused on reversing the tropes and clichés of 'black theatre', which were rooted, at the time, in popular entertainment forms such as clown shows, music-hall routines and circus acts. In this vaudevillian type of theatre, which I will from this point on refer to, generically, as the black review show, performers such as Josephine Baker, Chocolat the clown and Joe Alex were constrained to represent themselves as sexual objects, childish pranksters and physical athletes.[15] In Paul Colin's posters for the famous *La revue nègre*, staged at the Théâtre des Champs-Elysées in October 1925, Josephine Baker is depicted as a sexualised 'black Venus' in a shimmering white mini-dress, surrounded by lascivious black men, with exaggerated eyes, lips and teeth. Colin's image reduces the black performers to the body alone. Looking at them, there is no sense that these vaudevillians could ever put on a serious show or express profound emotion. Everything about them is comic, light, sexualised. Baker's buttocks, hips and thighs are as exaggerated as the smiles of the men who look less like real people than grotesque painted clowns. The semiotic of Colin's posters is clear: black performers are here to entertain the white world, to relieve its sadness, to inject it with sensuality.

Despite being performed by 'real' Blacks and not by white actors in black face, the review show in France between the wars fulfilled the same twofold function as the minstrel show had in the USA in the

15 For good contextualising studies of Josephine Baker in Paris, see Josephine Baker and Joseph Bouillon, *Josephine*, trans. M. Fitzpatrick (New York: Harper & Row, 1977); and Phyllis Rose, *Jazz Cleopatra: Josephine Baker in Her Time* (London: Chatto & Windus, 1990).

mid-nineteenth century.[16] It allowed white audiences to alleviate their anxieties about Blacks in their presence by making black identity knowable, locatable and consumable, and, at the same time, permitted them to cross the colour divide and to experience the seductive *frisson* of being black and primitive, albeit momentarily, and by proxy. In her study of negrophilia in Paris in the 1920s, the art historian Petrine Archer-Shaw is at pains to point out that French audiences who flocked to see *La revue nègre* at the Théâtre des Champs Elysées in 1925, or danced at the nightclub, Le Bal Nègre in Montparnasse in the 1920s and 1930s, had no interest in black identity in itself; they came 'to satisfy their desires' (2000: 13).

Regardless of the fact that the black review show was not as popular in the 1950s as it had been in the 1920s, the racist stereotypes it gave rise to had become fixed in the French collective consciousness, as a result of being recycled, constantly, in popular films, posters and advertisement campaigns.[17] Genet's decision to *détourner* the content and form of the review show was thus a measured choice. He was fully aware of the status of black performers in France, knowing that they were expected to supply a stock type of light entertainment which would reinforce the spectacle of blackness and pacify white concerns.

That Genet intended to use *The Blacks* as a vehicle for *détournement* is evident from his remarks in the 'Preface to *The Blacks*', and in the epigraph he attached to the published version of the play. In the former, Genet states that he only accepted the commission from the actor-manager Raymond Rouleau for the purpose of 'snub[bing] the [white] audience' (see the Appendix, in this book, p. 228). And in the latter, he deliberately sets out to problematise the rationale behind black performance by purporting not to know what blackness is: '[o]ne evening an actor asked me to write a play for an all-black cast. But what exactly is a Black? First of all what's his colour?' (1973a: 5).

Genet's question explodes, immediately, the racialised ideology of the black review show in France. Where white producers of shows like *La revue nègre* were happy to endorse the clichéd view of Blacks as eroticised primitives who were somehow ontologically equipped to express

---

16 For two excellent accounts of black-face performance in the USA, see David Roediger, *The Wages of Whiteness: Race and the Makings of the American Working Class* (London: Verso, 1991); and Eric Lott, *Love and Theft: Black Face Minstrelsy and the American Working Class* (Oxford: Oxford University Press, 1993).

17 This image of Baker has become a kind of popular icon. Carole Sweeney has shown how it is still used in advertisements on the walls of Parisian metro stations. See '*La revue nègre*: Négrophilie, Modernity and Colonialism in Inter-war France', *Journal of Romance Studies*, 1:2 (2001), 1–14: 1.

the poetry of the body, Genet puts black identity in brackets.[18] The foreword hints at what Roger Blin's specially devised acting style proved in performance: that blackness in white society defies naturalistic modes of representation. Although *The Blacks* situates itself within what French spectators at the time would have considered, erroneously, as a *bona fide* black cultural form, Genet's has no intention of perpetuating its logic: he wants to subvert it from the inside out.

Notwithstanding those odd moments that might have seemed incongruous – the drawing (rather than the raising) of the curtain, the presence of a white sheet draped over two chairs, and one of the cast, Newport News, dressed in blue jeans and a round-neck sweater, while the other black performers were in tattered evening wear – the opening images of Blin's production did little to disturb spectators.[19] The sight of blacks dressed in gaudy ball gowns and tails and 'dancing a minuet [. . .] to an air of Mozart' (*ibid*.: 9) was borrowed from the popular 'cake walk' dance, which had evolved from the slave plantations in the southern states of the USA to become a staple of vaudeville performance in France. Similarly, the presence of a white court, situated on the upper gantry of a stylised set, made from metal scaffolding, rope and white asbestos cloth, would not have been out of place at Les Folies Bergères, where colonialist dreamscapes were all the rage in the 1920s. In the iconic *La folie du jour*, staged in 1926-27, Josephine Baker played Tatou, a primitive slave girl, dressed only in pearls and a mini-skirt of bananas, who is saved from cannibalism by a doughty white explorer. At the start of Blin's production of *The Blacks*, the audience seemed to have been transported, yet again, to a surrealist Africa, where Blacks dressed in evening gowns mixed with the representatives of white, colonial 'civilisation'.

The audience would have been equally reassured by the presence of Archibald, the *compère*, who, like a perfect host, breaks off from the rest of the troupe, and introduces the 'exotic entertainment' for a polite soirée:

ARCHIBALD: Ladies and gentleman. . .(*The Court bursts into very shrill, but well-orchestrated laughter. It is not free and easy laughter. This laughter is echoed by the same but even shriller laughter of the*

---

18 *La revue nègre* was produced by Caroline Dudley Reagan, a white society woman 'who wanted to show Parisians "real" Negro music and dance'. See Dalton and Gates Jr., 'Josephine Baker and Paul Colin: African American Dance Seen through Parisian Eyes', *Critical Enquiry*, 24:4 (1998), 903–34: 911.
19 For detailed descriptions of Blin's performance, see Wallace Fowlie, 'The New Plays of Ionesco and Genet', *Tulane Drama Review*, 5:1 (1960), 43–8; Odette Aslan, '*Les paravents* de Jean Genet' and *Roger Blin* (Cambridge: Cambridge University Press, 1988) pp. 55–68; and Mark Taylor-Batty, *Roger Blin: Collaborations and Methodologies* (Bern: Peter Lang, 2007) pp. 137–57.

Negroes who are standing about Archibald. The Court, bewildered, becomes silent.). . .My name is Archibald Absalom Wellington. (*He bows, then moves from one to the other, naming each in turn.*) . . . This is Mr Deodatus Village (*he bows*). . .Miss Adelaide Bobo (*she bows*). . .Mr Edgar Alas Newport News (*he bows*). . .Mrs Augustus Snow (*she remains upright*). . .well. . .well. . . Madame (*roaring angrily*) bow! (*she remains upright*). . .I'm asking you to bow, Madame, to bow! (*extremely gentle, almost grieved*) I'm asking you Madame, to bow – it's a performance. (*Snow bows*). . .Mrs Felicity Trollop Pardon (*she bows*). . .and Miss Diop-Stephanie Virtue Secret-rose Diop. (*ibid.*: 10)

Within the standard economy of the review show, Snow's aggressive refusal to bow confirms that everything is not as it seems. Suddenly, the little details that did not fit in – the shrill laughter from the court, the masks that allowed 'the kinky hair' of the black actors to be seen by the audience, the presence of the chairs and white cloth – assume greater importance. The sense of the performance going awry is further exacerbated when Archibald inverts the usual dynamic of blackface performance and tells the audience that, on this occasion, black actors, and not their white counterparts, will black-up: '[a]s you see ladies and gentlemen, just as you have your lilies and roses, so we – in order to serve you – shall use our shiny black make-up' (*ibid.*: 10–11). In the performance at the Théâtre de Lutèce, this was emphasised by the performers rubbing their faces with handkerchiefs in an attempt to make them shine. Images such as these, along with the increasing insolence in Archibald's tone of voice, would have confused the audience in 1959. For while it would have been aware that something was amiss, it would not have known what to do or how to react. In Genet's script, the status of the play is only declared when Archibald steps forward and explains what is really at stake in the performance:

ARCHIBALD: Be quiet. (*To the audience.*) This evening we shall perform for you. But, in order that you may remain comfortably settled in your seats in the presence of the drama that is already unfolding here, in order that you may be assured that there is no danger of such a drama worming its way into your precious lives, we shall even have the decency – a decency learned from you – to make communication impossible. We shall increase the distance that separates us, a distance that is basic – by our pomp, our manners, our insolence – for we are also actors. When my speech is over, everything here – (*he stamps his foot in a gesture of rage*) here! – will take place in a delicate world of reprobation. (*ibid.*: 12)

Barely five minutes into the show, Archibald's direct address marks the moment of *détournement*. After it, the stock elements of the review show are turned on their heads and replaced by a more violent set of tropes and clichés, all of which are calculated to bring French fears about decolonisation into the open. Instead of titillating *danses sauvages*, ribald comedy and stereotypical colonialist fantasies, the audience is now presented with images of anti-colonial revolt, hymns to evil, and most controversially of all, the re-enactment of a ritualised rape and murder of a white woman. In Blin's production, Marie was played by Diouf, a black vicar, who was forced to wear a grotesque white mask with blond pigtails. What Genet's play shows – and Blin's *mise-en-scène* successfully brought out – is that black actors are not happy-go-lucky performers whose natural home is the stage; they are autonomous subjects desperate to escape from both the imprisoning walls of the theatre house itself and from the specific type of theatricality that their roles require.

Genet's negation of accepted forms of black entertainment stands in stark contrast to the Fifth Republic's attitude towards race relations. Where Blacks were represented as 'docile' and 'child-like' people, Genet on the other hand, presents them as subjects engaged in a self-conscious process of emancipation. Pre-empting the African-American theorist bell hooks's more contemporary (and subversive) notion of domesticity, Genet's Blacks are not content to uphold white mastery; rather, their aim is to undermine it by basing their revolt on knowledge, 'details, facts, observations, [and] psychoanalytical readings of the white "Other"' (hooks, 1997: 165).

In spite of this, however, it would be a mistake – and a serious one at that – to see *The Blacks* as offering an authentic expression of either black identity or desire. The content of the show is fake, a deliberate attempt on behalf of the actors to represent themselves according to how French culture, in an age of decolonisation, perceives them to be: '[w]e are actors and organized an evening's entertainment for you. We tried to present some aspect of our lives that might interest you. Unfortunately, we haven't found very much' (1973a: 76–7). In *The Blacks*, there is no consolation or redemption. Knowledge of the black 'Other' is impossible. Crucially, Genet's refusal to provide a 'truthful' representation of blackness does not mean, as some critics have argued, that the play is politically unhelpful.[20] On the contrary, Genet's reluctance to abandon

---

20 See Charles Marowitz, 'Notes on a Theatre of Cruelty', *Tulane Drama Review*, 11:2 (1966), 152–72: 169; Alfred Simon, *Les signes et les songes. Essai sur le théâtre et la fête* (Seuil: Paris, 1976), p. 257; and J. P. Little, *Les nègres* (London: Grant & Cutler, 1990), p. 84. This well-rehearsed argument has been repeated, most recently, by Mark Taylor-Batty, *Roger Blin*, p. 142.

the theatrical frame, at the very moment he deconstructs it, should be considered as a strategic move. In an era when the French State was desperate to 'police' African and West Indian immigrants by fixing them as objects of knowledge, epistemologically and spatially, the ambivalence that surrounds *The Blacks* is a technique for liberation, a tactic that redistributes the aesthetic and spatial politics of everyday life.

Deconstructing the frame, redistributing the sensible

In a series of articles written between 1996 and 2004, the UK theatre theorist Andrew Quick has suggested that the theatrical frame functions as a 'panoptic practice' (1997: 27). For Quick, the semiosis endemic to the frame domesticates the enigma of the actor's body by 'transforming it into a sign' (*ibid.*: 26; modified citation). By drawing attention to the way in which naturalistic theatre is 'a representational apparatus that asserts mastery over everything that exists beyond its limits' (*ibid.*), Quick suggests that the theatrical frame, tacitly, affirms and reproduces what I have been calling, after Rancière, the distribution of the sensible. Its function is to establish limits, to make the world knowable by confirming what is already there. Despite being firmly rooted in contemporary performance practice, Quick's analysis hints at an interesting parallel between theatre and French urban policy in the 1950s and 1960s. In both instances, the objective is/was to discipline and police unruly elements whose presence is/was both needed and yet feared. In the same way, however, that cities and their users, as Michel de Certeau (1984) and Michel Foucault (1997) have shown, resist the nightmare of total surveillance, so theatre's spatiality, the fact that it presents bodies in the present, means that its domestication of reality is always at risk of deconstruction. As Quick claims, if the coordinates of the frame are disturbed, as Genet does in *The Blacks*, then theatre has the potential to become a heterotopic space where sensible experience can be challenged and redistributed differently.[21] To understand fully how Genet's frame-breaking in *The Blacks* disrupts the disciplinary spatial practices used to police the black body in France, it is necessary to look in greater detail at the different ways in which he confuses epistemological limits and ontological borders in the play.

21 Erving Goffman, the sociologist and principal proponent of frame analysis, mentions *The Blacks* in his study *Frame Analysis* (London: Penguin, 1975), pp. 398–400.

As I mentioned earlier, *The Blacks* opens with a group of black performers, dressed in evening wear, dancing to a Mozart minuet around a makeshift catafalque, fashioned out of two chairs that are draped in a white sheet and covered with flowers. Above the black performers, on an elevated gallery, sits a white Court, played by black actors wearing garish white masks, each of which represents a figure from what we might call, after Louis Althusser, the ideological state apparatus of colonialism: a Queen, a Judge, a General, a Missionary and a Valet. In the half-masks and costumes designed by André Acquart for Blin's production, the White Queen had a sad expression; the Governor wore a colonial helmet and a white suit; the Judge, an ermine collar and satin robes; the Missionary, a white priest's gown with a cross painted on it; and the Valet, a courtier's livery with a ruffled shirt and a *commedia dell'arte* mask.

The action of the play starts in earnest when Archibald informs both the white Court and the white audience simultaneously that the performance they are about to watch is a representation of the ritualised rape and murder of a white woman, Marie, that has taken place before the show started: '[t]onight our sole concern will be to entertain you. So we have killed this white woman. There she lies. (*He points to the catafalque.*)' (1973a: 14). After numerous interruptions and procrastinations in which the cast comment metatheatrically upon their performances, the ritual re-enactment is finally staged when Diouf, a black vicar in drag, takes on the role of Marie. Despite the consternation of the white Court which mistakenly confuses the representation for reality, the ritual is revealed to be a ruse. There is no body in the catafalque. The ritual has been a performative trick, a device to entice the white Court down from its vertical position in the gallery onto the horizontal level of the stage so that its members can be murdered symbolically.

In keeping with the vertiginous theatricality of the play, the 'murder' of the white Court is not presented as a piece of dramatic fiction, a representation to believe in. It is deliberately theatricalised, a self-conscious play-within-a-play. Its 'real' purpose, so the actors say, is to conceal the trial of a black traitor whose execution is supposedly taking place offstage. This means, of course, that the spectators are unable to see it, and thus verify its dramatic truth. Like the revolution in *The Balcony*, the audience never knows if the execution is 'real' or not. When Newport News, a character who acts as a go-between between on-stage and off-stage spaces, returns with information about the execution and its effect on the black revolution (in whose name it was done), the actors playing the white Court are quick to take off their masks and to enter into what appears to be an authentic conversation with the black performers, their dramatic adversaries. The eagerness of the actors has a double effect, the result of which is to suspend any definitive meaning. Initially, their apparent candour endows both the off-stage revolution, and execution with a heightened sense of dramatic reality (if they are talking about it, then it must be dramatically true); and yet on the other hand, it immediately undercuts this by reinforcing the illusory quality of the performance that we are actually watching (their actions prove that nothing in this play is dramatically true).[22]

As in *The Balcony*, such dense metatheatricality produces a sense of confusion. The spectators no longer know if the actors are performing or simply using the play as a smokescreen to conceal a real act. To avoid potential misreadings, I am not suggesting here that the audience believes that an actual murder has taken place off-stage – that would be disingenuous – but rather that it *suspects* the actors of using the performance as a mask to articulate authentic emotions and feelings. In this context, it is interesting to note that in an interview with the novelist Marguerite Duras in *France-Observateur* in 1959, the actress Sarah Maldoror, who performed the role of Felicity, talked about discovering a sense of 'freedom' in the play and of 'distancing herself from what Whites thought of her' (March 1959; my translation). Understood in this way, the play could be seen, as many critics have proposed, as a one-sided ritual which attains its efficacy by allowing racially oppressed subjects to act out their real desires in front of a white audience, rendered powerless by the very rules of the theatrical game.[23] Although tempting, this reading overlooks theatre's essential and necessary commitment to artifice. Because the play *is* a play, re-realisation, while certainly gestured towards in *The Blacks*, is never fully achieved. The audience does not believe that the emotions expressed and fantasies represented *are* real; it suspects, though without reaching any definitive closure, that this *might* be the case. As such, it is more accurate to say that the play gives us the semblance of authenticity rather than authenticity itself. This makes the

22 See Derek Connon, 'Confused? You Will Be: Genet's *Les nègres* and the Art of Upsetting the Audience', *French Studies*, 50:4 (1996), 425–38; and J.P. Little, *Les nègres*, for a detailed discussion of the inconsistencies and paradoxes involved in Genet's representation of the off-stage revolution in *The Blacks*.
23 Some of the critics who discuss the play in terms of ritual are John Killinger, 'Jean Genet and the Scapegoat Drama', *Comparative Literature Studies*, 3 (1960), 207–21; Leonard Pronko, *Avant-Garde: The Experimental Theatre in France* (Cambridge: Cambridge University Press, 1962); and George Wellwarth, *The Theatre of Paradox and Protest: Developments in the Avant-Garde Drama* (London: MacGibbon and Kee, 1965. Richard C. Webb, provides an excellent overview of the critical literature dedicated to this aspect of the play. See 'Ritual, Theatre and Jean Genet's *The Blacks*', *Theatre Journal*, 31:4 (1979), 443–59.

play even more disturbing, since the strangeness of the actors is heightened. Blackness escapes all attempts to know it.[24]

A primary reason for the ambiguity that haunts *The Blacks* is caused by Genet's decision to cast black actors not as characters but as performers. As Chaudhuri (1986: 99–108) has persuasively argued, casting in *The Blacks* puts the theatrical frame in crisis. The audience stops responding to the actors as signs or substitutes, and reacts to them as real people; the performers *seem* to be playing themselves, speaking from their own experience. This explains, perhaps, why so many spectators felt disturbed and disoriented by the play in 1959. In an interview with Bettina Knapp, Blin describes how Ionesco felt so disconcerted by the production that he rushed out of the theatre mid-way through the show in a panic. As Blin explains it, Ionesco, 'as a white man [. . .] felt he was being attacked' (Knapp, 1963: 113). Interestingly – and this is confirmed by looking at the reviews at the time – Blin uses Ionesco's attitude as a metonym for the reaction of the Parisian audience in general. According to Blin, the spectators were 'shocked' by the play and 'frightened when confronted with a world they know really exists'. They 'sensed the great pleasure the actors took each time they insulted the whites' (*ibid.*).[25]

A good example of how Genet manufactures this mood of disturbing ambivalence is found at the very start of the play. After introducing himself and the actors by their proper names, Archibald provides the audience with the following information:

ARCHIBALD: When we leave this stage, we are involved in your life. I am a cook, this lady is a sewing maid, this gentleman is a medical student, this gentleman is a curate at St Anne's, this lady. . .skip it [. . .] Liars that we are, the names that I have given to you are false. (1973a: 14)

Archibald's statement exacerbates the potential confusion between actor and character that this ultra-iconic casting has produced. Initially, he

---

24 In this respect, those critics who see the play as a form of terror in the extent to which it connotes rather than denotes experience are correct. The terror is provoked because the actor who is patently and palpably there refuses to assume a specific identity. See Una Chaudhuri, 'The Politics of Theater: Play, Deceit and Threat in Genet's *The Blacks*', *Modern Drama*, 28:3 (1985): 362–75, John Orr, ' Terrorism as Social Drama and Dramatic Form', in J. Orr and D. Klaíc (eds), *Terrorism and Modern Drama* (Edinburgh: Edinburgh University Press, 1990), pp. 48–64; and Elinor Fuchs, 'Clown Shows: Anti-theatricalist Theatricalism in Four Twentieth-Century Plays', in A. Ackerman and M. Puchner (eds), *Against Theatre: Creative Destructions and the Modernist Stage* (Basingstoke: Palgrave Macmillan, 2006), pp. 39–57.
25 This sense of widespread shock among audience members at the Théâtre de Lutèce is confirmed by Odette Aslan, *Roger Blin*, p. 66, and Michel Corvin in Corvin and Dichy, *Jean Genet*, p. 1211.

appears to be setting up a conventional dramatic scenario by highlighting the unreality of the action – the fact that the actors are not who they purport to be. Yet by drawing attention to the actors' professions outside of the theatre, and by reminding the audience that what it is seeing is a representation ('the names that I have given you are false'), he places the vicarious logic upon which all naturalistic drama depends in crisis. Instead of existing as a play, *The Blacks* frames itself as a 'real event' staged by actual black actors who are using theatre as a mask to play themselves. This is intensified later in the play when the lovers Virtue and Village, in their attempts to represent the murder of Marie for the white Court, refer to a real world beyond the theatre:

> **VIRTUE:** Let me tell you that this evening's ceremony will affect me less than the one I perform ten times a day. I'm the only one who experiences shame to the bitter end...
> **ARCHIBALD:** Don't allude to your life.
> **VIRTUE:** (*ironically*). You've been infected by the squeamishness you've picked up from the Whites. A whore shocks you.
> **BOBO:** She does, if she's one in real life. There's no need for us to know about your personal likes and dislikes. That's *your* business...in your room.
> **VILLAGE:** This ceremony is painful to me. (*ibid*.: 31)

At such moments (and there are many of them), the performance, to use Michael Kirby's language, seems 'non-matrixed', the stuff of authentic emotion. The irony here, of course, as Chaudhuri cautions in her detailed reading of Genetian frame-breaking, is that 'authenticity' in *The Blacks* is rigorously plotted (1986: 77–108). The actors are merely repeating the words of Genet's script, and, as such, are as tightly matrixed in their performance as any naturalist actor would be.[26]

But to emphasise a point which I made in Chapters 3 and 4, Genetian authenticity is hardly Aristotelian authenticity. *The Blacks* is a performance where black actors self-consciously play out socially constructed ideas of blackness. In Blin's production, this was exacerbated in the 'voodoo' ceremony when the White Queen gave birth to miniature effigies of the court, and when the entire cast, with the exception of Newport News, danced to an African rhythm tapped out on tam-tam

---

26 An exception here is the actor James Earl Jones' decision to refer to the shootings of four innocent black children in Alabama in Frankel's production. See White, *Genet*, p. 507. For two interesting accounts of how the 1972 production of *The Blacks* at the University of Berkeley was received in the USA, see Jean Decock, 'Les nègres aux USA', *Obliques*, 2 (1972), 48–50; and Maurice Lecuyer, 'Les nègres et au-delà', *Obliques*, 2 (1972), 44–7.

drums at the end of the play. Tellingly, in Archibald's exhortations to the performers cited below, the onus is placed on imitating the sign, rather than the thing in-itself:

ARCHIBALD: (*severely*). The tragedy will lie in the colour black! It's *that* that you'll cherish, *that* that you'll attain, and deserve. It's *that* that must be earned. (1973a: 16; original italics)

ARCHIBALD: I order you to be black to your very veins. Pump black blood through them. Let Africa circulate in them. Let Negroes negrify themselves. Let them persist to the point of madness in what they are condemned to be, in their ebony, in their smell, in their yellow eyes, in their cannibal tastes. Let them not be content with eating Whites, but let them cook each other as well. Let them invent recipes for shin-bones, knee-caps, calves, thick lips, everything. Let them invent unknown sauces. Let them invent hiccoughs, belches and farts that'll give out a deleterious jazz. (*ibid*.: 42)

Since the actors are already black, or as Archibald says 'guilty prisoners playing at guilty prisoners' (*ibid*.: 32), we see them attempting to merge with an image that is patently *not* who they are. By self-consciously *re-presenting* blackness, the actors in the play void it of all substance: they make an absence appear. In the process, they force theatre to acknowledge its own culpability for the dissemination of racist images. They draw attention to the way in which the theatrical medium is both a method of production and an instrument of discipline.[27]

For these reasons, it might seem legitimate, as Elinor Fuchs has suggested, to read Genet's anti-theatricalist play as a Platonic critique of theatre (2006: 39–48). In the allegory of the cave, Plato famously rejected theatre because it seduced spectators into taking the simulacrum of truth for the truth itself, shadows for substance. As such, Plato demanded that mimetic theatre should be banned from the Republic, or *polis* on account of its corrupting influence. However, notwithstanding the very real similarities between the anti-theatricalism of Plato and Genet such a comparison only goes so far. Where Plato is interested in protecting the truth of the real, the place of light, Genet's metatheatrical theatre, as we saw in Chapter 3, is committed to shadows. He uses the stage to confuse binary distinctions between light and dark, real and fiction. What we are

---

27 Although he does not deal with politics or historical context, Mischa Twitchin's analysis of the phenomenological notion of the chiasmus is pertinent here in as much as it explains how theatre can show absence (electronic resource, accessed January 2008: see 'What Do We See in Theatre?').

confronted with in *The Blacks*, to twist Artaud's original metaphor, is a plague of representations that challenges the current distribution of the sensible.

Genet's deconstruction of Plato has important material effects. As Rancière has argued, Plato's rejection of theatre is not solely due to his disapproval of mimesis or simulation; it is caused by a deeper anxiety about people and things being out of place:

> In the third book of the *Republic*, the mimetician is no longer condemned for the falsity and the pernicious nature of the images he presents, but he is condemned in accordance with a principle of division of labour that was already to exclude artisans from any shared political space: the mimetician is, by definition, a double being. He does two things at once, whereas the principle of a well-organized community is that each person only does the one thing they were destined to do by their 'nature'. (2006: 42)

In Rancière's reading, Plato is anxious in the face of the stage because theatre disturbs the propriety of the *polis*. Unlike the good citizen who identifies himself with his place of work or position in the social/racial hierarchy, the actor exists on a duplicitous borderline: '[t]he mimetician brings confusion to this distribution; he is a man of duplication, a worker who does two things at once' (*ibid.*: 43). The mimetician is particularly subversive, continues Rancière, because she occupies the public stage, the space which only those schooled in proper wisdom and decorum are normally permitted to inhabit:

> [T]he mimetician provides a public space for the private principle of work. He sets up a stage for what is common to the community with what should determine the confinement of each person to his or her place. It is this redistribution of the sensible that constitutes his noxiousness, even more than the danger of simulacra weakening souls. (*ibid.*)

Like the noxious Platonic mimetician, the actors in *The Blacks* refuse to assume their proper place in the distribution of the sensible. By dislodging the theatrical frame that incarcerates bodies within an imaginary and real prison, they engage in concrete acts of dissensus which 'confront the established framework of perception, thought and action, with the inadmissible' (*ibid.*: 85). The erasure of blackness in Genet's play makes the black actors visible, but in a way that explodes the conventional racist *mise-en-scène*. Where white racism, as the black review show demonstrates, compels Blacks to become what they (supposedly) are, *The Blacks* permits them to become other than self. It positions them in a space of potentiality, a space, that is, where identity is contested and undone. In Genet's play, the stage no longer exists as *theatron*; it is positioned as a 'third space' or interval where the disciplinary mechanisms of the theatrical frame are nullified. In line with Rancière's ideas on theatre as both metaphor and practice, Genet uses the stage to create a public site, in which oppressed subjects can become visible and, at the same time, highlight their own excessive identities.

Within a France beset with racist anxiety and desperate to differentiate itself from its ex-colonial subjects, Genet's attempt to unsettle the space of theatre in *The Blacks* can be rightly defined as an urban practice in and by itself. For if the stage, as Condé's epigraph at the start of this chapter suggests, was a method for controlling the black body in the city (Blacks were permitted to be seen in theatres and concert halls), then to reorder the spatial rules of the stage is to allow for a very different type of metropolis. In keeping with the ideas of Lefebvre and Foucault, theatrical space in *The Blacks* is heterotopic, a concrete site where segregations and exclusions are undone in the here and now, and where black actors can escape, through the very act of performing, from the prison house that did so much to marginalise them within the space of metropolitan France.

As well as emancipating black actors, it is possible to imagine how Genet's reconfiguration of theatre/social space in *The Blacks* might have impacted, phenomenologically, on French audiences at the time. Because the spectator is unable to locate the black actor with any precision or confidence, space itself starts to float. The spectator is made to feel liminal; she no longer knows where she is or what she ought to do. In this slippage of reality, it is impossible to know how to react. For if we cannot ascertain the status of the message being communicated, then how can we defend ourselves from what it might be insinuating? The only solution is paranoia, which, as result of its persistent mood of doubt and gaping groundlessness, is no solution at all. What Genet's play manages to do is to provoke a confusion of limits, to erase the clearly delineated spatial and epistemological borders that French urban planners at the dawn of decolonisation were so concerned to keep in place in their attempts to separate improper foreigners from proper French citizens.

By doing so, Genet reverses the dynamics of the filth complex that I discussed earlier in the chapter (see pp. 137–42), and places the existential and racial integrity of the French spectators in question. What Genet appears to understand so well in *The Blacks* is that the filth complex is dependent upon maintaining clear limits, in keeping the gap between subject and object securely in place. This view is seconded by the post-Lacanian psychoanalyst Julia Kristeva in her influential study of abjection, *Powers of Horror: an Essay on Abjection*, in which she reminds us that abjection is primarily spatial. For Kristeva, abjection occurs when established limits are transgressed, and when the subject, '[i]nstead of sounding herself as to [her] "being", does so concerning [her] place: *Where* am I? instead of "*Who* am I?"' (1982: 8; translation modified; original italics).

Kristeva's words highlight the extent to which objects of filth in abjection are metaphorical. To feel polluted does not mean that the subject is frightened of being physically harmed through her contact with dirt; she is horrified, rather, because there is nothing but dirt to stop her from collapsing into the Other. To feel abject is to lose the object that defines the self; to be without limits; to fail to differentiate. Or as Kristeva remarks: '[i]t is thus not lack of cleanliness or health that causes abjection but what disturbs identity, system, order' (*ibid*.: 4). This explains why in *Powers of Horror*, the abject is always discussed in terms of a void, a vertiginous emptiness, 'a dark revolt of being' (*ibid*.: 1). To prevent herself from falling into this darkness, the subject, Kristeva proposes, uses abjection as a sort of existential barrier or frontier: 'abject and abjections are my safeguards. The primers of my culture' (*ibid*.: 2).

Like Kristeva's abject geometry, space in *The Blacks* is catastrophic for the white spectator. Since there is no longer a theatricalised black Other with, and against, whom she can define herself, she is made to feel *depaysée*. Her ability to use abjection as a protective device recedes; and she discovers, as Kristeva says, that the 'impossible constitutes [her] very *being*' (*ibid*.: 5; original italics). We are always already polluted by otherness. Historically, this is where the spatial and political significance of *The Blacks* resides; it deconstructs what de Gaulle, the good housekeeper, sought at all costs to eradicate: the blurring of racial boundaries. By doing so, *The Blacks* highlights the inherent relationality of all subjectivity: the fact that we cannot live without the Other. To attempt to do so is to exist in a permanent state of horror. Threatened by this agonistic form of being, the only solution – the only politically progressive solution – is to abandon all pretensions of propriety and to accept, as Genet did, that there is no homeland, no space to call one's own (see Chapter 1 in this book). In other words, the acceptance of abjection is the prelude to living with the wound, the recognition that opens the subject to internal and external foreignness.

As I have been arguing throughout this book, theatre is well suited to provoke the abjection or homelessness that the French nation-State was – and continues to be – so concerned to repress. Because of the necessary presence of the body, the fact that actors and spectators meet in real space, theatre is a badly constructed house; its foundations are always on the verge of internal collapse. To return to Quick, there is something in theatre's ontology that disrupts the sign's attempt to domesticate the real, to make the Other transparent. Kristeva, too, is aware of the disruptive power of performance, the sense in which it is allied to the production of abjection. Indeed, in *Powers of Horror*, she goes so far as to say that abjection is a form of 'true theatre without make up or masks' that 'shows me what I permanently thrust aside in order to live [. . .] There, I am at the border of my condition as a living being' (*ibid.*: 3).

Kristeva's theatricalised reading of abjection reinforces our awareness that all theatre, even when it is strenuously committed to upholding the dramatic illusion, is, to an extent, 'true'. In *The Blacks*, Genet exploits theatre's 'realness' by placing the white spectator in proximity to the foreign thing that supposedly threatens her identity as a clean and proper subject. In his play, the black actors are not, properly speaking, objects; they are ab-jects, phenomena that 'disappear' each time the audience tries to grasp them. In this relationship of alterity and void, the French spectator confronts her limits physically, as she is forced to experience, directly and in actual space, the black bodies that French urban planners wanted to render invisible. Placed in proximity to this Otherness, which stretches, as I mentioned in Chapter 3, the aesthetic frame to breaking point, the spectator experiences abjection: the object (or rather ab-ject) of fear is too close for comfort, so near that it can be touched. Although critics at the time did not, for obvious reasons, use Kristeva's concepts to account for their responses to the play, feelings of abjection and disorientation were widespread. Gabriel Marcel describes feeling 'confused', and accuses Genet of 'spit[ting] and vomit[ing] out [. . .] all that is honourable and worthy in the Christian West' (in Webb, 1992: 54). Al Alvarez defines the play as 'obscene' and notes that Genet 'piles blasphemy on blasphemy' (*ibid.*: 55). Alfred Simon remarks that *The Blacks* 'is impossible to swallow', and associates it 'with the exquisite smell of decay. . .and noxious scents' (*ibid.*: 61). And Jean Cau, writing in *L'Express*, reflects on an 'infinitely miserable feeling of being apart' and experiencing a sense of 'loneliness and banishment from the colour black' (*ibid.*). As these abject responses show, Blin's production fulfilled what Genet set out to achieve: to unsettle the white French spectator's sense of existential, racial and spatial being so that she no longer knew where she was or to what 'race' or nation she belonged to.

Disidentification

Erasing blackness is not the only way in which Genet subverts French identity in *The Blacks*. Like *The Mousetrap* in *Hamlet*, the play-within-the play of *The Blacks* is designed to make the French spectators feel guilty, to remind them of their whiteness.[28] This attempt to 'mark' identity explains Genet's insistence that the play be performed in front of an all-white audience:[29]

> This play, written, I repeat by a white man, is intended for a white audience, but if – which is unlikely – it is ever performed before a black audience, then a white person, male or female, should be invited every evening. The organizer of the show should welcome him formally, dress him in ceremonial costume and lead him to his seat, preferably in the front row of the stalls. The actors will play for him. A spotlight should be focused upon this symbolic white throughout the performance. (1973a: 6)

By ensuring that his play is watched by white French spectators, Genet blurs the gap between what theatre semioticians call 'scenic space' and 'audience space'.[30] The effect of this 'collapse' is to make any attack on the fake white Court appear as a symbolic assault on the French spectators themselves.[31] Hence when the white Court is 'murdered' at the end of the play, the audience has the impression that it too has been put to death, assassinated through performance. But what exactly does this death mean? And why does it seem so real?

Before we can begin to answer these questions, it is important to remember that the violence of whiteness resides in its ability to pass itself off as the invisible norm, the absent signifier against which all other colours are compelled to differentiate themselves.[32] As Steve Garner puts it, 'for decades, the gaze of white[ness] has been trained on those defined as Other, whether using the terminology of "race" or ethnicity' (2007: 5; translation modified). As long as whiteness remains unmarked, it is

---

28 Genet could be accused of overlooking important gender, sexual and class differences in his blanket depiction of whiteness. However, his admittedly totalising attack on whiteness is understandable within the context of the discourses on whiteness that emerged in France from the mid-1950s. As I have been arguing throughout this book, decolonisation was essentially an attempt to whiten France.
29 In the short text 'To a Would-be Producer' (1963), Genet famously refused to allow the play to be performed in Poland by an all-white cast.
30 For an in-depth study of the different semiotic spaces that constitute the total theatrical event, see Gay McAuley, *Space in Performance: Making Meaning in the Theatre* (Ann Arbor: University of Michigan Press, 2000), pp. 24–34.
31 Susan Taubes provides an early reading of this aspect of the play, but she does so according to the humanist language of the time. The aim of the performance was always more ambitious than simply wanting to make white people feel guilty. See 'The White Mask Falls', *Tulane Drama Review*, 7:3 (1963), 85–92: 97.
32 See, for instance, Theodore Allen, *The Invention of the White Race*, 2 vols (London: Verso, 1994); Richard Dyer, *White* (London: Routledge, 1997); and Ruth Frankenberg (ed.), *Displacing Whiteness: Essays in Social and Cultural Criticism* (Durham, NC: Duke University Press, 1997).

synonymous with universality, truth and nature. By contrast, to mark it, as Genet does in the play, is to expose 'its masquerade', to highlight its constitutive role in the production of political, cultural and ontological value. This is clearly evinced in the two examples below when Virtue experiences the temptation to betray her colour and stands beneath the White Queen echoing her words:

VIRTUE: (*softly, as if in a state of somnambulism*). I am the lily-white Queen of the West. Only centuries of breeding could achieve such a miracle! Immaculate, pleasing to the eye and to the soul! [...]. Whether in excellent health, pink and gleaming, or consumed with languor, I am white. If death strikes me, I die in the colour of victory [...] I am white, it's milk that symbolizes me, the lily, the dove, quicklime and the clear conscience, Poland with its eagle and snow! (1973a: 36)

THE QUEEN: [...] To the rescue, angel of the flaming sword, virgins of the Parthenon, stained-glass of Chartres, Lord Byron, Chopin, French cooking, the Unknown Soldier, Tyrolean songs, Aristotelian principles, heroic couplets, flowers, a touch of coquetry, vicarage gardens. (*ibid*.: 38)

By showing whiteness to be what Roland Barthes would call 'mythology' as opposed to biology, Genet's play performs a special kind of murder.[33] In this instance, violence is not inflicted upon the body, but upon the signifying system that allows Whites to regard their skin colour as a mark of their 'natural' superiority. As a consequence of this corporeal hailing, whiteness is blasted out of nature and placed in history, which, of course, opens it to the forces of contingency and death. Hence, the Governor's response to finding out that there is no corpse in the catafalque ('they kill us without killing us' (*ibid*.: 76) is equally applicable to the experience undergone by the actual French spectators. Like the white Court, they too have been subjected to a symbolic murder that has no need of an actual body. At the end of Blin's production, the symbolic assassination of whiteness was underlined when Newport News, in a departure from the original script, returned to the stage and placed a coffin before the audience.

The violence inflicted upon whiteness in *The Blacks* is complicated

---

33 Barthes deals with everyday life in France in the volume *Mythologies*, trans. A. Lavers (London: Paladin, 1986). Like The Blacks, several of his essays explore the political meanings and associations attached to whiteness and blackness. See 'Wine and Milk', pp. 56–8 and the long theoretical section 'Myth Today', pp. 109–59.

by the fact that Genet also invites the audience to disidentify with the white Court. Throughout the play, the members of the court are represented as grotesque tyrants, examples of Ubu-esque officialdom. Genet's decision to mask the court produces, as he does in *The Screens* with the *colons*, a form of Brechtian estrangement, in which the spectators are prevented from empathising with the representatives of their own culture. As a result of this complex interplay between proximity and distance, the audience is placed in an ethical and political 'nowhere', interpellated as white and European, and yet encouraged to respond, positively, to the justice of the black struggle. In keeping with the *promesse du bonheur* that is always present, in negative form, in Genet's late theatre (see Chapter 3 in this book), this interval or 'in-betweeness' is where the utopian politics of *The Blacks* are located. This disorientation allows for an experience of disidentification, which, by throwing the spectator's existing matrix of identity into question, opens her up to what Rancière names 'the cause of the Other' (1998).

The point of democratic politics, for Rancière, is to render visible the presence of a 'wrong', which can only be addressed through a fundamental redistribution of the sensible. While Rancière believes that the wrong can be corrected in specific circumstances and situations, it can never be fully satisfied or repaired. The wrong is infinite: to attempt to resolve it is to eradicate politics altogether: '[t]he wrong by which politics occurs is not some flaw calling for reparation. It is the introduction of an incommensurable at the heart of the distribution of speaking bodies' (1999: 19). For Rancière, the political wrong, embodied by those who momentarily represent 'the part with no part', is the antithesis to crude notions of identity politics. Where identity politics is predicated upon the assumption that identity exists, the subjects of the Rancièrian wrong are struggling to *derealise* themselves. They want to become other than self, to escape where and what they are and to reject any attempt to impose a definitive function or mode of being upon them. Importantly, Rancière believes that this commitment to dissensus is the cause and consequence of equality. By refusing to occupy a place or to identify with a fixed essence or self, the subject of the grievance discloses the emptiness of all social classes and hierarchies. This declaration of radical equality has major political consequences; it establishes relations and alliances between different parties and individuals who have nothing in common but their commitment to emancipation:

> Politics does not exist because men [. . .] place their interests in common. Politics exists because those who have no right to be counted as speaking

beings make themselves of some account, setting up a community by the fact of placing in common a wrong that is nothing more than this very confrontation, the confrontation of two worlds in a single world: the world where they are and the world where they are not. (*ibid.*: 27)

Politically, Rancière's concept of equality means that the subject does not identify with the Other as such (how could she?), but rather with her cause, with her struggle to attain visibility and speech. Furthermore, like Badiou's notion of the axiom of justice, equality, for Rancière, describes a process whereby each specific attempt at recognition is underpinned by an appeal to universality: 'Politics is the art of warped deductions and mixed identities. It is the art of the local and singular constructions of cases of universality' (*ibid.*: 139). The importance that Rancière attaches to the wrong means that disidentification or disappropriation becomes the determining factor in politics, the negative act that disrupts the solidity of the sensible and opens up new heterogeneous alliances between subjects who have nothing in common except their commitment to disaggregation and dispute:

> The feeling of injustice does not go to make up a political bond through a simple identifying that would appropriate the disappropriation of a wrong. In addition there has to be the disappropriation of identity that constitutes an appropriate subject for conducting the dispute. (*ibid.*)

Rancière's ideas elucidate the political rationale involved in Genet's desire to wound the white audience in *The Blacks*. From Rancière's perspective, Genet is doing more than simply seeking revenge on French culture; he is redistributing the sensible, and, by doing so, rupturing the racist logic of the time. Differently from poststructuralist readers of the play who regard Genet's refusal to define black identity as a concern to protect difference, Rancière allows us to see how blackness in the play is, by contrast, a marker of revolt, a specific historical signifier for a universal wrong.[34] Without ever knowing what blackness is (like the off-stage revolution that is never defined), the audience is encouraged to

---

34 It is interesting to consider Maryse Condé's views about what blackness stands for in the play. Responding to Genet's question in the prologue to the written text 'But what exactly is a Black?', Condé replied: 'It seems to me that, when you quote Genet, you should remember who Genet was. He was a kind of marginal, as you say, somebody who was outside society, outside the common world. So, for him, anybody outside society, outside the rules of the world, could be considered Black. That is to say, a Black could be a Jew. A Black could be a homosexual' (in Teleb-Khyar, 'An Interview with Maryse Condé and Rita Dove', *Callaloo*, 14:2 (1991), 347–66: 352).

cross the colour divide and to identify itself as black.[35] Importantly, this does not mean that the audience becomes 'white Negroes' *à la* Norman Mailer.[36] Rather, the object for the white spectator is to discover the impossible in identification and to ally herself with the Blacks' political quest to become other than self. As *The Blacks* demonstrates, this is achieved by fashioning a stage where equality is disclosed through a painful wound that throws identity into question, and which encourages the spectators to reject their existing alliances and allegiances. In the racist climate of post-imperial France in the 1950s and 1960s, this can be read as an invitation for the spectator to abandon the Gaullist consensus on French identity, and to forge alternative relationships with the foreigner workers in the 'hexagon' itself and with newly emancipated subjects in the former colonies. Without ever offering a message of hope or image of reconciliation, the negativity of Genet's play offers itself as a utopian space in which rigid definitions of racial identity are challenged by provoking an experience of wounding which reveals the presence of a wrong. Or, to put this in different, more provocative terms, Genet encourages us, the white spectators, to become like him, 'blacks with pink skin' (2004: 126).

Conclusion

In this chapter, I have attempted to show how *The Blacks*, when placed within its historical and sociological framework, becomes an early critique of decolonisation in France, rather than simply a semi-abstract work about anti-colonial revolt 'somewhere' in Africa. Although this changes the focus of the play's politics, it does not invalidate its revolutionary significance. The political thrust of *The Blacks* is found in the way it undermines the Gaullist consensus on what French identity in a

---

[35] In a fascinating article, Gisèle Child-Olmsted reminds us that, for Genet, class and race form part of the same struggle. See 'Black on White: Language and Revolution in Genet's Political Writings', Bougon (ed.) *L'Esprit Créateur*, 35:1 (1995), 61–9: 62. Genet hints at a similar alliance in 'Preface to *The Blacks*', when he mentions that 'abject poverty can only lead to revolt, and that already numerous agitators, Whites and Blacks, are raising awareness in their companions, and developing in them a taste for responsibility' (Appendix: 233).

[36] Mailer published a famous article on Gene Frankel's production of the play in *The Village Voice* in 1961. While he endorsed the play's violence, he criticised it, somewhat curiously, for not showing the 'truth of black experience'. What Mailer fails to see is that the 'truth of black experience' was the very thing that Genet was concerned to protect and challenge (May 1961, p. 14).

decolonised world was supposed to look like. Reflecting Genet's theory of aesthetic politics, political experience here is spatial experience. The heterotopic aspects of theatre are exploited for utopian purposes. Theatre becomes a site where new improper forms of subjectivity might come into being. As I showed, these new configurations of identity are dependent upon the disclosure of a wrong that invited French subjects to disidentify with the French nation-State and to hear the call of the immigrant Other. This ultimately is why *The Blacks* remains so vital for contemporary practitioners today, as the interviews with Ultz and Excalibah later in the book indicate (see Chapters 10 and 11 in this book).

6

Bringing it all back home: the battle of *The Screens*

It was a question of inflaming you, not teaching you. (Genet, 2003: 83)

Introduction

In contrast to the previous two chapters which investigated *The Balcony* and *The Blacks* by contextualising them historically, this chapter explores *The Screens*, Genet's last play, as a historical event in and by itself. The focus here is on mapping, through a study of newspaper reviews, audience responses and political reaction, the actual effects generated by Roger Blin's production of the play at the Odéon-Théâtre de France in April and May 1966. As I argue, Blin's production, although intentionally constructed as the antithesis of orthodox models of committed theatre, marked an important political turning point in French history.[1] In my reading, the

---

1 Blin's comments below underline Genet's anxiety about politics becoming more important than aesthetics in *The Screens*: 'He was aware of my political leanings, he knew I was attached to the Left far more than he was and he was fully aware of certain decisions I had taken. He also guessed that one of my reasons for being involved was to piss off those of the Right. We spoke about all that several times and he wrote me numerous letters, in one of which he said "whatever you do don't make my play

riots provoked by the play's treatment of the Algerian War called the Gaullist consensus on Algeria into question, and helped to prepare the ground for May 1968. In this way, I intend to provide empirical evidence for what I have been until now merely arguing for: that Genet's desire to wound his audience possessed real revolutionary potential.

The battle of *The Screens*

Midway through its run, at around 10.30 pm on 30 April 1966, Roger Blin's production of *The Screens* came to an abrupt and violent end when a group of about thirty *ex-parachutistes* and *ancien combattants*, associated with the extreme right-wing movement Occident, threw smoke bombs and bottles onto the stage before proceeding to attack the cast.[2] A riot soon ensued as the actors fought the protestors with chairs and batons. Two members of the cast were injured, one of whom was hospitalised. Order was finally restored when Jean-Louis Barrault, the respected actor-manager of the Odéon, addressed the audience and called for calm. The play recommenced with Genet's favourite actress María Casares uttering the appropriate line 'Causons' ('Let's talk').

The riot at the Odéon on 30 April was not an isolated incident, and for the remainder of the play's run, performances were routinely disrupted by fighting in the stalls, heckling from the front rows and bomb alerts. On 1 May, fifty or so young right-wing militants, including several students from the St Cyr military academy, pelted the cast with eggs and bricks. And on 7 May, during the last performance of the season, the Occident group attempted to set fire to the theatre. What Albert Dichy and Linda Bellity Peskine have called 'La bataille des *Paravents*' ('the battle of *The Screens*') was not confined to the theatre and spread throughout the neighbouring Latin Quarter (1991). Between these dates, on 4 May, a large right-wing demonstration against the play (one of whose organisers was Jean-Marie Le Pen, the future leader of Le Front Nationale), met at the Panthéon and marched on the Odéon. As the extreme right tried to enter the theatre, they were met by a large body of counter-protesters mobilised by the Union Nationale des Etudiants de France (UNEF), who

  an agent of the Left'" (*Souvenirs et propos*, L. Bellity Peskine (ed.) (Paris: Gallimard, 1986), p. 202; my translation)).
2 Occident was an extreme right-wing movement that was opposed to both the political left in France and to de Gaulle. It supported the US war effort in Vietnam and believed in European supremacy. It was officially outlawed in 1968.

had been active in orchestrating student opposition to the Algerian War. Genet and Blin watched the subsequent street battle from the balcony of the Odéon, which was begrudgingly protected by massed ranks of armed riot police. As the editor Paule Thévenin pointed out 'at that moment, the theatre was the street' (*ibid.*: 11; my translation).

The violence of the fighting, along with the heated and vociferous denunciations which appeared in the right-wing press (Genet was accused of being a deserter who had betrayed France and its Army) scandalised politicians and catapulted *The Screens* into the national consciousness. In October 1966 as the play geared up for its second run, a debate took place in the National Assembly in which several deputies, led by Christian Bonnet, proposed a motion to censor the play and to withdraw funding from the prestigious Odéon theatre. Amazingly, the motion was abandoned when the novelist André Malraux, de Gaulle's then Minister of Culture, reminded the parliament of the basic right of artists and theatre practitioners to explore whatever subject they deemed fit. In a speech which placed Genet's *esthétique du mal* in a lineage running from Goya to Flaubert, Malraux finished by pointing out that to censor *The Screens* would be to set a dangerous precedent, for it would affect not just the Odéon, but all state-sponsored theatres and *centres dramatiques* throughout France.[3]

But what was it about *The Screens* that produced such intense reaction? On the surface, the answer appears fairly straightforward. A mere four years after the Evian Accords were signed granting Algeria independence from France, Genet's satirical and cruel representation of the Algerian War was simply too much for nationalists and conservatives to stomach.[4] Ignoring the extreme sensitivity of the situation (the play's French premiere had already been delayed for five years on account of its explosive subject matter), Genet had produced, instead, a scatological comedy, which celebrated the victory of the Algerian rebels and set out to undercut the ideals and nostalgias of French imperialism.[5] To borrow the language of the *ancien combattants* who had published a collective

---

3 For a full transcript of the debate, see Corvin and Dichy, *Jean Genet*, pp. 971–80.
4 The fact that *The Screens* was always going to create a disturbance of some sort is evident from Jean-Louis Barrault's pre-emptive article 'Scandal and Provocation', published in *Les Cahiers Renauld-Barrault* in April 1966 and reprinted in Linda Bellity Peskine and Albert Dichy (eds), *La bataille des Paravents* (Paris: IMEC, 1991), p. 53.
5 Although Genet finished the final version of *The Screens* in 1961, Roger Blin had attempted to secure a theatre for its Paris premiere as early as 1959. According to Odette Aslan, this was at Le Vieux-Colombier. See *Roger Blin*, p. 69. Since no French theatre manager at the time was willing to stage it, the play premiered in Berlin in 1961 in a production by Hans Lietzau at Schlosspark-Theater. Other productions and versions of the play before 1966 took place in Vienna in 1963, and in Stockholm and London in 1964.

letter against the play in *Le Monde*, Genet had drenched France in 'a shower of shit' (May 1966). Nevertheless, the more one reflects on the battle of *The Screens*, the more it appears that its real significance resided less in its representation of the Algerian War than in its capacity to bring to light what the Gaullist consensus on Algeria was so concerned to repress: the emergence of new forms of revolutionary activism in France among students, young workers, and disaffected leftists.

The crucial point to grasp about 'the battle of *The Screens*' is that the students who fought in the streets were not acting 'as students', so to speak. Unlike earlier manifestations of student discontent organised by UNEF, the defenders of the Odéon had little interest in avoiding the draft to Algeria, reducing class sizes or liberalising conservative attitudes in French universities. Differently from the students on the campus at Antony in the south of Paris who, during 'The Love War' of 1965, had organised a sit-in against restrictions on visitor rights in same-sex dormitories, they were actively disidentifying with a consensual view of Frenchness promoted by de Gaulle.[6] In the aftermath of the Algerian War, this was based upon ideas of 'race' and clearly defined geographical boundaries. Instead of accepting the benefits of modernisation as their parents had done (see Chapter 4 in this book), the students at the Odéon were committed to defending more universalised notions of justice and equality. Siding with Genet and Blin in 1966, was to recognise the validity of Third World revolt and to reject France for a new earth, an earth where exclusionary images of national identity were rendered redundant. To gain some insight into the profound political significance inherent in the students' decision to defend *The Screens*, three further questions need to be explored. First, what type of crisis did Algeria provoke for France? Next, in whose name did de Gaulle attempt to manage that crisis? And finally, in what ways did *The Screens* reveal (or make appear) what the French nation-State wanted to occult?

Algérie française

It is well documented by contemporary historians that the Algerian War, which lasted from 1954 to 1962, traumatised France and produced

---

6 For a fascinating account of student politics in France in the 1960s, see Michael Seidman, *The Imaginary Revolution: Parisian Students and Workers in 1968* (Oxford: Berghahn, 2004).

a collapse in collective memory that has continued until the twenty-first century.[7] Unlike its colonies in Africa and Indochina, and protectorates in Morocco and Tunisia, all of which had been granted independence by 1960, Algeria was administered as a French region. It comprised three separate *départements*, and was inhabited by a large settler population, *les pieds noirs*. Similar to the Loyalists in Northern Ireland, *les pieds noirs* had developed deep economic and emotional ties with the country since the first wave of colonisation in the mid-nineteenth century. The exceptional status of Algeria was made more complex by the fact that Algerian 'Muslims' were not regarded, like other colonised peoples in the French empire, as subjects with their own autonomous national identity. On the contrary, they were legally recognised, in the Statute of 20 September 1947, as full French citizens, and granted the right to work in mainland France.[8] This was confirmed, even more emphatically, in Article 75 of the Constitution of 1958 which, as Shepard notes, 'recognized that all people born in Algeria – Muslims, Europeans, "natives" or "settlers" – were French nationals' (2006b: 151). Since Algeria had effectively been a part of France since 1848, the conflict waged by the Front de Libération Nationale (FLN) and Mouvement National Algerién (MNA) for independence was never labelled as a war per se; it was referred to euphemistically, like the revolution of May 1968, as a series of *événements*, or events which concerned France alone. The already difficult situation facing the French government was further exacerbated by the attitude of the French Army who had been humbled at the battle of Dien Bien Phu in 1954. In common with the *pieds noirs* who regarded Algeria as a part of France and themselves as proper French citizens, the Army was determined to keep *Algérie française* at all costs, and saw the conflict as a chance to win back military pride.

The presence of a large disgruntled settler population, supported by a sympathetic military, both of whom were ideologically and emotionally opposed to the claims of independence made by the FLN, threw France into a period of political and constitutional crisis. In May 1958, the hostility shown by the *pied noirs* towards what they had previously perceived to be a pro-independence gesture made by the Socialist Prime Minister Guy Mollet brought down the Fourth Republic, and eventually

---

7 In addition to Benjamin Stora, note in particular the work of Jim House and Neil MacMaster, *Paris 1961: Algerians, State Terror and Memory* (Oxford: Oxford University Press, 2006); and in a slightly different context, Henri Rousso, *The Vichy Syndrome: History and Memory in France Since 1944*, trans. H. Goldhammer (Cambridge, MA: Harvard University Press,1991).

8 I have put the word 'Muslim' in inverted commas since distinctions between Muslims and other ethnic groups in Algeria, such as the Berbers, were not recognised by the French State. One was either a European Algerian or an Algerian Muslim.

resulted, later that year, in de Gaulle's return to power after a decade or so in the political wilderness.[9] Initially, de Gaulle was supported by the *pieds noirs* and generals, who believed that the mystical figurehead of La France libre would, of all politicians, be the one most committed to keeping Algeria as part of France. Two years later, however, de Gaulle's decision to grant Algerians a referendum on self-determination (75 per cent of the population delivered a 'Yes' vote), led to a *coup d'état* in Algiers, and almost resulted in the war migrating to mainland France itself. If one can believe apocryphal accounts, some Parisians expected the imminent invasion of General Salan's paratroopers from the air. Although all-out civil war was avoided in France, it is no exaggeration to say that Paris was a city under siege between 1959 and 1962, caught between the in-fighting of the rival Algerian independence movements, the FLN and the MNA, and cowering under the bombs and assassination attempts of the Organisation de l'Armée Secrète (OAS).[10] In addition to this, the Parisian police force, headed by the ex-colonial administrator and Vichy official, Maurice Papon, had started to adopt increasingly heavy-handed tactics in the *métropole*. As the war intensified, Algerians and other North Africans were subjected to curfews, invasive surveillance techniques and random round-ups, or *rafles*. The discrimination against immigrant workers from the Maghreb reached its height on 17 October 1961, when the police massacred over one hundred innocent Algerians, who were marching against the war in a peaceful demonstration organised by the FLN in Paris. According to eyewitness accounts, the water in the Seine was stained red from the blood of the victims, many of whose bodies were thrown into the river from the bridges at Neuilly and Saint-Michel. When the PCF, UNEF and Confédération Générale du Travail (CGT) marched in support of the dead Algerians and in protest against the OAS attacks on 8 February 1962, the police, bolstered by the new special patrol group the Compagnies Républicaines de Sécurité (CRS), waded into the crowd with batons and *matraques*, and killed nine protestors on the steps of the Charonne metro station in the east of the city. On 13 February, a huge counter-demonstration against police brutality and right-wing violence took place in central Paris.

9 This is how Todd Shepard writes about de Gaulle's arrival in power in late May 1958 as Prime Minister: 'De Gaulle assumed power amid scenes of a popular uprising and in a context heavy with the possibility of an armed forces putsch. The general insisted that his moves were legal. Many others, however, posed trenchant questions, or expressed their outrage. François Mitterrand famously characterised those moves as a "'coup d'état'" (*The Invention of Decolonization*, p. 74).
10 The OAS worked against de Gaulle's government and tried to destabilise France on behalf of the colons and generals in Algeria.

The actions of the Army and settlers in Algeria, along with the police in the capital, divided metropolitan France ideologically, and reopened fresh wounds between the political right and left. For many on the left, the tortures and curfews practised by the Army and police were reminiscent of Nazi tactics against Jews and partisans which were condoned (and often supported) by the Vichy regime in France during the German Occupation of the country.[11] (In light of Papon's subsequent imprisonment in 1998, for ordering the deportation of hundreds of Jews between 1942 and 1944, this was a valid accusation.) Within this climate of right-wing intimidation and left-wing recrimination, the myth of the Resistance, which France had used to bolster its self-esteem, no longer seemed tenable, and the country was forced to come to terms with an unpalatable truth: that it was haunted by its own home-grown brand of Fascism. While it would be unfair to say, as Sartre and François Mitterrand insinuated, that de Gaulle, too, was a Fascist, his charismatic form of leadership, characterised as it was by a mystical faith in an organic nation-State, nevertheless had distinct Bonapartist overtones.[12]

If the Algerian War disclosed the power of the political right in France, it also revealed a deep malaise in official left-wing politics. The Socialist (SFIO) and Communist parties had been slow to support Algerian independence and only came out in favour of the FLN when it appeared that the victory of the latter was all but assured. Their lukewarm response to the FLN's anti-colonialist struggle was not lost on young French militants, many of whom felt increasingly alienated from mainstream left-wing politics and had turned instead to more dynamic Third-Worldist models of revolutionary change. For the authoritarian centrist de Gaulle, the Algerian War proved that the nation-State was dangerously divided and in urgent need of unification. De Gaulle's solution was simply to repress the memory of Algeria. No official monuments or celebrations were commissioned to mark the end of the war (the war was not recognised as a war by the French State until 1999); an amnesty on war crimes in Algeria was announced as early as 1968; the massacre of 17 October 1961 was repressed until 2001 when Bertrand Delanoë, the Mayor of Paris, laid a wreath of remembrance on the Saint-Michel bridge; and there was a draconian policy of censorship imposed

---

11 Some degree of the panic felt by the left in the face of this resurgence of the extreme right in France is attested to by Sartre's decision to help to found Le Front d'Action et de Coordination des Universitaires et Intellectuels pour un Rassemblement Antifasciste (FAC) in 1961–62 (The Action and Co-ordination Front of University Staff and Intellectuals for an Anti-Fascist Movement).
12 For a good discussion of Sartre's attack on de Gaulle during the Algerian War, see David Drake, *Intellectuals and Politics in Post-War France* (Basingstoke: Palgrave Macmillan, 2002), pp. 121–7.

on books, films and television programmes which provided an alternative perspective to the Gaullist consensus on Algeria. This censorship continued well into the 1970s, and affected works such as Henri Alleg's *La question*, Frantz Fanon's *The Wretched of the Earth*, the Vérité-Liberté Collective's *Octobre à Paris*, Jean-Luc Godard's *Le petit soldat*, and, most famously, Gillo Pontecorvo's *The Battle of Algiers*, all of which were produced between 1958 and 1966.[13]

Censorship was not the only tactic used by de Gaulle to repress the memory of Algeria. Something more palatable and mythical was needed to overcome the guilt and turmoil. And from 1958 onwards, de Gaulle attempted to regain France's lost grandeur by turning towards Europe and embarking on a feverish policy of economic and technocratic modernisation. De Gaulle's comments at a press conference in 1961 are a brutal reminder of where France's new priorities lay: 'Algeria is costing us [...] more than it is bringing in [...] Now our great national ambition has become our own progress, the real source of power and influence' (de Gaulle, in Stora, 2001: 107). De Gaulle's words were ruthless, but entirely responsive to the needs of French capital. Between roughly 1955 and 1985, France experienced, as the historian Benjamin Stora claims, 'the most extraordinary development it had ever known' (*ibid.*: 91). Growth was particularly high in the period just before and immediately after the war, and the widespread economic benefits it delivered allowed the French to patch over what Soria describes as 'the psychic scars' caused by the loss of Algeria (*ibid.*: 114–15). Committed to reinventing itself as a decolonised capitalist State, the last thing that France wanted was to be reminded of its colonial past. The historian Todd Shepard notes:

> With the advent of the notion that decolonization was a tide of History, however, French élites came to see Algerian independence as necessitated by the logic of history itself. No longer the exception among European overseas possessions, Algeria now became the emblematic example [...] The lessons these French officials drew were not limited to France. Just months after Algerian independence, de Gaulle pointed to the United Kingdom's failure to decolonize fully as a sign of its lack of commitment to building Europe – one key reason, the French president explained, why Britain should be kept out of the European Community. (2006a: 7)

Shepard's analysis shows how, for de Gaulle, defeat in the colonies was transformed into a moment of national victory. The loss of Algeria

---

13 For a more in-depth study of censorship in fiction and film during the Algerian War, see Philip Dine, *Images of the Algerian War: French Fiction and Film 1945–1992* (Oxford: Clarendon Press, 1994).

gave France the excuse to extricate itself from its costly imperialist past and to embrace, instead, a new managed future, in which the nerve-centre of capitalist expansionism was henceforth situated in Europe.

The attack on consensus

Although Genet always insisted that his play was the very opposite of *théâtre engagé*, there is no doubt that *The Screens* was deliberately calculated to shatter historical amnesia. In an interview with the magazine *L'Algérien en Europe* Genet explained that the objective behind the 'violent stage images' in the play was to shock the audience into a new awareness about its imperialist past (May 1966). Likewise in 'Letters to Roger Blin', he talked about forcing a confrontation with the nation's 'true history', which, as he was careful to remind Blin, was forged in 'crime':[14] '[s]hame is less prone to being shaken than glory [...] A people solely distinguished by periods of glory or men of virtue would inevitably be subject to analysis and reduced to nothing, save a receptacle. The crimes of which a people is ashamed constitute its real history' (1972: 19).

The main thrust of Genet's attack in *The Screens* was directed against the *colons* (the colonists) and the Army, both of whom, in the 1961 script and in Roger Blin's 1966 production, are represented as grotesque tyrants, devoid of sympathy and intelligence. Sir Harold, a caricature complete with red hair, a false moustache and huge painted-on freckles, is willing to sacrifice his son for his roses, 'to save my son's patrimony I'd sacrifice my son' (1987: 74–5); Monsieur Blankensee wanders through his estate with a huge prosthetic cushion strapped to his stomach as a way of impressing his workers '[m]y pad is the chief element of my glamour' (*ibid.*: 85); and the Vamp's only regret as she leaves Algeria is that she will be unable to show her legs to the Arabs: '[n]evertheless, they did know how to look at my thighs. From a distance, of course. (*She laughs.*) Mustn't touch' (*ibid.*: 180). Adopting the same techniques he used in *The Blacks* for representing the white court, Genet shows little concern in *The Screens* in trying to understand the complexities involved in the political and ethical choices made by the settler population in

---

14 In the context of *The Screens*, it is difficult not to associate Genet's reference to shame and guilt with the systematic torture of Algerian militants and civilians by the French Army.

Algeria. By depicting them as pantomimic imbeciles and by inviting the audience to laugh at them, Genet simply assumes that they are politically wrong and ethically unjustified.

He makes the same assumptions in his depiction of the Army. Unlike the filmmaker Pontecorvo, who, for all his political engagement, was unable to resist glamorising the paratroopers in his movie of 1966, *The Battle of Algiers*, Genet goes out of his way to insult them. In Blin's production, for instance, the paratroopers, the pride of French masculinity, are obsessed with mirrors and soft skin, and, according to Genet's rehearsal notes, ought to march like Bluebell Girls. And in Scene Fifteen, in what was the most provocative moment in Blin's production, a group of inept French soldiers fart in the face of their dying Lieutenant so that he can go to his death with a whiff of France in his nostrils:[15]

ROGER: Put him down gently, with his back against the rock. And do your job silently. The enemy's in the neighbourhood, but thanks to us in the hostile darkness and countryside there'll be a Christian death chamber with the smell of candles, wreaths, a last will and testament [. . .] (*To the Lieutenant*): Sir, you won't go down amongst the dead without harmony and a little local air [. . .] Sir, open your ears and nostrils. . .Fire!

Roger himself goes and places his ass above the Lieutenant's face. Nestor slaps his own face with his finger and makes a farting sound. (*ibid.*: 153)

It is not difficult to see what is being signified by this provocative image. Blin and Genet are associating France with the smell of shit, and puncturing, in the process, the myth, so dear to many *ancien combattants*, that the paratroopers would have triumphed on the military plane if only the politicians had let them do their job properly. Somewhat predictably, Genet's message was not lost on his contemporaries and the 'farting scene' provoked much outrage and anger among right-wing extremists and journalists, who accused him of disrespecting the dead and dishonouring the Army. In an attempt to placate the right-wing protestors in 1966, Blin placed the scene in the wings and removed the French tricolour flag from the stage for the last week of the play's run.

Given its focus, it is astonishing that the play provoked so little serious political debate even in left-wing publications such as *L'Humanité*,

15 For comprehensive descriptions documenting Blin's production of *The Screens* in 1966, see Odette Aslan, *Jean Genet: théâtre de tous le temps* (Paris: Seghers, 1973) pp. 98–101); and *Roger Blin* pp. 68–104; Maria Delgado, *'Other' Spanish Stages*, pp. 106–12; and Mark Taylor-Batty, *Roger Blin*, pp. 158–86.

Libération or *Combat*. While the quasi-totality of reviewers writing in these papers assumed that *The Screens* was an attack on colonialism, no one thought to see it as a work that posed incisive questions about the logic of decolonisation in metropolitan France. Indeed, for many commentators schooled in Brechtian and Sartrean models of engagement, Genet's refusal to provide any overt support for the FLN proved beyond any doubt that the play's significance was poetical rather than political. Pierre Kyra, the reviewer for *Combat*, concludes that: '[i]t is evident that the play puts colonialism on trial, but as the work of a poet, the argument has a metaphysical dimension: the enemies before us are two versions of the same human nature, distressed, separated and torn asunder by the play of appearances' (in Webb, 1992: 67). The nub of Kyra's review explains why so many critics felt justified – as indeed they still do – in defining *The Screens* as an essentially absurdist or nihilistic work that uses the Algerian War as a ploy for Genet to explore his unique brand of metaphysics grounded in abjection and negation.[16] However, by reading *The Screens* in this way, contemporary reviewers of all persuasions, as they did with *The Blacks* in 1959, failed to ask the obvious questions. Namely, why should Genet have chosen to locate his private obsessions in the public realm of Algeria? And what was the reason behind his savagely comic attack on the *pieds noirs* and the Army? To adopt the terminology of psychoanalysis here, it appears that Genet's critics were involved in the same process of foreclosure as Gaullist politicians. Instead of reflecting on what the play's representation of Algeria signified for contemporary France, they were concerned to repress the issue altogether, which they did by responding to *The Screens* as either mere aesthetics or puerile infantilism. Roger Gellert, the Paris-based correspondent of the *New Statesman* described the play as 'an endless bundle of fun. . .laid on with a dirty great trowel' (*ibid.*: 66); and Gilles Sandier of the magazine *Arts* experienced it as 'a funeral poem in which the major themes of Genet come together [. . .]: the liturgy of filth, the celebration of evil, sex, hatred, death' (*ibid.*: 70). Interestingly, only two reviewers touched upon the play's pressing historical relevance. Lamine, the correspondent who interviewed Genet in *L'Algérien en Europe*, mentions how the nationalist outrage about the play acted 'as an alibi' that 'helped the spectators' to extricate themselves from the deep 'malaise' which Blin's production had put them in (May 1966). And Gabriel Marcel, the conservative reviewer for *Les Nouvelles Littéraires* concludes a contemptuously hostile article, entitled 'Le procès de Genet' ('Genet on trial'), by warning readers of the play's 'toxic quality':

---

16 See for instance Christopher Innes, *Avant Garde Theatre*, p. 111–17.

The work will surely provoke passionate debate. And, of course, by itself, this is an excellent thing. Nevertheless, I hope that by recommending the play in this way, its essentially toxic quality is not underestimated, especially as regards its impact on young people – this text risks reactivating the cancerous process whose symptoms are all around us. (in Bellity Peskine and Dichy, 1991: 62; my translation)

As with all symptomatic readings, Marcel's says both more and less than what it purports to. What Marcel is confirming here – although he is unable to state it outright – is that the politics of Genet's play are not dangerous because they are about the Algerian War, but because they threatened to aggravate an already inflammatory situation in the hexagon itself. As Marcel mentions in his review, he was concerned, above all, with the play's impact on French students. The presence of the word *procès* (trial) in the title of Marcel's argument is salient; it suggests, if read against the grain, that what *The Screens* is actually doing is instigating an ethico-political tribunal and questioning the rationale behind France's desire to forget, so quickly, its former attachment to Algeria.[17] The aptness of this reading is underlined by Genet's own comments about the play. In a letter to Blin in 1966, he explained that his decision to write about the Algerian War was trigged by a desire to reflect on, and ultimately rethink, the significance of French and European identity in a post-imperial world:[18]

> The Algerian war? I don't know about you, but I for one am not Algerian. While I do hope (to say the least) that the Algerians win it, it is perhaps also because it is good to see a people rebel when they have been humiliated for such a long time [. . .] The Algerian war seemed to be an obvious way of taking stock, both of myself and of those around me (as a Frenchman) or rather as a European. (Genet, in Bougon, 1998: 137–8; trans. Susan Marson)

17 Interestingly, Genet posits himself as a witness in the final pages of his final book *Prisoner of Love*, the implication being that he wants to put the western world on trial for its politics (see pp. 374–5).
18 This diverges considerably from the view of François Regnault who, in his book with Bernard-Marie Koltès, on Patrice Chéreau's production in 1983, argues that the play is neither for nor against France, but rather is a sort of negative, sacred carnival. See *La famille des orties: esquisses et croquis autour des Paravents de Jean Genet* (Paris: Editions Nanterre/Amandiers, 1983) pp. 27–45. Like David Bradby and Maria Delgado, by contrast, I believe that *The Screens* is very much against Europe, which, in the context of the Gaullist reconfiguration of French national identity, is ostensibly the same as being against France. See Bradby and Delgado (eds), *The Paris Jigsaw: Internationalism and the City's Stages* (Manchester: Manchester University Press, 2002), p. 5. Genet's comment in the main text would appear to support this view.

Taking the above words into account, it seems reasonable to suggest that what Genet was trying to do with his play was to make visible the fault-line – the wound – that the Algerian War had opened in French society. As I described above, Algeria was always more than a localised struggle for national independence; it was a signifier for a new way of thinking about French national identity in an era of decolonisation. Where the Gaullists and extreme right clashed, ideologically and ultimately momentarily, over what that identity should be, Genet's invitation to 'take stock' offered a more radical alternative. Like various militant student groups such as the Union des Jeunesses Communistes Marxistes-Léninistes (UJCml) or the Liaison des Etudiants Anarchistes (LEA), *The Screens* questioned the ethical values of western society. By subjecting French and European imperialism to coruscating critique, it offered a trenchant attack on both nationalism and capitalism, and suggested, implicitly, that they should be left behind. To that extent, those critics who saw Genet's representation of the Algerian War as pretext are half-right: they intuited, correctly, that the play was not an accurate or anecdotal representation of the Algerian War of independence, and that its ambition transcended the narrow limits of *art engagé*. Their readings are less convincing, however, when they endeavour to locate the 'truth' of the work in the author's own personal obsessions. Building on *The Balcony* and *The Blacks*, *The Screens* interrogates what Frenchness and Europeaness were – and could become – in an era of decolonisation.[19] One of the ways in which the play was able to achieve this in 1966 was by bringing the ideological tensions and generational divisions caused by the Algerian War into the open. Blin's production showed that the problems associated with the name of Algeria had not ended with the cessation of hostilities; they had simply migrated into mainland France itself.

That the migration of the 'Algerian problem' to France is no mere metaphor is underlined by looking at demographic factors. The end of the Algerian War saw one of the largest people movements in modern times, as over one million *pieds noirs* were repatriated to France between 1962 and 1963. This was soon followed by the arrival, *en masse*, of over 100,000 Algerian 'Muslims' who used their status as French citizens to find work and asylum in France. As Maxim Silverman points out, this 'upsurge' in immigration from Algeria was 'so intense that it led to the Franco-Algerian agreement of 10 April 1964 by which numbers would

19 This is underlined in the essay 'That Strange Word', when Genet talks of wanting to stage the play in a graveyard in the very heart of Paris. For a politicised reading of this essay, see Carl Lavery, 'Theatre in a Graveyard: Site-Based Performance and the Revolution of Everyday Life', in Finburgh et al., *Performance and Politics*, pp. 95–105.

be limited and reviewed trimestrally in consideration of the economic situation in both countries' (1992: 43). The influx of Algerian 'Muslims', along with increased numbers of Moroccans and Tunisians entering the country, provoked an identity crisis in mainland France, as many of those who had arrived were, as I explained earlier, *bona fide* French citizens. De Gaulle's solution to this was to institute the Ordinance of 21 July 1962 which was used to refuse citizenship rights to Algerian 'Muslims', and to reconfigure French national identity so that it became synonymous with being white, European and Catholic (that is to say, not Algerian).[20] As such, to stage a play about Algeria in Paris in 1966, and to lay bare the hypocrisy of the French nation-State towards 'Muslims', who until 1962 had been considered as French citizens, was to pose fundamental questions about the revolutionary ideals of *liberté, égalité* and *fraternité* – the very things, in other words, that the Gaullist practice of decolonisation, with its emphasis on exclusion and forgetting, was in the process of occulting.

Within this context, the action of the students on 4 May 1966 is highly significant. As opposed to the extreme right who sang the French national anthem, *La Marseillaise*, the young defenders of the Odéon blasted out *The Internationale*, a gesture which symbolised both their disidentification with France *and* their commitment to an international Socialist future. The students' willingness to listen to Genet (the theatre was packed every night) and to defend his play indicates that his critical perspective on Algeria was not the solitary utterance of a solipsist or nihilist, as some claimed. Rather, it was the work of a historically sensitive playwright whose rejection of imperialism's mix of nationalism and capitalism tallied with the revolutionary desires of a young generation politicised by the repressions and atrocities it had witnessed in Paris and Algiers during the Algerian War. As Kristin Ross has brilliantly shown in *May 68' and Its Afterlives,* Algeria was a rallying cry for a political sequence based on anti-capitalism, anti-Gaullism and anti-Americanism:

> At the most general level, the end of the [Algerian] War saw the birth of a new form of political thought and subjectivity in France, whose accomplishment was the great political, philosophical, and intellectual ruptures of the end of the 1960s. Algeria defined a fracture in French society, in its

---

20 Officially, the ordinance of 21 July 1962 'requir[ed] French citizens from Algeria with official civil status to apply for French nationality before 1 January 1963' (Shepard, *The Invention of Decolonization*, p. xv). In reality, it allowed the government to renege on the Evian Accords and to refuse citizenship to 'Algerian Muslims' regardless of their legal entitlement. Shepard, supplies an insightful discussion of the consequences of this ordinance (*ibid*.: 229–47).

identity, by creating a break between the official 'humanist' discourse of that society and French practices occurring in Algeria and occasionally within France itself. (2002: 38)

Ross's comments enable us to see that 'the battle of *The Screens*' was much more than a battle against right-wing censorship and/or a banal attempt by left-wing students to settle scores with fascist adversaries.[21] Rather, it stemmed from a widespread sense of disaffection among French youth with the French nation-State in the wake of the Algerian War. The students who defended the play at the Odéon were fighting for a political truth process; they wanted to put both French imperialism and western capitalism on trial. This larger political significance of the episode would appear to be borne out, moreover, when it is recalled that Daniel Cohn-Bendit, the student's spokesperson in May 1968, was one of the defenders of the play, along with other anarchists from the Nanterre campus. And also that in the days after the riots at the Odéon, radical students formed the UJCml and the Trotskyite, Jeunesse Communiste Révolutionnaire (UJC), both of which played a key role in organising revolutionary energies in the months before and during May.[22]

While it is, of course, impossible to determine its historical significance in any definitive sense, it seems plausible to suggest that the 'battle of the Odéon', like other key political events such as the Situationist International's takeover of the student union at the University of Strasbourg in 1966, the strike at the SAVIEM lorry factory in Caen in January 1968 and the decision of militant students on 22 March to occupy the administration building on the campus at Nanterre in the same year, played a major role in contributing to the build-up of pressure that finally exploded in May 1968. Turning to Rancière's terminology, we might say that the mobilisation of the students in April 1966 produced a stage where left-wing revolutionaries could display their own disidentification with nationalism and capitalism and encourage other disaffected groups and movements to join with them in a moment of dissensus.

Viewed from this Rancièrian perspective, 'the battle of *The Screens*'

21 Throughout the 1960s, right-wing and left-wing students were involved in violent clashes in the Latin Quarter and at the campus at Nanterre.
22 The theatre and film director Patrice Chéreau who staged *The Screens* in 1983 at Le Théâtre des Amandiers at Nanterre also helped to defend the play. See Odette Aslan, *Roger Blin*, p. 244 and Paul-Louis Mignon, *Jean-Louis Barrault: le théâtre total* (Monaco: Rocher, 1999), p. 275. Interestingly, Chéreau did much to bring the work of Bernard-Marie Koltès to public attention. As David Bradby has pointed out, Koltès is, of all contemporary French playwrights, the one closest to Genet stylistically, thematically and politically. See 'Genet, the Theatre and the Algerian War', in Read and Birchall, *Flowers and Revolution*, pp. 156–72: 169–70.

was a watershed moment in French political life, an incident which, on the one hand, looked back to the anti-imperialism of Algeria, and, on the other hand, pointed forward to the anti-capitalism of May 1968. In retrospect, left-wing action at the Odéon is arguably best approached in terms of synthesis and praxis; it allowed the two radical strands of the student movement to come together and to fight against a common enemy: the capitalist nation-State. The influence that the 'battle of *The Screens*' had on militant action in May 1968 is further revealed when geography is taken into account. Not only did the students in 1968 occupy the iconic Odéon theatre, but they also refused to let the CRS enter the Latin Quarter by barricading the major streets and arteries of the Left Bank. Just as they had done in 1966, but on a macro level, the students in 1968 transformed a sector of the city into a theatre of struggle, a site where the exclusionary logic of the Gaullist State was contested and refused.

Although Alain Badiou usually reserves the term for great seismic shifts brought about by the revolutions of 1789, 1871, 1917 and 1968 (2005: 39–40), the 'battle of *The Screens*' has all the hallmarks of what he would consider to be a political event. As well as negating the existing state of the situation by wagering on, and contributing to, a revolutionary future that no one at the time could have imagined or foreseen, the students were willing to wager on the Badiouian axiom of equality, the unrepresentable truth of justice which defies representation and conceptual knowledge. As Peter Hallward explains:

> When the enslaved call for freedom, for instance, or the colonized for liberation, or women for equality, the declaration of freedom or liberation or equality is itself primary or unconditioned, and not a matter of investigation or confirmation. Equality is not something to be researched or verified but a principle to be upheld. (2003: 228)

By rejecting the Gaullist consensus on Algeria, the students at the Odéon were not simply supporting Genet's right to freedom of speech, and nor were they solely concerned to pledge their allegiance to the cause of Algerian workers in France. Rather, they were acting in tandem with what, for Badiou, is the determining factor of a political event: the sense in which it is radically inclusive and universally valid: '[a]n event is political if its material is collective, or if the event can only be attributed to a collective multiplicity [. . .] We say that the event is collective to the extent that it provides the vehicle for a virtual summoning of all' (2005: 141). In this way, and without really knowing what they were doing, the students were contributing to the development of a new political sequence which looked towards a revolutionary horizon. Mirroring

Genet's own trajectory in the wake of his experience of the wound, the students deserve to be regarded as 'militants of truth', willing to fight for a universal or axiomatic cause which was no longer theirs alone. Just as crucially, they were ready to assert non-identity in order to create something beyond narrow and exclusive notions of Frenchness. Where France retreated into the hexagon, they sought to create a new earth. In Badiou's language, they affirmed the 'void of the situation', that is to say, the unrepresentable nothingness which produces a new world from the negation of the status quo.

Politics of the void

As the argument above proves, there is little doubt whatsoever that *The Screens* was transformed into a political event in 1966 as the result of its chance encounter with a particularly fraught historical moment. Not every production of the play, for instance, has provoked the same degree of animosity and tension as Blin's staging.[23] Nevertheless, while insisting upon the primordial role played by socio-historical context here, it is also important that we do not underestimate the political potential inherent in the performance itself. In proposing this, I do not wish to contradict the logic of the argument I have been following throughout this book and conflate aesthetic politics with political aesthetics. I am simply contending that if the work had not opened wounds theatrically, then no event would have taken place at the Odéon theatre at all. Like the notion of aesthetic politics I advanced towards the end of Chapter 3 (see pp. 99–101), this is a different way of saying that theatre is an activity that produces the possibility of politics, as opposed to being synonymous with a political act in and by itself. In the final section of this chapter, I want to clarify, further, the relationship between aesthetic and political events by showing how the 'battle of *The Screens*' was caused by Genet's 'oblique attempt to provoke a politics' by 'illuminat[ing] the void' (Genet, 2003: 103).[24]

23 When Patrice Chéreau staged the play in Paris in 1983, it provoked no political controversy whatsoever. However, in early 1991, the director Marcel Maréchal cancelled the original production date of the play at the Théâtre de la Criée in Marseilles in order to calm divisive religious and political tensions in the city that had been provoked by the preparations for the first Gulf War.
24 In his writing, Badiou is generally concerned to distinguish political events from aesthetic events. For a further discussion of this, see *Rhapsodie pour le théâtre* (Paris: Imprimerie Nationale, 1990) and 'Théâtre et philosophie', *Frictions: Théâtre/écritures* 2 (2000), 133–41. However, contemporary theatre theorists who engage with Badiou's

Reading the reviews of *The Screens* by conservative critics such as Gabriel Marcel and Jean-Jacques Gautier, one is struck by the remarkable violence of their language. Marcel complains that Genet is the 'least morally equipped of all contemporary playwrights' to deal with the Algerian War, and describes the play's language 'as the most systemically excremental' that 'he has ever heard on the French stage' (in Bellity Peskine and Dichy, 1991: 61–2; my translation). Similarly, Gautier explains that 'everything in me revolted and reared up [. . .] at this heap of filth' (*ibid.*: 65; my translation). In these accounts, the performance seems, somehow, to have bypassed the intellect and to have insinuated itself into their bodies directly. Marcel and Gautier seem under attack, personally victimised by the performance and ready to see things that were not there. What they are expressing, in other words, is what Jacques Lacan would call *jouissance*, excessive and painful affect. Marcel's metaphors are of sickness and disease. According to him, the play is a kind of cancer threatening to spiral out of control and to consume the French body politic from within. Gautier's language, by contrast, is largely scatological. His reference to 'filth', 'spit' and degradation is indicative of a sense of abjection; he sees the play as a foreign element, a threat to everything decent and civil in France (*ibid.*).

Intriguingly, other more sympathetic critics also use a language of affect to describe their experience. Writing in *Preuves*, Jacques Carat specifies how the horrors of war were 'composed in front of our eyes' (June 1966; my translation); Robert Abirached describes undergoing 'a rain of blows', which left him with a profound sensation 'of remorse and angst' (June 1966; my translation); Catherine Valogne in *Tribune de Lausanne* compares the play to a happening and describes the encounter between text, actors and spectators as a 'shattering explosion' (September 1966; my translation); and Jean Dutourd in *France Soir* says, explicitly, that the performance 'wounded' him (April 1966; my translation). Likewise in a roundtable debate with Roger Blin organised by La Maison du Spectateur in June 1966, the audience expressed its disgust at the 'odious' nature of the play, with Monsieur Vignaux, an ex-Army Officer, commenting that if he had witnessed anything like the infamous 'farting scene' in Algeria, he 'would have taken out his revolver' and shot the perpetrators. When Maurice Mercier, the organiser of the talk, tried to explain, calmly, the aesthetic rationale behind Genet's images he was shouted down as the room dissolved into a bedlam of recrimination

theory of aesthetics, often argue for theatre as a political event in itself. For two good revisionist essays see Adrian Kear, in 'Thinking out of Time: Theatre and the Ethic of Interruption', *Performance Research*, 9:4 (2004), 99–110; and Janelle Reinelt, 'Theatre and Politics: Encountering Badiou', *Performance Research*, 9: 4 (2004), 87–94.

and *délire*. In the examples mentioned, it is notable that spectators and critics of the play were not affected, as Ionesco was in Blin's production of *The Blacks*, by a sense of vertiginous ambivalence. Rather they were wounded through a preponderance of theatricality, as they watched the narrative unfold in front of them in a series of concrete stage images.

Thematically and formally, *The Screens* marks a major departure from the ambiguous metatheatricality dominating *The Balcony* and *The Blacks*. Whereas the latter problematised Aristotelian notions of plot, character and space by deliberately deconstructing the gap separating the fictional from the real, *The Screens* invests in an epic form of storytelling with a discernable beginning, middle and end. In Blin's production, more than sixty actors were required, and a flotilla of mobile screens was used to point, indexically, to different places and loci. Like the scenic constructivism of Vsevolod Meyerhold, Blin divided the stage into multiple levels and presented it as a kind of enormous canvas or landscape in which characters dressed in fabulous costumes, and (sometimes) wearing prosthetic masks, walked through a field of colour and dazzling light. As Genet explains in the essay 'That Strange Word', the blatant artificiality of the work was a deliberate attempt to contest the realist logic of cinema and to think spatially in terms of physicalised hieroglyphs and ideograms (2003: 103–7).

The plot of *The Screens* is based on two parallel, but interpenetrating narratives. First, the existential adventures of the Nettle family (Saïd, Leïla and the Mother); and second, the epic struggles of a colonised people to free itself from European rule. The plot unfolds in three phases. The first stage starts with Saïd's marriage to Leïla, the ugliest woman in the village, and ends in Scene Nine, when he assumes his outcast identity in prison.[25] Stage two runs from Scene Ten to Fifteen and merges the Nettle's family commitment to a metaphysics of loss with the Arab community's revolt against the settler population. And the final stage, from Scene Fifteen to Seventeen, highlights the fundamental incompatibility between these two antithetical concepts of revolution. As opposed to the Mother who enters the world of the dead, and Leïla who disappears altogether, the rebels, after their success in defeating the Europeans, organise themselves into a disciplined Army and imitate the structures and thought processes of the coloniser. In Badiou's terms, a non-event has taken place; the State has simply reorganised itself under a different regime. That nothing has fundamentally happened, either politically or existentially, is underlined in the denouement when Saïd is shot by the

---

25 I am referring here to the standard English version of the play that I have used in the main text.

military guards for disobeying orders. In the text used in Blin's production, the play ends ambiguously with only the dead on-stage, and the Mother and Kadidja wondering where Saïd has gone:[26]

THE MOTHER: Saïd!... I'll simply have to wait for him...
KADIDJA: (*laughing*): Don't bother. He'll no more be back than will Leïla.
THE MOTHER: Then where is he? In a song? (1987: 201)

Saïd's refusal to reappear among the dead shows that his commitment is not to the new order, which has reneged on the radical energy of the revolution; rather, he has aligned himself with the void, and thus wagered on the community to come. His possible re-emergence in a song is equivalent to the *promesse de bonheur*, which lies at the heart of Genet's utopian notion of aesthetic politics. Recalling Genet's point about Rimbaud going further than Marx in the search for justice (see Chapter 3, p. 88), Saïd is a kind of militant poet whose song keeps the very source of politics alive. As Joseph McMahon, one of Genet's earliest commentators realised 'the force that Saïd embodies is undying' (1963: 231). Likewise, but in a more politicised vein, Michel Deguy reminds us that Saïd 'incarnates the absolute refusal of the western model of [the State]' (1972: 55; my translation and addition).

In spite of being set during the Algerian War of independence, Genet's treatment of history in *The Screens*, as Hamdi Hémaïdi has claimed, is fundamentally paradoxical (2001: 36). No reference to Algeria is made in the text, either in the stage directions or by the characters; and nor is there any mention of key historical events, battles or personalities. As I noted earlier, Blin's most concerted attempt to fix the play historically occurred during the 'farting scene' when he placed a tricolour flag on the stage. On the few occasions when the war is represented in the play, it is usually highly stylised, such as when Kadidja exhorts the Arabs to merit the 'world's contempt' in Scene Twelve (1987: 101). Or when the Mother accidentally and comically strangles Pierre, a Legionnaire who is lost in the desert in Scene Thirteen. Taking the opposite stance to Pontecorvo, Genet has no interest in exploring the military aspects of the Algerian War; he presents us with a poeticised struggle between a colonised Arab population and a mixed European settler community

---

26 In the 1961 version of the play, Kadidja ends the play with a more definitive statement about Saïd's whereabouts. To the Mother's question, 'Where is he, then?', she replies 'With the dead' (Genet in Corvin and Dichy, *Jean Genet*, pp. 1249–50; my translation). As usual, Corvin provides the best account of the mutations and variations undergone by the text in performance (*ibid*.: pp. 1226–89).

located 'somewhere' in a dreamlike North Africa. The time period in which the action takes place is equally vague. In his copious instructions in the published script, most of which Blin attempted to carry out, Genet advises that the European colonisers should be dressed in costumes of the 1840s, and that the Legionnaires ought to wear Stetson hats (*ibid.*: 91). The intention here, as in *The Balcony* and *The Blacks*, is to transcend particularity, to write a play that is both about, and not about, the Algerian War.

In *The Screens*, the aesthetic strategy of Genet and Blin is not guided by a concern to copy reality, but rather to enchant or to put a spell on the audience. For them, *poesis* is more important than mimesis. In a letter written to the director Antoine Bourseiller in 1969 as he was preparing to stage *The Balcony* in Marseilles, Genet defined enchantment in the following way:

> Every type of theatrical representation, every spectacle is an enchantment. The enchantment that I am speaking about has no need of mirrors, sumptuous costumes or baroque furniture: it comes to pass in a voice which breaks on the wrong word. The necessary thing is to find the word and the voice; it (enchantment) is in a gesture which is out of place, in a little finger which makes the wrong move; as when a Noh actor, built like a taxi-driver, puts on his make-up in public, takes the fan in a (certain false) way, drops his shoulders, puffs out his chest and gives you goose bumps by transforming himself in front of your eyes into the first Shintoist woman, etc.
>
> I sought to make my text appear false, so that a kind of enchantment was born from it [. . .] I don't know much [about theatre], except perhaps this: you have to surprise yourself. What I mean is: to stand aside from the thing you are representing. (Genet, in Corvin and Dichy, 2002: 903–4; my translation)

In parallel with his notion of obliqueness (see pp. 85–8 in this book), enchantment is created when the text appears false, and when the theatrical signifier is held as far apart as possible from the actual referent. This accounts for three of Genet's most celebrated theatrical instructions. First, that on-stage gestures in *The Screens* should be as artificial and plastic as possible: 'don't let the Arab worker light a cigarette: the match flame not being able to be imitated on stage; a lighted match, in the audience or elsewhere, is the same as on-stage. To be avoided' (1972: 40). Second, that the images and signs depicted in *trompe l'œil* on the mobile screens need to be confronted with the material reality of the objects that they supposedly represent: '[n]ear the screen there must always be at least one real object (wheelbarrow, bucket and bicycle, etc.), the function of which is to establish a contrast between its own reality and the objects that are drawn' (1987: 10). And finally, that the actors must renounce the real world and consent to live in a poeticised universe with its own logic and laws:

> Therefore the actors and actresses must be induced to put aside cleverness and to involve the most secret depths of their being; they must be made to accept difficult endeavours, admirable gestures which however have no relation to those they employ in their daily lives. If we maintain that life and the stage are opposites, it is because we strongly suspect that the stage is a site closely akin to death, a place where all liberties are possible. The actors' voices, moreover, will come only from the larynx: this is a difficult music to find. Their make-up will, by transforming them into 'others', enable them to try any and every audacity: as they will be unencumbered by any social responsibility, they will assume another, with respect to another Order. (1972: 12)

In *The Screens*, Genet wants to evoke the Algerian War poetically, to make it palpable as a sensible idea, as something that is being artificially constructed in the present. Hence the importance to the play of the light-weight mobile screens which, in Blin's performance, allowed the actors to build the architecture of the show in front of the audience. In *The Screens*, Genet's desire for poetry is dependent upon theatre showing its own mechanisms, in accepting its autonomy and alterity. As the director Charles Marowitz reflected on Peter Brook's experimental workshop version of the play in London in 1964: 'one last observation on *The Screens* – in the work of no other writer is the external life of the play quite so essential' (1966: 169).

A good example of the painful affect produced by Genet's decidedly non-genteel aesthetic of enchantment is found in Scene Twelve when Kadidja returns from the dead – she has just been shot by Sir Harold's son for refusing to keep her mouth shut – and calls on the Arabs to commit crimes against the French settlers. Holding a lighted candle in the dimmed auditorium, the actress playing Kadidja addresses a prayer to evil on an empty stage:

KADIDJA: [. . .] Evil, wonderful evil, you who remain when all goes to pot, miraculous evil, you're going to help us. I beg of you evil, evil, and I beg you standing upright, impregnate my people. And let them not be idle! (*She calls out in a tone of authority.*) Kaddur! (1987: 97)

Kadidja's prayer is quickly answered, and from the wings an actor playing an Arab revolutionary emerges and responds to her question – 'What have you done for Evil to prevail?' (*ibid.*) – with the following remark:

KADDUR (*in a hollow, but proud tone*): Their muzzles are still hot – put your hand on them – look: I picked up two revolvers. (*ibid.*)

In a complete departure from naturalistic theatre, Kadidja asks the revolutionary to show her his crime, which he does by drawing the revolvers on a blank screen with a stick of charcoal:

> KADDUR *very quickly draws the revolvers on the screen with a charcoal pencil. Then he goes to the left side of the stage. The drawing should represent the objects monstrously enlarged.* (*ibid.*; original italics)

Kaddur's act is the catalyst for a tumult of bodies and props to invade the stage space. After it, a group of revolutionaries emerge from the wings and proceed to draw, serially, their crimes against the coloniser on the screens. These include the rape of a young *pied noir*; the murder of a policeman; the slaughter of cattle; the dynamiting of a lemon plantation; a cry of anger; and the disembowelling of a soldier. In Blin's production, the frenzied drawing continued until three blank screens were covered with a mass of shapes, lines and colours. The violence communicated, directly, through the mass of *art brutiste* images was compounded by the gestures and movement of the actors, who delivered their lines, and carry out their tasks, at top speed.

In Scene Twelve, as a result of the physicality of the action, the spectator is placed at the centre of a savage *sensorium*, in which she is bombarded by a riotous choreography of bodies, movement and sound. Words take on the weight of the things, and ideas are physicalised. In this reconfiguration of the sensible, the Algerian War, the thing that France wanted to keep out of sight, is made 'present' through a matrix of plastic signs and symbols. In keeping with the notion of enchantment, the war, of course, is not represented iconically or frontally; it is evoked, obliquely, by actions and gestures which have been deliberately stylised and constructed. As in *The Balcony* and *The Blacks* (but differently) the spatial proximity of the actors – their liveness – has an important role to play here. Because the actors share the same space as the spectators, it is impossible to forget their physicality. They present as much as they represent, and, by doing so, compromise the fictionality of the dramatic sign. Paradoxically, however, it is this troublesome doubleness, embodied by the awkward 'thereness' of the actor's body, which produces the spectator's emotional and imaginative investment in the play.

In his earliest essay on theatre aesthetics, 'Letter to Jean-Jacques Pauvert', Genet argues that if theatrical performance is to be effective it needs to avoid 'the dreary sadness of a theatre that too exactly reflects the visible world'. Instead, it should exist as 'a profound labyrinth of active symbols' (2003: 36). This is closely linked to Genet's famous statement that 'theatrically speaking, [there] is nothing more effective than the Elevation of the Host' (*ibid.*: 38). What Genet is proposing here is that communion is produced via a process of transubstantiation, in which the body of Christ is consumed in and through the physical presence of an object, the communion wafer, which is blatantly *not* the thing it represents. Strangely, the effectiveness of the mass as a performance event is dependent upon the congregation, the audience, being able to hold two incompatible ideas in mind at the same time: ostensibly, that the communion wafer is both a wafer *and* the body of a God. In the mass, as in theatre, efficacy resides in the symbol's difference from the idea or thing it represents. The store which Genet sets by this oblique process is illustrated by his comments at the end of 'Letter to Pauvert' when he describes the 'formula' for a theatre that would 'delight him':

> A young writer told me of having seen in a public garden five or six little kids playing at war. Divided into two troops, they were preparing for attack. Night, they said, was coming. But it was noon in the sky. So they decided that one of them would be Night. The youngest and frailest, having become an element, was then the master of the Combat. 'He' was Time, the Moment, the Ineluctable. From very far way, it seemed, he came, with the calm of a cycle, but burdened by twilight sadness and ceremony. As he approached, the others, the Men, became nervous, anxious... But the child, in their opinion, came too soon. He was ahead of himself: of one common accord, the Troops and the Chiefs decided to suppress Night, who became once again a soldier in a troop... (*ibid.*: 40)

As with the Catholic mass, the 'playground theatre' referred to above and the Algerian War in *The Screens* is simultaneously there and not there, a continually evoked but always veiled presence which disturbs the vicarious pleasures of theatre-going. This strange duality, what we might define as 'concrete spectrality', prevents the spectator from consuming the war as a dramatic object and thus achieving a sense of catharsis through imaginary identification. *The Screens* is not a play which helps the French nation to mourn and forget the loss of Algeria; it is a play that keeps the idea of Algeria at the forefront of consciousness by, perversely, not representing it. The distinction that Hans-Thies Lehmann makes between the televisual gaze and the theatrical gaze is pertinent here:

> Inherent to the curious gaze in theatre is the expectation that it will 'at one point' see the other. But this gaze does not reach for ever more distant

unreal spaces but circles inside itself, pointing inwards, towards the clarification and visibility of the figure that nevertheless remains an enigma. Therefore this gaze is accompanied by a sense of lack instead of fulfilment. Naturally this hope cannot be fulfilled because plenitude only persists in the question [...] not in the 'present' reality of the object. The figure of the other in theatre always has a reality only of arrival, not presence. (2006: 172)

Lehmann's comments explain how the gaze in theatre is always disappointed. Because the eye is unable to penetrate the dense corporeality of the body placed in front of it – what Lehmann terms the 'enigma' – the spectator remains aware that what she is seeing is a 'virtuality', and not a simulacrum (ibid.: 171). It is thus up to the audience to summon the imaginative effort necessary to transform this theatrical 'virtuality' into a dramatic 'reality'. However, because of the presence of the actor's body, the work of the imagination is never completed. As a medium of dramatic representation theatre is a failure. The spectator's desire always remains unfulfilled, since the actor arrives either too early or too late to become an ethereal sign. Bizarrely, theatre's failure to transform itself into a pure image is what produces its success. The more the actor's body resists the efforts of the spectator to derealise it, the harder the imagination has to work. Consequently, the audience, as demonstrated by the reactions of critics such as Gautier and Marcel, starts to see images and think ideas that are not there. A form of hallucination takes place, as the mental labour required to make an on-stage image take on the semblance of reality endows it with an uncanny aura that no other medium can rival. Crucially, the object of this hallucinatory experience is never embodied in performance; it remains always within the mind, a product of the spectator's own desire.

Within this context, it is plausible to say that the painful affect produced by *The Screens* is caused by Genet's capacity for making the war 'appear' without making it 'visible'. As such, the title of the play is ironic. *The Screens* is a work that represents the Algerian War by screening it, by keeping it hidden and approaching it obliquely. The objective behind this suggestive opacity is to dislocate the audience spatially and emotionally. Instead of purging the trauma of the Algerian War, Genet brings the war back home to mainland France by planting it in the minds of the spectators as a ghost that refuses exorcism. As in *The Balcony* and *The Blacks*, Genet's success in *The Screens* is dependent, once again, on exploiting the spatial ontology of theatre, in making the war present through the materiality of fleshy bodies and real objects that are not what they purport to represent, and always point beyond themselves. To describe this in terms of the central metaphor of this book: Genet wounds the audience in order to show, like Rembrandt and Giacometti, that 'every man is worth as much as every other'. This revelation that bypasses knowledge is, as I have been arguing in this chapter, the catalyst that allowed a new political sequence to emerge.

Fittingly, the shift from aesthetics to politics that occurred in Paris in 1966 did so in a largely oblique manner. The failure of right-wing spectators and journalists to work through the wound provoked by Blin's production at the Odéon caused them to demonstrate against the play. This, in turn, led disaffected students and left-wing revolutionaries to mobilise in its favour and to show their solidarity with Genet. In so far as the defenders of *The Screens* were willing, unlike their nationalist opponents, to affirm non-being in their attempts to create a more egalitarian world, Genet's desire 'to illuminate the void' was transposed from the theatre to the streets of Paris itself. Without confusing aesthetics and politics, *The Screens* can be accurately defined as one of those rare cases when a theatrical event gave rise to a political event. The emptiness disclosed by the aesthetic, in other words, placed the rationale of an entire society in question and insisted upon action. The consequences of that action were revealed two years later on the same Parisian streets.

Conclusion

By concentrating on historical factors, I have attempted to uphold a double argument in this chapter. First, I tried to show how Roger Blin's production of *The Screens* at the Odéon-Théâtre de France in 1966 caused a political event which contributed to a process of dissensus, which finally culminated in the events of May 1968. It could be argued of course that any play about Algeria was bound to create controversy within the volatile climate of France in the mid-1960s, yet to say that is to ignore the way in which Genet's play was deliberately constructed to open wounds. His technique for achieving this was to insist on poetic evocation rather than naturalistic representation. In this oblique way, Genet allowed the war to insinuate itself into the imagination of the spectators, and, as a consequence, managed to produce a political result which no deliberately committed work on Algeria could ever hoped to have achieved.

Closely related to this (and in keeping with the overall objective of the book), I also tried to explicate how theatre's unique distribution of space played an integral role in allowing Genet to wound his audience in 1966. By insisting on the uncanny presentness of performance, the sense in which actors are always involved physically in what they do, Genet was able, quite literally, to restage the Algerian War on home soil, and so create a provocative act of spatio-political dissensus. To that extent, Genet, once again, exploited the heterotopic aspects of theatre to disturb the dominant spatial practices of the Fifth Republic, which were concerned to protect the borders of the hexagon from being breached by foreign elements. By bringing Algeria into a privileged arena of French cultural life (and we ought not to forget that the Odéon was – and still is – one of France's most prestigious theatres), Genet issued a direct challenge to the Gaullist consensus on French national identity and thus articulated a desire for a different France which many on the political left shared.[27] This, for me, is where the utopic dimension of the play, and indeed of Genet's late theatre in general, resides.

---

27 Casting María Casares in the role of the Mother would also have linked the play to the political situation in Spain at the time. Casares had fled Spain at the end of the Spanish Civil War and was the daughter of the Republican politician Santiago Casares Quiroga. As Maria Delgado and David Bradby indicate: 'Collaborating with Camus, Vilar, Barrault, Sobel and Lavelli, [Casares'] view of theatre as a public service links her to the great social directors of the era but [. . .] her own career is in many ways indicative of a cultural policy which has facilitated the presence of bodies habitually inscribed as "other" within the dominant discourses of power' (*The Paris Jigsaw*, p. 18).

7

Conclusion: Genet our contemporary

> Possibility is the privileged mode of utopian thought. Indeed, it is the modal condition of politics in general. Hence the ineliminability of utopia from politics. (Osborne, 2006: 36)

In the crucial text 'Preface to *The Blacks*' (see the Appendix in this book, pp. 227–34), the reader finds Genet ruminating on the possibility of aesthetic defeat. Where the successful artwork, Genet claims, should transcend particularity, he accepts that *The Blacks* is too reliant upon its specific historical context to endure:

> What will become of this play when contempt and disgust have disappeared on the one hand, and on the other, the powerless rage and hatred that constitute the basis for the relationship between people of colour, and Whites? In other words, when humans bonds are consolidated between the two? It will be forgotten. I accept that it only has meaning today. (Appendix, p. 227)

Reading these words some fifty years after the event, it is difficult not to feel a sense of poignancy. As we know all too well, Genet's confidence in the future was misplaced. Despite a brief moment of hope from the late 1960s through to the mid-1970s, racism simply took new forms and migrated *en masse* from the global South to the global North. That Genet himself realised this is apparent in his commitment to armed insurrection in the 1970s, and in the equivocal but inescapable melancholy that haunts his last book, *Prisoner of Love*. Menaced by the 'military–industrial–entertainment complex' of the West, Genet's black and Arab revolutionaries are portrayed as heroic but doomed figures, whose fight for a different world is as futile as 'fir[ing] bullets at the Milky Way' (1992: 7).

In today's France, divided by racism, and increasingly paranoid about the presence of the large North African population in its major cities, Genet's late theatre has lost none of its profound political and aesthetic significance. Indeed, if anything, its power seems to have intensified, a fact which is borne out by the recent interest in staging his work in Paris since the attacks on New York and Washington on 11 September 2001, and the subsequent invasions of Afghanistan and Iraq by US and UK troops.[1] Two decades after his death, Genet remains the poet of the dispossessed, the writer who, more than any other western artist of the age, charted and supported the rise of a militant Arab world. It is easy to see why Genet's virulent attack on western values should provoke such consternation for some. At a time when those values are simultaneously globalised and felt to be under threat, plays like *The Blacks* and *The Screens* are uncompromising and unrestrained. Their aim is to inflict pain upon western spectators, not to offer images of multicultural reconciliation.

What impact does this have on the argument that I have been developing in this book? On the one hand, it seems to imply that Genet's utopianism is the least relevant aspect of his work, the element which remains trapped within the 1960s, and which arguably reached its apex in the revolutionary month of May 1968. Viewed from this perspective, it appears that the meaning of his theatre resides, more and more, in what one might term its 'resistant anger'. That is to say in its relentless attempt to force France (and Europe) to confront what it continues to foreclose: imperialist guilt in a neo-imperialist present. In a France beset with stringent immigration policies, riots and discontent in the *banlieus*, and President Sarkozy's ultra-conservative and aggressively defensive notion of national identity, Genet's plays, like Michael Haneke's astonishing 2005 film *Caché*, disclose the presence of an alternative history. They remind us that France is a haunted country, whose present discontents can be traced back to its refusal to deal with events in the 1950s and 1960s. Recalling Rustom Bharucha's argument (see pp. 2–3 in this

---

1 For a good discussion of recent productions of Genet's theatre in France since 2001, see Carl Lavery, 'The State of Genet studies', *Contemporary Theatre Review*, 15:4 (2005), pp. 470–5: 471–2.

book), Genet's late theatre forces us to take a stance; it shocks us out of the complacent amnesia and sterile ahistoricism tirelessly manufactured by the society of the spectacle, and expresses, instead, a deep sense of hostility against the convenience of 'forgetting'.

Yet, for all of that, I am nevertheless reluctant to give up so easily on the utopian arc that I have attempted to trace in this book. The problem with memory work, indeed with mourning in general, is its contention that the past can be somehow redeemed and set right. This has dangerous consequences. After a brief period of interruption and hiatus, it assumes that society will get down to business as usual. This is the very thing that Genet is against. For Genet, individual and social being is built upon a wound that resists healing. The only progressive way of living with the wound as I have shown in the previous pages, is to acknowledge its presence and to wager on the equality it discloses. The anachronism of the wound, its stubborn refusal to be subtlated ontologically (and thus historically), is precisely why the strong utopianism of Genet's late theatre endures. Genet is not interested in improving or reforming the State, he wants to explode it. His commitment, as I argued in Chapter 1, is to a deterritorialised world, to a *utopos*. Contrary to those theorists and poets who would try 'to get us back into place', this *utopos* ought to be celebrated. The nowhere is also and necessarily the everywhere. The world, in other words, is simply one – it belongs to all of us. In an age when the possibility of a different horizon remains remote, it seems to me that the vitality of Genet's theatre, the very reason why it has had such an enormous impact on a diverse array of theatre makers such as Lindsay Kemp, Bernard-Marie Koltès, Kazuo Ohno, Peter Sellars, La Carnicería Teatro, The Wooster Group and Ron Athey (to name but a few), is because it reminds us that the possibility of becoming other than self is ever present.[2] By negating the world we are in and revealing the gaps in the Symbolic order of global capital, Genet 'lifts' what Badiou, in his politicised reading of Jacques Lacan, calls the 'barrier on *the impossible*' (2008: 45; my translation; original italics). In doing so, his late theatre is an antidote to existential depression and political stasis, even if it does compel us to acknowledge, always, the melancholic presence of an infinite wound.

Genet's simultaneous investment in both ecstasy and loss is precisely why his theatre remains so intensely relevant; his commitment to an always impossible sense of becoming compels us to gamble on

2 For more details on Genet's influence on contemporary theatre and performance makers, see Carl Lavery and Paul Woodward, 'Jean, Ron, Franko and Me'; Martin Hargreaves, 'Dancing the Impossible'; and Dominic Johnson 'Perverse Martyrologies: An Interview with Ron Athey', *Contemporary Theatre Review*, 18:4 (2008), 503–13: 513.

non-being and to act upon the artwork's *promesse du bonheur*. In the language of Rancière, he encourages us to supplement aesthetic politics with political aesthetics and so force a new world into being through a poeticisation of sensible experience. In this respect, it is fitting that the final page of Genet's last book should be left deliberately 'transparent' (Genet, 1992: 375). Like the blasted architecture of his theatre with its fissures, gaps and holes, the empty last page of *Prisoner of Love* is a reminder of the protean capacity of the wound, an invitation, both poetic and political, to reconfigure self and world. The decidedly spatial aspect of this textual practice confirms, yet again, the relationship existing between Genet's late theatre and his post-1968 political commitment. In both cases, the point was – and still is – to produce new spaces, spaces of revolution.

In the final section of the book, I address Genet's contemporary political significance by looking at his key influence on modern directors in Spain, the USA and UK. Reflecting my methodological commitment to anachrony in this study, my intention is to broaden the book's historical and geographical remit, and to grasp how Lluís Pasqual, JoAnne Akalaitis and Ultz and Excalibah have attempted to make Genet's late plays politically relevant for audiences in different socio-political contexts than the one discussed in the first two parts of this study.

PART III: **Interviews**

8

Interview with Lluís Pasqual

Llu's Pasqual is one of Europe's foremost theatre and opera directors. He is best known for his dazzling collaborations with the designer Fabià Puigserver, with whom he reinvented classic Spanish and European plays for contemporary audiences in Catalonia and elsewhere from the mid-1970s onwards. This interview deals with Pasqual's productions of *The Balcony* in 1980 and 1981 before going on to explore where Genet's contemporary significance resides.

CARL LAVERY: How did you become interested in Genet's work?
LLUÍS PASQUAL: I was drawn to Genet for literary and political reasons. My first encounter was through the novel *The Thief's Journal*, some of which is set in Barcelona. Since Genet's novels were banned under Franco, I had to cross the border and buy it in Perpignan. I was blown away by *The Thief's Journal*; it represented a story that I knew well – the story of Barcelona in the 1930s – but from a completely different angle. It turned reality on its head. When I decided to stage *The Balcony* at the Teatre Lliure in Barcelona in the late 1970s, my reasoning was purely political. [1] Although Franco had died and we were in a period of transition in Spain and

---

1 For an excellent account of the production; see Maria Delgado, *'Other' Spanish Stages*, pp. 192–4.

Catalonia, my intention was to remind people of his regime, to make sure that we didn't forget just how terrible life had been under his dictatorship. The production was an exercise in remembrance, in not-forgetting.

CL: Did Genet come to Barcelona to see the production as he had done with Víctor García's version of *Las criadas* in 1969?

LP: He didn't come to see it, but he did know about it. When I was rehearsing the play in Barcelona, I couldn't get the rights. I wanted to stage it in Catalan, but the only rights for the play were in Spanish. A literary agent in Madrid informed me that the sole way to resolve the situation was to obtain the playwright's personal permission. So being young and fearless, I tried to contact a woman in Paris who represented Genet's estate. I managed to get through eventually, but unfortunately he wasn't there. He was always travelling, and often his friends and representatives had no idea where he was. So I left my telephone number and naïvely asked if Genet could contact me when he returned. About four or five days later, I received a phone call from Genet at the theatre in the middle of rehearsals. He asked me visit him, so that we could speak about the production and arrange the rights. So I dropped everything and went to Paris to see Genet. After a couple of days of talking with him, he granted me the permission. In the years after that, we kept in regular contact. We'd meet in airports or train stations. His death affected me deeply. I hadn't looked for a relationship with him, but one had developed. He was very kind to me, and acted as a teacher. I think he was willing to do this because he had a great affection for Spain and its people.

CL: That's very different from his normal reputation.

LP: With me, he was more or less like a grandfather. He was very gentle and polite. In Berlin on the day of Tito's death, he told me that he preferred the Spanish under Franco to what they had subsequently become. He thought that democracy had de-energised them; they had nothing to fight against. I found that a little difficult to accept at the time. I'd just been through the miserable crappiness of the Franco years and couldn't share his vision. For me – for Spain – Franco's death was a real relief; it was as if a pressure valve had been released. But now I understand Genet's point. He realised that vitality is found in the process of struggle, not in achieving it necessarily. He was always saying incredibly complicated things like that.

CL: Did he talk much about theatre?

LP: No, hardly at all. Mostly, we talked about architecture. He said that it was another person who had written his plays. When I was staging *The Balcony*, he encouraged me to do whatever I wanted to do, and endorsed the changes I made in the opening four scenes. As you doubtless know, I had a young boy dressed as a girl in the opening scene with the Bishop rather than a female prostitute; and I also changed the sadomasochistic scene with the beggar into a scenario in which the beggar is 'punished' by a smartly dressed woman who appears to be on her way to communion. She hits him with a bunch of flowers. When I knew him he was crazy about house building.

CL: That's quite a contradiction isn't it? He's usually thought of as a vagabond.

LP: The houses were never for him. However, you're right in a way. Genet's life and work are built on ambiguity and contradiction. At the very heart of Genet's poetics, is the gesture. He thinks – he believes – that the life of a human being is caught in the endless repetition of the same gesture. This fixity is what we need to escape from. He was interested in upsetting stereotypes and suspending meaning – in other words, in not getting trapped in a gesture or image. The deliberate cultivation of ambiguity allowed him to do that.

CL: Was that the political driving force behind your two stagings of *The Balcony* in Barcelona and then in Paris at the Odéon-Théâtre de l'Europe in 1991? In the programme note for the Paris production, you said that *The Balcony* was 'a cubist play', a play in which 'undecidability undermines every formal system by constituting the miniscule crack through which life remains vital, fragile and stubborn. Ultimately, this crack, is what makes everything explode' (in Corvin and Dichy, 2002: 1156; my translation)

LP: It's funny but I don't remember writing that. Genet is like Beckett, he's too intelligent to state that there is one truth. I have often thought that the key to Genet's thinking lies in that perverse comment he made in *The Thief's Journal* about betrayal being the very epitome of love. Things are always dialectical for him; he's interested in reversing the status quo.

CL: Can you talk about how the unconventional use of space in your productions of *The Balcony* might also have reversed expectations?

LP: In Barcelona, we experimented with a traverse staging by splitting the audience in two and performing the play in the space between them. The idea was to create a theatre machine, in which the reactions of the spectators on one side of the stage were mirrored by the reactions of those on the other side. In Paris, we used the space differently. The Théâtre de l'Odéon is a classic proscenium-arch theatre, with boxes, plush seating, velvet curtains, and so on. It has a long and illustrious history and used to be the home of the Comédie Française. But to me, it looked like a brothel – it was the perfect 'maison de luxe', exactly the type of whorehouse that Madame Irma would have worked in. So I decided to put the audience on the stage and to place the actors in the auditorium. We also changed the doors and the lighting of the theatre so that everything inside was a garish red and green. The Odéon was transformed into a seedy brothel or porno film-set. Outside on the façade of the building, we advertised the play with an enormous red neon sign. The locals weren't happy with this at all; for them, we'd made the theatre and their neighbourhood into a dodgy bar or crass bordello. It was funny. We'd made a bourgeois space, both inside and outside the theatre, into a kitsch space, a sort of false whorehouse. Everything looked fake.

CL: It's interesting how the inside and outside blur in Genet's plays. Do you have the impression that there's a perpetual struggle with and against theatre itself in Genet's work? He seems both to love theatrical images and to hate them at the same time.

LP: Yes. Genet loved the theatre but he also had to destroy it. He was obliged to wreck his own work. The reason for that goes back, I think, to his attitude towards the French language. In French theatre, there is a strong emphasis placed on creating a beautiful text. All of the great French playwrights – Molière, Racine, Claudel, Koltès – are poets. France is the only country I know where you hear people praising the text in the interval. Genet wanted to break this language apart. His revolution in theatre was typically perverse. First, he wanted to create his own poetic universe; and then he did his utmost to negate it. In that respect, he's like all the great playwrights. Chekhov and Shakespeare are the same. They make a world, and then they undo it, linguistically and structurally. The aim is to avoid speaking a single truth.

CL: So is that what you meant in the programme note about Genet being a cubist playwright?

LP: Let's take another example. If you have a broken mirror, you can't reflect a single object in its entirety or totality. Rather the object is fractured and multiple. It's very difficult to achieve that kind of multiple vision without falling into chaos. But when it does work, meaning becomes a process, a quest. The spectator puts the shards together. Nothing is fixed in this type of theatre. That's why two great directors, Giorgio Strehler and Peter Stein, were unable to get to grips with *The Balcony* and *The Blacks*, respectively. They wanted to make the plays too political, too Marxist. You just can't do that with Genet. His theatre reserves all moral judgements – something unexpected always prevails. Think, for instance, of the essay 'Four Hours in Shatila' where he describes entering the camps of Sabra and Shatila the morning after the massacre of Palestinian women and children by the Lebanese Christian militia in the 1980s.[2] A political writer would simply express his moral outrage at the carnage in front of him. But what does Genet do? He immediately starts to talk above love and male beauty, without for a moment forgetting that death is everywhere around him. That's why he can't be used for simple political purposes. There's no moral judgement.

CL: But isn't that precisely what makes Genet such an important political writer for us today? By refusing clichés and stereotypes images, he redistributes the world differently and shows us the possibility of/for change.

LP: Lorca is the same. In his play *El público* (*The Public*) which I staged in 1986, there's a very tender love scene, and one man says to the other 'if you were a cloud, I'd like to be the soft breath of wind that would move you' (or something like that). In the stage directions, however, Lorca specifies that the words have to be delivered ironically. By doing this, he destroys the tenderness he had created – he shatters his own illusion. Like Genet's, Lorca's politics are found in the constant movement and oscillation between two extreme poles. As opposed to the cliché or congealed image, the movement caused by this oscillation is life itself – it can't be represented or pinned down.

CL: Genet's politics then lie in their capacity for transgressing fixity. Is that why Genet was so important for you and other practitioners, like Nuria Espert and Víctor García, who attempted to resist Franco's authoritarian desire to put everything and everyone in their proper place?

LP: Yes, completely. Genet's vision is the opposite of Franco's. He's always trying to create a sort of anxiety, which is ultimately the basis of/for individual freedom and self- reinvention, whereas Franco wanted to stultify that anxiety. But let's be clear about this: I staged *The Balcony* after Franco, and Nuria and Víctor performed *Las criadas* under Franco. The two plays are different. *Las criadas* is certainly about politics because it's about power, yet it is not as politically explicit as *The Balcony*. *Las criadas* is more allegorical and abstract, but I agree, in the main, with your hypothesis about the 'transgression of fixity'. In *Las criadas*, too, everything is about movement – the key thing

2 See Genet, *The Declared Enemy*, pp. 208–28.

is to change our vision of the world by reversing our perception of what appears to be a stable and self-evident reality.

CL: The notion of movement is intriguing. One of the original titles for *The Screens* was *Ça bouge encore*, which translates, roughly, as *It's Still Moving*.

LP: In my opinion, *The Screens*, of all Genet's plays, is the one which is the most politically relevant today. Not only does it talk about European imperialism, but it addresses the extent to which colonisation is a kind of total occupation of self. And yet, it's very rarely performed, especially outside of France. The problem is that, for many people in Europe and the US, Genet is wrongly perceived to be part of a dated theatrical aesthetic, which includes the work of people like Jerzy Grotowski, the Living Theatre, Fernando Arrabal and the Theatre of Panic.

CL: There have been attempts – successful attempts, to my mind – to reinvigorate Genet's work. I'm thinking, in particular, of *The Blacks Remixed*, where Genet's play was given a hip-hop remix (see the interviews with Ultz and Excalibah, chapters 10 and 11, in this book). Do you think that this remixed approach is perhaps the key to reviving Genet for today's audiences?

LP: It's difficult to say as I didn't see the production. But it seems to me that Genet's theatre is built on a tense relationship with what might be called a gay or queer aesthetic – a type of theatre which is camp, kitsch and always in bad taste. The German filmmaker Rainer Werner Fassbinder got it exactly right in his 1982 film *Querelle*. If you lose sight of that side of Genet, which happens when you try to make ballets or operas out of his plays, then you weaken the power of the work. Genet's theatre, as I mentioned previously, is built on a fault-line. You think you are getting a very campy, queer play and then suddenly he calls you to attention in a manner that is very high art, very modernist.

CL: A final question. In this book I've been arguing that Genet's theatre is not a theatre against colonisation as such, but more specifically a theatre against decolonisation. His late theatre is a challenge to the Gaullist consensus of the 1950s and 1960s, and its political significance, I believe, pertains to its critique of European attitudes towards immigrant workers and ethnic minorities. I'd like to get your opinion on that.

LP: In that respect, Bernard-Marie Koltès is Genet's inheritor. Similar to Genet, Koltès presents us with a world which, on the one hand, is radically specific (it's obvious that it's about French society), and then, on the other hand, he shows us something universal, which transcends geography, and even history. Who can say what the deal in *The Solitude of the Cotton Fields* is actually about? For both of them, politics is more than politics – it's about sexuality, bodies and justice. There is also the sense in which both of them use language to challenge our reality, to put things in movement. In the monologue in Koltès's *Roberto Zucco*, the central protagonist Zucco talks about wanting to go to Africa to see the snow. That image is hardly what you expect when you think of Africa. Usually, we associate Africa with heat, the desert, flies, and so on, not snow. And by that token, we are back once again to the idea of movement, to the unrepresentable energy which resists representation. I think that Genet supported the Black Panthers and the Palestinians because he thought that Europe was fake, a sort of Disneyland with its castles, museums and culture. Europe for him was dead, an image. The key political line in Genet's theatre occurs when Madame Irma, in her discussion with the Police of Chief in *The Balcony*, talks of needing a single word of truth which she associates with looking at her wrinkles in the mirror or washing out her mouth. Here there is something unrepresentable, something to do with movement and with life. This is what Genet's politics are about: the desire to avoid getting fixed definitively. To answer a question you posed earlier, this is why, I think, that Genet was attracted to the Spanish under Franco. In their resistance, their desire to be Other than what they were constrained to be, he saw signs of life in movement. For him, that was a sort of truth; the Spanish were breaking out of prison.

9

Interview with JoAnne Akalaitis

JoAnne Akalaitis is a US theatre director and founder of the influential avant-garde theatre company Mabou Mines. In this interview, I talk to her about her two widely praised productions of Genet's work, *The Balcony* with the American Repertory Theatre in Cambridge, Massachusetts in 1985–86, and *The Screens* at the Tyrone Guthrie Theatre, Minneapolis in 1989–90.

CARL LAVERY: The first question I want to ask you is how did you get into Genet?

JOANNE AKALAITIS: I happened to catch a production of *The Maids*, and it just amazed me. I thought it was wonderful. Then I saw *The Screens* in Paris in the 1960s, and although I couldn't understand what the actors were saying – it didn't matter – it was thrilling. I read his novels and became even more attracted to his revolutionary voice. It's a long history I have with Genet.

CL: So you saw Blin's production of *The Screens*? Were you there in the riots?

JA: No one was rioting when I was there but it *was* the famous one with people throwing dead rats on stage, and the actors fighting the paratroopers. I was stunned by it.

CL: Was it the way that it looked?

JA: Well, it was everything. It was an event. There are very few theatrical events in modern theatre history. And this was clearly one of them. I knew I was present at something that was going to be very important in cultural history. When I went back to Paris some years ago on my way to Palestine, I saw the theatre version of Genet's essay 'Four Hours in Shatila', at the Odéon theatre.[1] It was a beautiful production and I was touched by it. In the lobby there was an exhibition celebrating Genet's career and they had all these set models from the 1966 production. I was moved to see that.

CL: Do you think there's something in the script that allows it to become an event or was it simply the meeting of a given production with a certain cultural–historical moment?

JA: I think both of these things are true. Although the socio-political situation was different, my production of *The Screens* in 1989 at the Guthrie Theatre in Minneapolis was still an event, and there are several reasons for that. First of all, in my view, Genet is the first western playwright to write about Arabs and a revolutionary culture in a way that is not clichéd or necessarily easy to swallow. Politically, that's different and new. Second, there's the whole spectacle aspect of the show – it's visually so rich. It goes on and on, and you get lost in this strange landscape, but you don't care because it's so odd and dreamy and, at the same time, violent. And third, there's the character Saïd who is an outcast from everything and everyone. You don't get that kind of extreme character very often. He's really out there. Watching the play is like entering a completely different universe with its own values and rules. When the play opened I was nervous about the Midwest and its religious values, etc. But everyone 'got' it.

CL: What led you to stage *The Screens* in Minneapolis?

JA: Well, luckily through the great vision of my late colleague Garland Wright. He was the artistic director at the Guthrie at the time and asked me what I wanted to do, and I said, 'I want to do *The Screens*'. He told me, 'You'll have to wait two years', which I did, and then he supported it, and the theatre bankrolled the whole thing. I mean it was probably the most expensive production they've ever done and he supported it from day one. One of the reasons why it succeeded is that we had a workshop – I think it was three weeks long – and it was wonderful. I knew after the workshop that we could do the play.

CL: You've talked in interviews about Genet's stage directions being important to you. Why is that?

---

1 *Quatre heures à Chatila* was staged at the Odéon-Théâtre de l'Europe in 1991. It was directed by Alain Milianti and adapted by Jérome Hankins.

JA: Yes, I have used 'Letters to Roger Blin' in rehearsal. Obviously not all of them, because some of the letters give very detailed notes about costumes and movement. The stuff I found useful is when he talks about the play being a kind of festival or explosion without anything coming before and after it. I was also fascinated by his comments about acting, about how it should be so intense and focused.

CL: Do you think actors 'get' Genet. He's notorious for confusing them, for not giving them anything psychological to hold on to?

JA: Oh, well my students don't find him a problem. They've done incredible work on *The Balcony*. Basically it allowed their imaginations to flower. At first it was hard. They were kind of mad and hostile, and then I said, 'Well this is an opportunity for you to do anything you want'. And they did. They did wonderful work. I've taught it twice, maybe three times now, and I'm very impressed with how Genet unleashes a lot in young people. A major reason for that is the sexuality; it's wild. It's forbidden sexuality, dangerous and taboo. There's great energy in experimenting with that. One of my students did a site-specific performance of the Judge's scene in *The Balcony* in a tiny little room with only three people to see it, and I thought it was incredible. I mean it was unbelievable. I saw people doing things in there that they would never be able to do in some other play because they were given licence to do it.

CL: Perhaps it's just trained actors then? I've talked to the UK director Terry Hands about this, and he believes that Genet is difficult for professional actors because he demands a physicalised approach to performance (Lavery, 2006c: 203–4).

JA: I never had any problems with the physicalised approach, but I did have other problems. Some of it has more to do with heterosexual men having difficulties with his politics. Genet, like Strindberg, empowers women in a way that very few playwrights do. I think men are threatened by that, by the challenge it poses to them. It's very 'out'. In a way, it's so obvious, but I didn't quite get it until I did *The Balcony* and I thought, 'Why are these actors so mad at me?' And then I realised: 'Oh, it's because they're straight guys and they hate getting dressed up in these outfits and having women do them'. What I'm saying is that Genet's troubling for actors because he's troubling for straight, heterosexual society. *The Balcony* was obviously difficult for a Harvard audience; it's too theatrical and playful. It makes a mockery of patriarchy. I didn't feel that with *The Screens*, though, because, in some ways, it's very universal and its epic quality kind of sweeps you in.

CL: But *The Screens* is offensive too, isn't it?

JA: Yes, that's right. In *The Screens* there are images of rape and murder. At the Guthrie we covered the windows of the theatre with graffiti-like pictures that the actors had been working on throughout rehearsals. One was an image of a woman with blood dripping from her vagina and all the feminists in Minneapolis rose up and were very offended. My response was, 'Look, I'm a feminist and I think there is nothing wrong with showing images of violence towards women on stage'. Violence is committed against women every day.

CL: It's interesting, though, that the violence is also accompanied by this huge sensuality and eroticism.

JA: Well, of course. Most of us are quite normal and lead banal lives and Genet allows us access to a very dark side of ourselves that we couldn't possibly get to except for the theatre. That's why his work is so attractive.

CL: In his writings on theatre he speaks of wanting to 'wound the audience'. Does that make sense to you?

JA: He talks in such oblique and odd sentences. Like when he says, 'theatre is a place akin to death where all liberties are possible'. I know what he means by that intuitively, and I can work with it. But I don't try and analyse it or break it down rationally. I can't explain it. I 'get' it in some kind of deep unconscious way. You know, the negative void, the glamour of evil, the seduction of death. All of that – it's very profound and beyond understanding. But it's something we all know and recognise when we see or feel it.

CL: Yes, in *The Screens* he makes death seem very beautiful.

JA: Oh, it is beautiful. It is beautiful because everyone is together, the Arabs, and the French. And in our production at the Guthrie, Philip Glass wrote the most beautiful piece of music for it – it's called *The Land of the Dead*. It's a string quartet thing and all these dead people are crawling in a big net above the audience. And I just thought 'Wow, I get it. I get what Genet's doing, I get it'. And we managed it.

CL: And then Saïd becomes a song, doesn't he? He troubles the harmony of the dead.

JA: Personally, I think the end is a big mess. One of the things I feel about Genet is that he overwrites or sometimes writes in a very sloppy way. He's not careful. But he's a genius. It all seems to come so easy to him, and he's just spinning it out, line after line. Some of my students are doing *The Maids*, and I said, 'Well you'll have to cut the play, it's overwritten'. They get it. They are going to cut it. In a way, Genet's overwriting is fine because we're here to fix it up. As far as I'm concerned the two greatest playwrights of modern times are Beckett and

Genet. And they're very, very different. Beckett is absolutely rigorous and unbelievably clear and Genet is sloppy and rude, and somehow adolescent.

CL: Yes, and strangely both of them feel more politically relevant than ever.

JA: I agree. And did you know that Genet detested Brecht's work? He hasn't a good thing to say about it. I don't like Brecht either. There's no longer an audience for his type of work. But I think you're right about Genet, especially because of the emergence of Islam in the world. It's unprecedented. I mean politically and culturally it's unbelievable. And Genet saw this, he saw this many, many years ago. And it wasn't just because he wanted to have boyfriends from Morocco and stuff like that, it's because he actually grasped what was happening. He understood the first African rebellions, too, the revolutions in the Third World. He's one of the great modern political playwrights: there's no doubt about that (see Figures 1 and 2, pp. 213–14).

1 *The Screens*, Tyrone Guthrie Theatre, Minneapolis, Minnesota, 1989–90. Directed by JoAnne Akalaitis

2 *The Screens*, Tyrone Guthrie Theatre, Minneapolis, Minnesota, 1989–90. Directed by JoAnne Akalaitis

10

Interview with Ultz

In October and November 2007, a hip-hop version of *The Blacks* (*The Blacks Remixed*) was performed at the Theatre Royal Stratford East in East London. The play was commercially and critically acclaimed and was one of the most exciting productions of Genet's work to have taken place in recent years. In this interview, I talk to the director Ultz about the production, before going on to reflect, more generally, on his experiences of staging Genet.

CARL LAVERY: Did the Genet estate have any objections to you remixing *The Blacks*?
ULTZ: There was a little hiccup at the start. Joanna Marston has always stood by me, and she said you can stage *The Blacks* on the condition that you don't add music or change the words. Obviously, that was going to be a problem with the hip-hop version that we'd planned! So Excalibah and I went to see her and explained what we wanted to do, and why we wanted to use Robert David MacDonald's translation. We had some tea and biscuits and it resolved itself very amicably. She came to see the show in Stratford and really liked it.
CL: Why did you use the MacDonald translation?
UL: Mainly because I dislike the Frechtman translation which is, for the most part, gobbledegook. I knew MacDonald from my time as assistant designer at the Glasgow Citizens Theatre. And I knew he

had translated a potted version of the text for a Genet season at the Citizens in 1982. In the late 1990s when I knew we were going to be staging the play in South Africa and Sweden I approached him to translate the missing bits. He gave me permission to swap words and phrases around to allow for the rhythms of the local dialects. I told him about my idea for Stratford but sadly he died before we put it on so we didn't have his input.

CL: Why did you decide to put *The Blacks* on at Stratford?

UL: You can't really just do *The Blacks*. You have to have a reason for it. There needs to be a catalyst. That's, perhaps, why it's always seemed more vital in the USA than here. When I staged it at the Market Theatre in Johannesburg 2001, we just missed our timing by a couple of years, because the Zeitgeist was to promote a 'Rainbow Nation'. If we'd done it just after apartheid had ended, it would have been really provocative. Imagine it: it's the end of white rule, and there is a bunch of Blacks on stage talking about the need to create a black revolution and to rid themselves of their oppressors. That would have been wild. However, it was still an important thing to do. There are enough black people in South Africa who feel that the place is owned by Whites, even if there is a nominal black government.

But to answer your question more directly: there were two basic reasons why I wanted to stage it at the Theatre Royal Stratford East. First, I am an associate artist at Stratford so I am always trying to think up projects that are suited for the people we have trained. I wanted to do something with Excalibah and Kyza who played Amistad in the show. But, of course, it was good timing, too. It was the two hundredth anniversary of the end of the slavery, and the fiftieth anniversary of Ghana's independence. It seemed like now or never. We were right to do it. I mean everyone was wondering about why neither the Queen of England nor the British government had apologised for our role in the slave trade. That's why in the production we had Tameka play the white Queen as Queen Elizabeth II, and also why Ville Saint Nazaire/Newport News was called Amistad, after the title of the Steven Spielberg movie. We were able to use the play to show that black people are still angry about history. There's something else too, something that was a major factor in both of my productions of the play. At The Market Theatre you have a particular local dialect, and you've got actors who were brought up in the townships. They have a shared working-class background. And so you were able to tap a distinct group feeling. They were part of a tight-knit community. Here at the Theatre Royal, we are interested in plays that celebrate street dialect. Excalibah is local, and a high proportion of the performers we train are brought up in the borough. It seemed to me that we stood a good chance here of creating a unified black voice, of expressing an injustice that actually meant something. But the tone here was very different from the one in South Africa.

CL: In what way?

UL: In South Africa, the cast was more politicised. That was inevitable. The actors, like everyone in the country, had been involved in massive political change. Also the theatre was run at the time by the great John Kani. I wanted him to play Archibald, but he managed to charm his way out of that. He was saving himself for Peter Brook's *King Lear*. The actor who eventually played the part in South Africa was a great leader in the townships, a political spokesman and teacher.

CL: A friend of mine who saw the production in Sweden on 11 September 2001 was amazed by it. The black revolution stunned him and the audience – it seemed prophetic.

UL: Yes, that's right. There were a lot of dazed people in Stockholm that night. Coincidentally, when we staged the play at the Theatre Royal, we started from the premise that Newport News/Amistad was a Black Muslim. We wanted him to carry a backpack, but in the end we didn't push that. When I staged *The Screens* at UC Davis in 1999, I used the play to teach the students about Arab terrorists. We were able to look at both sides of the situation then. It was thought to be a good thing to do. I don't think you could stage *The Screens* at the moment in the USA – it's so obviously on the side of the local Arab population in Algeria.

CL: Could you expand on that?

UL: *The Screens* urges the spectators to take the side of the revolutionary Arabs in the play. We are encouraged to recognise the justice of the revolt. We are not allowed to do that today. It would be seen as unpatriotic. Of course the play is about a revolution that happened in the past, but it's still relevant for us. Its energy is transhistorical, isn't it? It's totally against the State, any State.

CL: *The Blacks* works like that too, thought, doesn't it? It's about post-colonialism as much as colonialism.

UL: Totally, the play is so divisive. I'm sure Excalibah told you about the problems he and the rest of the cast had rehearsing it. It's emotionally difficult for the actors. They have to explore their hatred of the colour white, and some of them have a white parent, grandparent or partners.

CL: Do you think that perhaps Genet was tapping into something in the 1950s and 1960s that we are only just getting now?

UL: Yes, I do think that. *The Blacks* is incredibly ahead of its time, isn't it? When he was writing it in Paris in the late 1950s, there wouldn't have been any leading black performers, and there would only have been groups of black immigrants around train stations and marginalised places like that, wouldn't there?

CL: Well, I'm not sure about that. Immigration in France in the 1950s started to change and there were more and more black people coming into the country, especially students. On top of that, there was Les Griots, the all-black troupe for whom Genet created the play. What I would say, however, is that *The Blacks* is clairvoyant, to an extent. Genet is writing on the eve of decolonisation and the subsequent mass immigration into the country.

UL: OK. That's interesting – I can see what you mean. After all, the Notting Hill riots took place in the UK in 1958. It's definitely a play for white people who are confronted with a black community living among them. Interestingly, when I staged the production at The Market Theatre for an all-black audience, we used the white dummy that Genet specifies in the short note at the start of the play. He was carried down the aisle at the start of the performance and the whole show was played to him.

CL: What happened? I've often wondered what Genet meant by that?

UL: The dynamic is very different. Basically, you play to the rest of the audience saying 'look what I am doing to this "person"'. You are effectively getting everyone, cast and audience, to focus on, and unite against, this symbolic figure. The atmosphere changed again, of course, when we took the play to Stockholm, where we had an exclusively white audience. I know I'm generalising terribly, but in Sweden they have a slightly patronising relationship to immigrants. They don't have the same guilt that we have about colonialism. Sweden didn't colonise Africa or deal in the slave trade like the UK, USA and France. Because of that, the Swedish audience didn't really 'get' the tension in the play. It couldn't comprehend the aggression. There was no history of slavery there. Subsequently, they don't understand it when second-generation immigrants turn around and hate them. All they say is 'but we invited you here, you should be so grateful'.

CL: After the success of *The Blacks*, would you like to go back to *The Screens*, and stage it professionally?

UL: Totally. I discovered some great visual images from staging the play at UC Davis. I'd love to do it again. Did you know that I learned classical Arabic to understand it better? I thought to myself I can't do *The Screens* unless I know as much Arabic as Genet did. I had an Arabic teacher in London and, because in those days Algeria was dangerous for Europeans, as it still is, I decided to explore the rest of North Africa. My original intention – the point of my first trip – was to make a pilgrimage to Genet's grave in Larache. But I never got there. I stayed in Morocco on and off for four years. Being there allowed me to see how the whole play is rooted in Arab culture, the ways in which people breathe, move and relate to each other.

CL: You make it sound like a realist play. What does being in Morocco add to the production?

UL: Well, it's hard to be specific. But it means you can study the customs of the Arab world and Islam – the rituals of eating and drinking, of praying. The customs regarding dress – how to tie the burka, and what you wear underneath! The priorities in relation to your family and your community, how to make the guttural sounds of the language and the gestures that go with that – and so on. *The Screens* is a play about village life in Algeria. For me, it is a realist play of sorts. We might think it's strange to see a guy, like Saïd, dressed in a red jacket, or the Mother wearing different coloured shoes, but people in extreme poverty don't always wear grey rags! Genet wasn't inventing anything; he was just copying what he saw in the street. I tried to use some of these gestures and sounds in my production at Davis. I wanted the actors to embody a different world, to live a different culture. In fact, I sometimes think that you need to perform *The Screens* on red earth. There has to be the dust and you have to be able to drink every so often because it's so hot.

CL: JoAnne Akalaitis also said that Genet is the only western playwright who understood the Arab world (see p. 212 in this book). It sounds like you'd agree with that.

UL: Absolutely. I don't think Genet is exoticising or fantasising Algeria, he's just depicting it. It's all real, on one level.

CL: That also sheds interesting light on why Roger Blin's production provoked such controversy in Paris at the Odéon. From what you say Genet is bringing Algeria into Paris isn't it he? That must have been difficult for French audiences.

UL: Yes. That must have been quite an affront at the time in Paris. And although I said earlier that you couldn't stage *The Screens* in the US after 11 September, you can, of course do it, especially if you want to cause the same sort of outrage. The play is all about terrorism – it makes you understand why people commit these acts of violence. I'm thinking of that moment in the play when Kadidja makes her prayer to evil and the revolutionaries come forward and spray-paint their crimes on the screens.

CL: And yet, despite that there are also moments of great hope and affirmation in Genet's plays. Perhaps, it's to do with the colour and the scale?

UL: For all the difficult emotions felt by the actors in *The Blacks Remixed*, there was a real sense of solidarity and affection in the Theatre Royal during the run. There is a cathartic process at work in Genet. Despite all the anger and aggression, the play takes you somewhere else, somewhere more positive. That doesn't mean that it stops you questioning the world or induces a state of apathy, but there is more to the play than a simple cry of hate. Genet allows us to work things through, to experience stuff we normally repress.

11

Interview with Excalibah

This interview is a companion piece to my conversation with Ultz. In it, I talk to the DJ, musician and writer Excalibah who co-directed *The Blacks Remixed* and played the role of Archibald, the MC.

CARL LAVERY: I know you best as a DJ and hip-hop artist. How did you get involved in this project?

EXCALIBAH: I'm on the Board of Directors at the Theatre Royal Stratford East and have been since I was 18. I also did a lot of youth theatre there. One of my first shows was *Da Boyz*, which I helped to conceive and compose with Ultz. Ultz wanted to do a modernised version of *The Blacks* in a contemporary urban setting. Then he asked me if I wanted to co-direct with him. I'm half-Black, and I don't think he felt right directing a company of black actors in a play this divisive, as a white man. It goes against the whole ethos of the play.

CL: Why do you decide to remix the play with hip-hop music?

EX: It's to do with the aggression that hip hop has. Hip hop comes from struggle; it comes from being oppressed, and it speaks out against oppression. We tried to merge the anger of gangster rap, with the social commentary that you find in songs like Grandmaster Flash's 'The Message'. We felt that this was exactly what Genet was doing. I'm sure that French spectators in the original production in Paris must have been amazed to hear black people talking so aggressively and eloquently on the stage. Carl Ramsey, a local poet, was our lyrical adviser on the show. He also played the role of the Judge. We would give him a chunk of text from the original, and he'd look at how it worked across the different translations. Then we'd say something like 'we need two verses and a chorus'. We'd come up with the chorus together, and Carl would write the verses. Normally, I'd composed the music in advance. A lot of the energy, obviously, was hostile – and we used hard, sparse and aggressive snare drums at those moments. However, some of it was sweet and loving, like the 'Gentle Blackbirds' song that Virtue sings to exorcise the black male spirit from the preacher, Diouf, so that he can be inhabited by the white woman's spirit. The lyrics to that song were already in the play. What we needed to do was to get the rhythm and the mood right. With Rosie Wilson (Virtue), we would sit in the dressing room and improvise melodies and delivery until we found the right fit. We tried out about six or seven melodies, and in the end came up with what I think is a charming, pretty song.

CL: How long did the process take?

EX: It was about a year from when we first sat down. We had an intense two months before we went into production, when we really worked on it. But we'd been doing little workshops across the year.

CL: And the performers were hip-hop artists and poets rather than professional actors, weren't they? You obviously wanted people who knew how to deliver the lyrics emotionally rather than just represent emotion, as perhaps a professionally trained actor might.

EX: The cast was a mixture. We had two 'proper' actors, but they also had other skills. The Valet, Ashley, is an excellent break-dancer and rapper. The Governor General (Nathan Clough) is an actor, too. Tameka Empson, the Queen, is a stand-up comedian, Kat François (Felicity) is a slam champion of poetry, Rosie Wilson is lead singer with The Gorillas, Carl is a lyricist, and Nolan Weekes (Village in our show) is an actor and lyricist. We knew we had to have Tameka. She was crucial to the whole thing. She was on the BBC comedy show *3 Non-Blondes*, and is brilliant at improvising. That's why we had the moment in the play when we break the frame and get the Queen to talk directly to the audience. That's the only non-scripted bit of the show. We never knew what was going to happen. Sometimes the audience didn't respond, and at other times, they would speak for ten minutes, and really engage with her. It was funny for the cast too – we hadn't heard the material before, and lots of it was great, really great.

CL: I remember it as a tough experience. Most of the people where I was sitting were black, and I felt uncomfortable watching it with them.

EX: It's not meant to be an easy ride. We wanted the play to serve a dual purpose. To speak to the black community and to affect white spectators. But I'm still unsure if we achieved the second objective. The main audience that comes to this theatre is black. The Theatre Royal Stratford East is known for promoting black and Asian work. Perhaps, we were guilty of preaching to the converted. I had a meeting with Dominic Cooke, the artistic director at the Royal Court Theatre, a month or so after the show had ended, and he said 'you need to do it here. This is the type of place where it should be staged'.

CL: At the Royal Court?

EX: Yes, because you get a white middle-class audience there. It would have shocked more people if we had staged the play at the Royal Court. The whole feeling would have been different: more tense, more aggressive and threatening.

CL: That's interesting. When the play was first staged in the UK, it was performed at the Royal Court.

EX: But there were also really important things about staging the play in Stratford. At the Theatre Royal, black people knew what they were seeing right away. They were aware of the reality behind the clichés – the fact that black men, in a white world, play at being hard and unemotional. They have to swagger. They can't afford to be emotional preachers, like Diouf. Whereas maybe white people only saw the reality of the cliché on the way home in the car. Reflecting on the play, they might have understood how the white mainstream constructs black 'emotion' as real. The difference between some of the audience who 'got' it immediately and others who needed some time to think about it was worthwhile in itself. There was real tension in the theatre. You said you felt uncomfortable and lots of my white friends felt the same.

CL: How did the cast feel about the play? I mean Genet is a white playwright writing for Blacks.

EX: The cast found it difficult and we nearly had a *coup d'état*. There were lots of emotional meetings in the green room with actors not being happy with what they were portraying. They wanted to comment on the situation in a more uplifting and positive way. To show that black people know what pleasure is and can have fun, too. But I think the play does have hope. Even though the White Queen says that they'll be waiting in the earth for thousands of years to come back, there's a real sense at the end of the play in Village and Virtue's dialogue that new images of blackness can be created.

CL: One of the reasons why I liked your production so much is that it expressed a very contemporary 'truth'. You managed to highlight what I think the show is about: the difficulty of being black in a supposedly post-imperial world. *The Blacks Remixed* is not a play about Africa; it's a play about black people in white cities. You managed to bring out that side of the play very successfully.

EX: Joanna Marston, who manages Genet's literary estate in the UK, came to Stratford to see the show. She loved it, and said afterwards that 'the spirit of Genet is here tonight in this building'. Her comments vindicated our decision to remix the show. We set out to remain true to the spirit of Genet, and hopefully we did that by updating the form and the language (see Figures 3 and 4, pp. 225–6).

3 *The Blacks (Remixed)*, Theatre Royal Stratford East, London, 2007. Directed by Ultz and Excalibah

4 *The Blacks (Remixed)*, Theatre Royal Stratford East, London, 2007. Directed by Ultz and Excalibah

APPENDIX: 'PREFACE TO *THE BLACKS*'[1]

Translated by Clare Finburgh[2]

What will become of this play when contempt and disgust have disappeared on the one hand, and on the other, the powerless rage and hatred that constitute the basis for the relationship between people of colour, and Whites? In other words, when humans bonds are consolidated between the two? It will be forgotten. I accept that it only has meaning today.

What tone would a Negro use to address a white audience? Several have done it. Whether charmers or protesters, they highlighted their own particular temperament. For my own part, when speaking to a Black, I know what to say and how to say it: I always identify the specific individual, and adapt myself to that individual accordingly. But if I had to address an audience of Blacks, I would contradict what I have just said. In front of them, I would have too acute a feeling that Whiteness wishes to speak to Blackness. One has to be completely mad,

---

[1] First published in Corvin and Dichy, *Jean Genet*, pp. 835–43.
[2] The translator is indebted to Christophe Brault and Michel Corvin for having elucidated the meaning of Genet's more opaque comments, and for having reassuringly confirmed that a difficulty in comprehending his texts is not because of the translator's incompetence, but because of Genet's consciously abstruse style.

or a complete coward to accept such a dialogue. What am I saying? It wouldn't be a dialogue, it would be a rant. And still, speaking is nothing: where would I, a white man, find the emotion capable of generating the myth that would overwhelm them? Theatrical expression is not a speech. It does not address a human's rational faculties. It is a poetic act that seeks to affirm itself as a categorical imperative, in front of which reason puts itself on hold, without, however, surrendering. I believe it is possible to find the unique expression that would be understood by all humans. But instead of leading societies towards ever increasing mutual understanding, transformations in History harden around them a crust of singularity, to the point where our primary preoccupation will be to crack this crust, under which a human being is longing to be free.

Around last December, Raymond Rouleau informed me of his intention to create a theatre troupe that would comprise solely Blacks. I am not aware of his reasons. In truth, I paid little attention to it, feeling I knew that he saw in them wonderful stage objects that had, until then, been unexploited in Europe. When he asked me to write a play for his troupe, I accepted. 'Yes', I said to myself, 'the Blacks shall play. But they will put on a show that will snub the audience'. For, hardly had the idea of a theatrical performance by Blacks been formulated, than the example came to mind of what must not be followed, against which I had to fight: Katherine Dunham.

We still remember her ballets. Were they irreproachable from the point of view of the aesthetics of music hall? It is possible. They were danced by Blacks alone, but what did these Blacks show? Where were they from? What were they ambassadors of? Of which sovereign empire? Pale, faded, they issued from a world without earthly power, without roots, without pain, without tears, a world that does not even want these things; a world of basic life forms that refuses to try to realise itself. Through them, we never got to know the ordeal of a Negro world which is realising itself less and less. Not its rage, nor its abject poverty, its anger, nor its fear. I was embarrassed to the point of feeling sick by these athletic Blacks who had agreed to show the audience – primarily American – a form of entertainment that would gratify it, where they would appear bursting with talent, with skill, with beauty, and all this in order to present themselves in inoffensive postures, whilst at the same time they would be refused the simple boldness of brushing the elbow of a Yankee citizen. Not only their show never insulted us, but their misery and despair never featured in it. Instead, everything sang of what we call *joie de vivre*, and reassured us basely of everything we know about life and about the entire black population, by telling us that nothing could wound them profoundly, because their joy was so fresh. They betrayed themselves, and everyone else. I do not know if I shall be bold enough to affirm that every act – and every gesture – born in humiliation must take on the colour of revolt. But we must regard an art born in humiliation, domestication, one that refuses to account for abject poverty, as poor and pitiful. It is not so much that I hold this view for reasons of facile magnanimity; it is a demand for a type of art which can only have vigour if it relies on the reality from which it has derived, and bears witness to it.

So, were they adopting an attitude of quite beautiful magnanimity by responding to the Whites' enmity with a smile, to their contempt with an abundance of talent; by showing these hostile or indifferent Whites that 'I am a man like any other', in other words, a man who has taste, skill, even genius; by going to the point of offering them talent and genius? Perhaps, in the particular realm of art, one will tell me, it was a show of intelligence to offer possibilities for conciliation. I don't buy that. The attitude of these Blacks fell within the province of seduction, prostitution, the kind of exhibitionism to which favoured slaves resort: Aesop writes fables to amuse his master, who pinches his ear, then moves on to another form of entertainment.

Art is the slave's least ignoble refuge. But it must not remain disinterested and destined only to amuse his lordship during his rest time. It is justified if it incites active revolt or, at the very least, if it introduces into the soul of the oppressor the doubt and unease of his own injustice. We would of course not know how to appreciate the charms of the slave's art, the gentleness, the sadness that highlighted nothing but nostalgia for a lost paradise. A revolt broke out in Kenya: would we dare to imagine the Kikuyus seeking to charm the English with dances? Yes, perhaps with lascivious dances designed to weaken the apoplectic oppressor and to bring him more easily to mercy. But not to be applauded by him. Would we dare to imagine them reduced to being strolling players returning to the stage to take a bow, thereby losing their souls, their severity, their violence? To persuade other tribes to join them in the revolt, they might put on propaganda shows. But in this case, they use such subtle disguises, that we can grasp neither their meaning nor their formal beauty, because they are not addressed at us.

The play you are about to read therefore has no intention of inciting revolt amongst the Blacks. A demand of this order could not come from a white conscience via a work of art. [The only effective commitment would be direct action.]³ This play is [therefore] not created for

---

3 The Pléiade edition of the 'Preface' features square brackets containing material which Genet had crossed out in his manuscript.

them. [Let me explain myself.] Whether I like it or not, I belong to the white community. A whole combination of cultural factors ties me to the Whites. Wanting to write for the Blacks would derive from that moral abjection that involves taking interest magnanimously, with understanding, in the weak; absolving one's conscience; abstaining from any effective action. It means claiming morality and worthy sentiment for oneself, while the people whom one supports must struggle in abject poverty, up to their necks in it, in dishonest compromise. Minorities have to attain their freedoms themselves. We must be wary of our enthusiasm for magnanimous causes, since it quickly makes us appear complacent. Very quickly, we become sure of ourselves, and set in the aspic of a very satisfying moral comfort. For, all things considered, it is quite pleasant to support the oppressed with words, spoken or scribed, when at the same time we profit from the benefits of the oppressive community, and from the gratitude of the oppressed. I do not say that we must systematically refuse to give aid to the oppressed, but that it would be vain if, at the same time, we did not exert ourselves against the dominating power we serve, from which we profit, in which we participate; in other words, against ourselves. It would therefore be a nasty activity, turned against oneself, that would aim to set us free from the crust about which I spoke earlier. Even if he does not revel in it, the oppressor does not disassociate himself easily from the image of an oppressed person reduced to servility. What purpose, then, would oppression [otherwise] serve, other than to give him an idea of his own strength through the weakness of those who recognise and revere this strength? This image simultaneously reassures and charms him. It is only an image, and it is this image that the oppressed will attempt to transform. What if this image, which is essentially in the oppressor's head, suddenly worried him?

Conversely, I had the right to try and wound the Whitess, and through this wound, to introduce doubt. In fact, I think it is necessary that a scandalous act make them question themselves, worry them with regard to this real problem that causes no conflict in their souls.

From the moment I accepted the principle of a play written by a White and played by Blacks, I wanted the play to be performed by them alone (on the necessity of the theatrical work, there is plenty to say). Since a play is a poetic act, I no doubt felt obliged to write it in response to an internal need, as a means to express my own personal drama, which I then attempted to channel towards an end that would be external to me. The starting point, the trigger, was provided for me by a music box, on which four liveried clockwork Negroes were bowing before a little princess made of white porcelain. This charming curio dates from the eighteenth century. Could we seriously imagine a modern-day replica, four white servants bowing to a black princess? Nothing has changed. So, what goes on in the souls of these obscure characters that our civilisation has accepted into its imagery, but only ever when they play the somewhat clown-like part of an ornate leg to a pedestal, a carrier of ladies' trains, or a server of coffee in a costume? They are made of material; they have no souls. If they have souls, they dream of eating the princess.

These figures do not represent all Africa, you will tell me. If I questioned them, could they not answer on behalf of all Africa? I fear precisely that they could. For a white conscience, they only represent Africa in that they symbolise the state in which our imagination delights in dragging them, fixing them. Don't tell me there are black scholars, doctors, engineers, that some of them are French citizens, British subjects; I knew that. I also know that even if they had had white servants, our relationship will still continue to be symbolised by the charming motif on the eighteenth-century music box.

Several hundred thousand black slaves live their mindless existence in abject poverty, exhaustion and hunger. Their revolt against dreadful basic living conditions will gradually make them aware of their reality, and of the fact that they are equal to other human beings. By winning at the real level of social protest, they will succeed in recognising themselves as equal to the rest of humanity which, little by little, after one surrender and then the next, will no doubt lose its arrogance. When these people are at the heart of glorious revolt, in the heat of the action, we no longer need to look after them: they are saved. They will never again enter our imagery in the form of submissive, smiling and shifty lackeys. But at the end of the day, how do we see Blacks?

Put this way, furthermore, the question means nothing. Even the most obtuse European is capable of imagining them in their abject poverty, in their situation as slaves. But how do we 'experience' Blacks? We no doubt see them as cattle, as livestock that must yield, but which must still provide our Christian humanitarian consciences with reassuring justification. This is it: Negroes are inferior, cowardly, lying, shifty, lazy and naïve; in other words, incapable of raising themselves to the level of intellectual reflection. Have I not just defined the servant in theatrical comedies? With the one difference, that the classical servant still belongs – owing to the colour of his skin and to his features – to the community from which, due to a mysterious fact, he is cut off for a time, but that he will regain if, for example, he becomes rich, while the Black will be eternally banished from it.

So, when they are not engaged in the heat of active revolt, is this what Blacks are? And what do my four figurines have in common with

Negroes who think, and with those who are condemned to forced labour in African mines and plantations? The question is important. Basically, the psychology of the oppressed is determined by that of the oppressor, in this case the colonialist, who is born of capitalist and racist politics. Colonialists are at their most merciless when they base their acts on feigned liberalism and grant the oppressed one or two favours. So what will happen? Not capable of persuading – they lack a dialectical method relative to ours; they lack our language and the material means that give weight to all argumentation – the oppressed will try to charm us. Very soon and very quickly, they will develop the feminine virtues of seduction: we are talking about the servant – or his decorative replica, the actor. Negroes serve and charm us. We are delighted by their availability. But stripped of everything, what will the actor condemned by our implacable will to be nothing more than an actor, then play? In fact, the actor will never kill the master because, mercifully, his acts are only ever played, his knife artificial. So what will they vent their anger against?

I have not said that Blacks are actors by nature, but quite the opposite: that in our own minds they become actors as soon as they are looked at by Whites. And they are always actors because as soon as we see them, before we even see them, we imagine them by using the categories I indicated earlier. Since we refuse to see them in their reality, as people who revolt – otherwise, our attitude towards them would be different – we must presumably perceive them as playing. This playing at the same time de-realises them, and makes them conform to the idea that it pleases us to have of them. What have I said, other than this? When we see Negroes, do we see anything other than distinct and dismal ghosts born of our desire? But what do these ghosts think of us? What role do they play?

This must really be what these ghosts think, ruminate: that they are ghosts who already exist, or that we force them to become, and that we are only prepared to applaud when they play buffoons, because this is all they represent in our dreams of emasculating an entire race by refusing it the right to reality. If I do not highlight the politics which conspire to drive them to be nothing more than this, it is because these politics are already implicated in the gaze that the Whites impose on them. Added to this, is the fact that this comedy of seduction of the master by the slave will not take place without a revolt at the heart of the seduction itself. Is it perhaps after we have revelled in delights which are all too derisory and shameful, that a revolt will arise?

It is in my own language that I express myself; it is on my own language that I wish to act, and it is from my own language that I await images, metaphors, that will assist me in defining the Blacks who, in the secret of their souls, seek themselves, search for their own identities with the help of metaphors that will make them into something I do not know. My language, pride of my race and of my people, intended to enable the ultimate definition of myself. I cannot think that they do not hate it, at the very moment when they take the trouble to learn it. Can the figures that will rise up out of this language be anything other than the projection, there on the stage, of those ghosts into which I wish to transform real Negroes?

This play is written in a bourgeois world. It shows that world what it has obtained from a whole race when that race comes into contact with it. Intent upon wounding this world, the race uses its most reliable weapons. It goes without saying that in a socialist universe, such a play and such an author are improbable. No more than in a humiliated world. No more than in the black world.

For a long time, my situation was that of one humiliated. Do not be surprised that now that my humiliation is ended – ultimately a victory in itself – I show what becomes of the humiliated. I know the danger. Will I not colour with my own particular despair the state of an entire race that knows a different kind of despair, that lives a different kind of despair, of a different order?

We are no longer really speaking about the pug-nosed lackeys in sky-blue silk breeches. We are talking about quiet strippers of mangroves, calm dockers, nice miners. But what then happens inside their heads? I know that contact with the world of warehouses, mines, etc., does not encourage dreams and does not develop a taste for seduction. Fair enough. But when they have a moment's rest, how might they have hopes and dreams? I know that this much abject poverty can only lead to revolt, and that already numerous agitators, Whites and Blacks, are raising awareness in their companions, and developing in them a taste for responsibility. I very much fear that a black proletariat will have to go through the stage of theatrical comedy, because comedy is such a powerful dominant attraction in the white world which, to the point of religious symbolism, has given the colour black to the devils in its hell. That black symbolises evil. . .?

It is therefore also possible that my own particular kind of despair informs me, better than anyone else, of the despair of an entire race. Will I be sufficiently capable of transcending my own personal drama in order to describe another, more general one? But above all, I hope that people do not confuse a lyrical outburst with a political demand. Even if they both have to work towards the same goals, they must not be listened to in the same way. Must real Negroes exalt their blackness? How should I know? What, then, is this blackness that I have not lived, that intuition will never understand? If I stipulate such a demand, it is to the ghostly Negroes desired by the Whites. Humiliation that is lived by an individual to the point of despair can be transcended in a work of art. It can be a source of freedom. If this triumph remains secret, it enables the artist to seize the real world, to be recognised by others. But a group of people living in humiliation cannot extricate itself in this way. Despair that is transcended in a work of art can only enable the triumph of a few individuals who, in this way, can break away from the oppressed group of people, with no benefit to the group itself, which will only attain salvation by means of effective revolt in the realm of real events.

This play is written not *for* Black, but *against* Whites. Would I still show in the play the resentment of a man who was condemned to humiliation and despair? Wouldn't this play be not a magnanimous act, but the explosion of a nasty soul? Well, who knows? But let us first not speak too badly of nastiness, or rather, of cruelty, if it is against me that it is exerted. In any case, it has this in its favour: more definitely than a generous sentiment, it can be at the origin of a magnanimous work of art, since it will no doubt continue to inspire the imagination.

REFERENCES

Primary works

Where possible I have used standard English translations of Genet's work. All other translations, with the exception of the 'Preface to The Blacks', are my own. These are noted in the main text. In the references to Genet's own texts, I have used the original publication date to order the bibliography rather than the date of the edition I have cited in the main text, although that too is supplied below.

Novels
Our Lady of the Flowers [1944], trans. B. Frechtman (London: Panther, 1966)
Miracle of the Rose [1946], trans. B. Frechtman (London: Penguin, 1975)
Querelle of Brest [1947], trans. G. Streatham (London: Faber & Faber, 2000)
Funeral Rites [1948], trans. B. Frechtman (London: Panther, 1971)
The Thief's Journal [1949], trans. B. Frechtman (London: Penguin, 1965)
Prisoner of Love [1986], trans. B. Bray (Hanover, MA: University of New England Press, 1992)

Plays
Deathwatch [1947], trans. B. Frechtman (London: Faber & Faber, 1989)
The Maids [1947], trans. B. Frechtman (London: Faber & Faber, 1989)

Splendid's [1947], in M. Corvin and A. Dichy (eds), *Jean Genet: théâtre complet* (Paris: Gallimard, 2002), pp. 215–44
Elle [1955], in M. Corvin and A. Dichy (eds), *Jean Genet: théâtre complet* (Paris: Gallimard, 2002), pp. 445–69
The Balcony [1955], trans. B. Wright and T. Hands (London: Faber & Faber, 1991)
The Blacks [1958], trans. B. Frechtman (London: Faber & Faber, 1973a)
The Screens [1961], trans. B. Frechtman (London: Faber & Faber, 1987)
Le bagne [unpublished], in M. Corvin and A. Dichy (eds), *Jean Genet: théâtre complet* (Paris: Gallimard, 2002), pp. 757–811

Films (and unreleased scenarios)

Un chant d'amour [1950] (London: Connoisseur Video, 1991, 25 min.)
Mademoiselle [1966] (Santa Monica: MGM/UA Home Video, 2002, 103 min.)
La nuit venue, unedited filmscript, Genet archive, Institut Mémoires de l'Edition Contemporaine, Caen, 1976
Le langage de la muraille: cent ans jours après jour, 2 vols, unedited filmscript, Genet archive, Institut Mémoires de l'Edition Contemporaine, Caen, 1981

Ballet

'adame Miroir [1949], in *Fragments of the Artwork*, trans. C. Mandell (Stanford: Stanford University Press, 2003), pp. 1–7

Correspondence and letters

'Lettres à Bernard Frechtman' [1957–62], in M. Corvin and A. Dichy (eds), *Jean Genet: théâtre complet* (Paris: Gallimard, 2002), pp. 905–51
'Letters to Roger Blin' [1966], in *Reflections on the Theatre and Other Writings*, trans. R. Seaver (London: Faber & Faber, 1972), pp. 7–60
'Lettres à Roger Blin' [1966], in M. Corvin and A. Dichy (eds), *Jean Genet: théâtre complet* (Paris: Gallimard, 2002), pp. 845–77
'Lettres à Antoine Bourseiller [1969], in M. Corvin and A. Dichy (eds), *Jean Genet: théâtre complet* (Paris: Gallimard, 2002), pp. 901–4
'Claudel, poète trahit sa réligion', unedited letter sent to Patrick Prado from Madrid, Genet archive, Institut Mémoires de l'Edition Contemporaine, Caen, 1970

Essays on aesthetics

'J'ai été victime d'une tentative assassinat', *Arts*, 617 (May 1957)
'To a Would-be Producer', trans. Bernard Frechtman, *Tulane Drama Review*, 7:3 (1963), 80–1
Fragments of the Artwork, trans. C. Mandell (Stanford: Stanford University Press, 2003)

Political articles and interviews

'Entretien avec José Monléon' [*Triunfo*, November 1969], in M. Corvin and A. Dichy (eds), *Jean Genet: théâtre complet* (Paris: Gallimard, 2002), pp. 966–70
'The Palestinians', trans. M. Dobson, *Journal of Palestine Studies*, 3:1 (1973b), 3–34

The Declared Enemy: Texts and Interviews, A. Dichy (ed.), trans. J. Fort (Stanford: Stanford University Press, 2004)

References to Genet

Abel, L., 1963, *Metatheatre: A View of Dramatic Form* (New York: Hill & Wang)
Abirached, R., 1966, 'Sur *Les paravents*', *Nouvelle Revue Française* (1 June)
——, 1978, *La crise du personnage dans le théâtre moderne* (Paris: Grasset)
Anciens Combattants (anon.), 1966, 'Au théâtre de France', *Le Monde* (2 May)
Aslan, O., 1972, '*Les paravents* de Jean Genet', in D. Bablet and J. Jacquot (eds), *Les voies de la création théâtrale*, 3 (Paris: CNRS), pp. 11–105
——, 1973, *Jean Genet: théâtre de tous le temps* (Paris: Seghers)
——, 1986, '*Les paravents*', in D. Bablet and J. Jacquot (eds), *Les Voies de la création théâtrale*, 14 (Paris: CNRS), pp. 295–316
——, 1988, *Roger Blin* (Cambridge: Cambridge University Press)
Barber, S., 2004, *Jean Genet* (London: Reaktion)
Barrault, J.-L., 1991, 'Scandale et provocation', in L. Bellity Peskine and A. Dichy (eds), *La bataille des Paravents: Le Théâtre de l'Odéon 1966* (IMEC: Paris), p. 53
Barthes, R., 2002, '*Le balcon*', in J. Rivière (ed.), *Ecrits sur le théâtre* (Paris: Seuil), pp. 270–1
Bataille, G., 1993, *Literature and Evil*, trans. A. Hamilton (London: Marion Boyars)
Bélanger, P.-L., 1995, 'L'éthique de la trahison. *Les paravents* de Jean Genet', in G. Sicotte and P. Popovic (eds), *Misères de la littérature* (Montréal: Université de Montréal), pp. 11–31
Bellity Peskine, L. and A. Dichy (eds), 1991, *La bataille des Paravents: Le Théâtre de l'Odéon 1966* (IMEC: Paris)
Bermel, A., 1976, 'The Society as Brothel: Genet's Satire in *The Balcony*', *Modern Drama*, 19:3, 146–55
Bersani, L., 1995, 'The Gay Outlaw', in *Homos* (Cambridge, MA: Harvard University Press), pp. 113–81
Bharucha, R., 2003, 'Genet in Manila: Reclaiming the Chaos of the Times', *Third Text: Critical Perspectives on Contemporary Art and Culture*, 62, 15–28
Bickel, G., 1988, *Jean Genet: criminalité et transcendance* (Saratoga: Anma Libri)
Blin, R., 1986, *Souvenirs et propos*, L. Bellity Peskine (ed.) (Paris: Gallimard)
Boisseron, B. and F. Ekotto, 2004, 'Genet's *The Blacks*: "and Why Does One Laugh at a Negro?"', M. Hanrahan (ed.), *Genet*, special issue of *Paragraph*, 27:2, 98–112
Borie, M., 1981, *Mythe et théâtre aujourd'hui: une quête impossible? Beckett, Genet, Grotowski, Le Living Theatre* (Paris: Nizet)
Bougon, P., 1993, 'Politique et autobiographie', *Le Magazine Littéraire*, 313 (September), 67–70
——, 1997, 'The Politics of Enmity', S. Durham (ed.), trans. Susan Marson, *Genet: In the Language of the Enemy*, *Yale French Studies*, 91:1, 141–58
——, 1998, 'Translation, Tradition and Betrayal: From Political Commitment to Literary Freedom in *Les paravents* (Preceded by a Reflection on What Remains of a Larousse Dictionary in Colonial Politics)', trans. Susan Marson, *Parallax*, 7, 4:2, 129–44
Bougon P. and J.-M. Rabaté, 1995, 'Genet et la politique: entretien de Patrice Bougon et Jean-Michel Rabaté', *Etudes Françaises*, 31: 3, 103–10
Bradby, D., 1984, *Modern French Drama 1940–1980* (Cambridge: Cambridge University Press)
——, 1988, 'Blacking Up: Three Productions by Peter Stein', in W. G. Sebald (ed.), *A Radical Stage: Theatre in Germany in the 1970s and 1980s* (Oxford: Berg), pp. 18–30

—, 1997, 'Genet, the Theatre and the Algerian War', in B. Read and I. Birchall (eds), *Flowers and Revolution: A Collection of Writings on Jean Genet* (London: Middlesex University Press), pp. 156-72

Bradby, D. and M. Delgado (eds), 2002, *The Paris Jigsaw: Internationalism and the City's Stages* (Manchester: Manchester University Press)

Brook, P. and J. Halpern (eds), 1979, *Genet: A Collection of Critical Essays* (New Jersey: Prentice Hall)

Brustein, R., 1964, *The Theatre of Revolt: An Approach to Modern Drama* (Boston: Little, Brown & Company)

Bullaro, G., 1997, 'Genet: Gay Deceiver or Repressed Homosexual', in B. Read and I. Birchall (eds), *Flowers and Revolution: A Collection of Writings on Jean Genet* (London: Middlesex University Press), pp. 73-84

Carat, J., 1966, '*Les paravents* ou l'immonde féconde le monde', *Preuves*, 184 (June)

Case, S. E., 1997, *The Domain-Matrix: Performing Lesbian at the End of Print Culture* (Bloomington: University of Indiana Press)

Cetta, L., 1974, *Profane Play, Ritual and Jean Genet: A Study of His Drama* (Alabama: University of Alabama Press)

Chalaye, S., 1998, *Du noir au nègre: l'image du noir au théâtre de Marguerite de Navarre à Jean Genet (1550-1960)* (Paris: L'Harmattan)

Chaudhuri, U., 1985, 'The Politics of Theater: Play, Deceit and Threat in Genet's *The Blacks*', *Modern Drama*, 28:3, 362-75

—, 1986, *No Man's Stage: A Semiotic Study of Jean Genet's Major Plays* (Ann Arbor: UMI Research Press)

Chesneau, A., 1973, 'Idée de révolution et principe de réversibilité dans *Le balcon* et *Les nègres* de Jean Genet', *PMLA*, 88:5, 1137-45

Child-Olmsted, G., 1995, 'Black on White: Language and Revolution in Genet's Political Writings', P. Bougon (ed.) *L'Esprit Créateur*, 35:1, 61-9

Cixous, H., 1975, 'Le rire de la Méduse', *L'Arc*, 61, 39-54

Clark, T., 2008, 'Becoming Everyone: The Politics of Sympathy in Deleuze and Rorty', *Radical Philosophy*, 147, 33-44

Coe, R., 1968, *The Vision of Jean Genet* (London: Peter Owen)

Connon, D., 1996, 'Confused? You Will Be: Genet's *Les nègres* and the Art of Upsetting the Audience', *French Studies*, 50:4, 425-38

Corvin, M. and A. Dichy (eds), 2002, *Jean Genet: théâtre complet* (Paris: Gallimard)

Creech, J., 1997, 'Outing Genet', S. Durham (ed.), *Genet: In the Language of the Enemy*, *Yale French Studies*, 91:1, 117-40

Critchley, S., 1999, 'Writing the Revolution: The Politics of Truth in Genet's *Prisoner of Love*', in *Ethics, Politics and Subjectivity: Essays on Derrida, Levinas and Contemporary French Thought* (London: Verso), pp. 30-50

Curtis, J. L., 1974, 'The World Is a Stage: Sartre Versus Genet', *Modern Drama*, 17:1, 33-41

Davis, C., 1994, 'Genet's *Journal du voleur* and the Ethics of Reading', *French Studies*, 68:1, 64-7

Decock, J., 1972, '*Les nègres* aux USA', *Obliques*, 2, 48-50

Deguy, M., 1972, 'Théâtre et réalisme: le cas des *Paravents*', *Obliques*, 2, 51-5

Delgado, M., 2003, *'Other' Spanish Stages: Erasure and Inscription on the Twentieth Century Spanish Stage* (Manchester: Manchester University Press)

—, 2006, '*Las criadas*, Genet and Spain', in C. Finburgh, C. Lavery and M. Shevtsova (eds), *Jean Genet, Performance and Politics* (Basingstoke: Palgrave Macmillan), pp. 143-57

Derrida, J., 1990, *Glas*, trans. J. Leavey, Jr. and R. Rand (Lincoln: University of Nebraska Press)

—, 2004, 'Countersignature', M. Hanrahan (ed. and trans.), *Genet*, special issue of *Paragraph*, 27:2, 7-42

Dichy, A., 1997, 'Jean Genet: Portrait of the Artist as Warrior', in B. Read and I. Birchall (eds), *Flowers and Revolution: A Collection of Writings on Jean Genet* (London: Middlesex University Press), pp. 21–5

Dollimore, J., 1995, *Sexual Dissidence: Augustine to Wilde, Freud to Foucault* (Oxford: Oxford University Press)

Donohue, W., 1974, 'Genet's *The Screens* at Bristol', *Theatre Quarterly*, 4:1, 74–90

Dort, B., 1979, 'Genet: The Struggle with Theatre', in P. Brooks and J. Halpern (eds), trans. R. Goldfarb, *Genet: A Collection of Critical Essays* (New York: Prentice Hall), pp. 114–28

——, 1980, 'Genet et Pirandello ou d'un théâtre de la représentation', *Lendemains*, 19, 73–83

——, 1988, 'Une extraordinaire jubilation', in J.-B. Moraly (ed.), *Les nègres au Port de la Lune: Genet et les différences* (Bordeaux: Editions de la Différence), pp. 103–9

——, 1993, 'Le théâtre: une féerie sans réplique', *Magazine littéraire*, 313, 46–50

Duras, M., 1958, 'Entretien avec Sarah Moldoror', *France-Observateur* (20 March)

Durham, S., 1995, 'Genet's Shadow Theatre: Memory and Utopian Phantasy' in *Un captif amoureux*', P. Bougon (ed.), *L'Esprit Créateur*, 35:1, 50–60

——, 1997, 'Genet's Deaths', S. Durham (ed.), *Genet: In the Language of the Enemy*, *Yale French Studies*, 91:1, 158–84

——, 1998, *Phantom Communities: The Simulacrum and the Limits of Postmodernism* (Stanford: Stanford University Press)

——, 2004, 'The Divided Event: The Aesthetics and Politics of Virtuality in *Funeral Rites*', M. Hanrahan (ed.), *Genet*, special issue of *Paragraph*, 27:2, 59–76

Dutourd, J., 1966, *France Soir* (23 April)

Duvignaud, J., 1959, 'Roger Blin: aux prises avec *Les nègres* de Jean Genet', *Lettres Nouvelles* (22 October)

Eldridge, L., 2005, 'Genet's *The Maids*: Performativity in Performance', *Studies in Theatre and Performance*, 25:2, 99–113

Eribon, D., 2001, *Une morale du minoritaire. Variations sur un thème de Jean Genet* (Paris: Fayard)

Esslin, M., 1968, *The Theatre of the Absurd*, 2nd enlarged edn (London: Penguin)

Federman, R., 1979, 'Jean Genet: The Theater of Hate', in P. Brook and J. Halpern (eds), trans. F. Abetti, *Genet: A Collection of Critical Essays* (New Jersey: Prentice Hall), pp. 129–45

Finburgh, C., 2002a, 'Facets of Artifice: Rhythms in the Theatre of Jean Genet, and the Painting, Drawing and Sculpture of Alberto Giacometti', *French Forum*, 27:3, 73–98

——, 2002b, 'Jean Genet and the Poetics of Palestinian Politics: Statecraft as Stagecraft in "Quatre heures à Chatila"', *French Studies*, 56, 4:4, 495–509

——, 2004, 'Speech without Acts: Politics and Speech Act Theory in Genet's *The Balcony*', *Genet*, special issue of *Paragraph*, M. Hanrahan (ed.), 27:2, 113–29

——, 2006, '"Micro-treatise on a mini-politics" Genet, Individualism and Collectivity' in C. Finburgh, C. Lavery and M. Shevtsova (eds), in *Jean Genet, Performance and Politics* (Basingstoke: Palgrave Macmillan), pp. 79–91

Forbes, J. and M. Kelly (eds), 1995, *French Cultural Studies: An Introduction* (Oxford: Oxford University Press)

Fowlie, W., 1960, 'The New Plays of Ionesco and Genet', *Tulane Drama Review*, 5:1, 43–8

Francovich A., 1969, 'Genet's Theatre of Possession', *The Drama Review*, 14:1, 25–45

Fredette, N., 1993, 'Genet politique: l'ultime engagement', *Etudes Françaises*, 29:2, 83–102

——, 1995, 'Jean Genet: les pouvoirs de l'imposture', *Etudes Françaises*, 31:3, 87–101

——, 2001, *Figures baroques de Jean Genet* (XYZ: Montreal)

Fuchs, E., 2006, 'Clown Shows: Anti-theatricalist Theatricalism in Four Twentieth-Century Plays', in A. Ackerman and M. Puchner (eds), *Against Theatre: Creative Destructions and the Modernist Stage* (Basingstoke: Palgrave Macmillan), pp. 39–57

Gaitet, P. 2003, *Queens and Revolutionaries: New Readings of Jean Genet* (London: Associated University Press)

Gautier, J.-J., 1991, 'A l'Odéon: *Les paravents* de Jean Genêt [sic]' in B. Bellity Peskine and A. Dichy (eds), *La bataille des Paravents le théatre de l'odéon 1966* (Paris: IMEC), p. 65
Gennaro, M. de, 2003, 'What Remains of Jean Genet?', *Yale Journal of Criticism*, 16:1, 190–209
Grazia, E. de, 1993, 'An Interview with Jean Genet', *Cardoza Studies in Law and Literature*, 5:2, 307–24
Giles, J., 1991, *The Cinema of Jean Genet: Un chant d'amour* (London: BFI)
——, 2002, *Criminal Desires: Jean Genet and Cinema* (The Persistence of Vision) (London: Creation)
Goffman, E., 1975, *Frame Analysis* (London: Penguin)
Goldmann, L., 1979, 'The Theatre of Genet: A Sociological Study', in P. Brooks and J. Halpern (eds), trans. P. Dreyfus, *Jean Genet: A Collection of Critical Essays* (New York: Prentice Hall), pp. 31–46
Gourgouris, S., 1998, 'A Lucid Drunkenness (Genet's poetics of revolution)', *South Atlantic Quarterly*, 97:2, 413–56
Goytisolo, J., 2002, 'Postface: ambiguïté politique et radicalité poétique', in J. Neutre, *Genet: sur les routes du sud* (Paris: Fayard), pp. 329–40
Graham-White, A., 1970, 'Jean Genet and the Psychology of Colonialism', *Comparative Drama*, 4:3, 208–16
Grossvogel, D. I., 1965, *The Blasphemers: The Theater of Brecht, Ionesco, Beckett and Genet*, 2nd edn (Ithaca, NY: Cornell University Press)
Guattari, F., 1989, 'Genet retrouvé', in *Cartographies schizoanalytiques* (Paris: Editions de Galilée), pp. 269–90
Guicharnaud, J. with J. Guicharnaud, 1979, 'Jean Genet: the Glory of Annihilation', in P. Brook and J. Halpern (eds), *Genet: A Collection of Critical Essays* (New Jersey: Prentice Hall), pp. 98–113
Hanrahan, M., 1997, *Lire Genet: une poétique de la différence* (Montréal: Presses de l'Université de Montréal)
——, 2004, 'Introduction', M. Hanrahan (ed.), *Genet*, special edition of *Paragraph*, 27:2, 1–6
Hansberry, L., 1961, 'Genet, Mailer, and "the New Paternalism"', *Village Voice* (1 June)
Hardt, M., 1997, 'Prison Time', S. Durham (ed.), *Genet: In the Language of the Enemy, Yale French Studies*, 91:1, 64–79
Hargreaves, M., 2006, 'Dancing the Impossible, Kazuo Ohno, Lindsay Kemp and *Our Lady of the Flowers*', in C. Finburgh, C. Lavery and M. Shevtsova (eds), *Jean Genet, Performance and Politics* (Basingstoke: Palgrave MacMillan), pp. 106–16
Harvey, R., 1997, 'Genet's Open Enemies: Sartre and Derrida', S. Durham (ed.), *Genet: in the Language of the Enemy, Yale French Studies*, 91:1, 103–16
Hayman, R., 1979, *Theatre and Anti-Theatre: New Movements since Beckett* (London: Secker & Warburg)
Hémaïdi, H., 2001, '*Les paravents* de Genet: écriture de l'histoire/écriture de l'abjection', *L'Esprit Créateur*, 41:4, 25–36
Hopkins, D.J., 1998, 'Misunderstanding *Los biombos*: A Response to Irresponsible Press', *Theatre Forum*, 13, 84–5
Hubert, M.-C., 1996, *L'Esthétique de Jean Genet* (Paris: Sedes)
Hughes, E., 2001, *Writing Marginality in Modern French Literature* (Cambridge: Cambridge University Press)
Innes, C., 1993, *Avant Garde Theatre 1892-1992* (London: Routledge)
Jablonka, I., 2004, *Les vérités inavouables de Jean Genet* (Paris: Seuil, 2004)
Kennelly, B., 1995, 'A paraître/apparaître, Genet and his press', *French Review*, 68:3, 466–76
Khélil, H., 2001, *Figures de l'altérité dans le théâtre de Jean Genet. Lecture des Nègres et des Paravents* (Paris: L'Harmattan)
Killinger, J., 1960, 'Jean Genet and the Scapegoat Drama', *Comparative Literature Studies*, 3, 207–21

Knapp, B., 1963, 'Interview with Roger Blin', *Tulane Drama Review*, 7:3, 111–25
——, 1967, 'Interview with Roger Blin', *The Drama Review*, 11:4, 109–10
——, 1968, *Jean Genet* (New York: St. Martin's Press)
Koltès, B.-M. and F. Regnault, 1983, *La famille des orties: esquisses et croquis autour des Paravents de Jean Genet* (Paris: Editions Nanterre/Amandiers)
Lacan, J., 1993, 'Sur *Le balcon* de Genet', *Magazine Littéraire*, 313 (September), 51–7
Lamine, 1966, 'Entretien avec Jean Genet', *L'Algérien en Europe* (1–15 May)
Lane, C., 1997, 'The Voided Role: On Genet', *Modern Language Notes*, 112:5, 876–908
Laroche, 1997, H., *Le dernier Genet* (Paris: Editions du Seuil)
Lavery, C., 1997, 'Alienation Effects in Jean Genet's *Les nègres*', in C. Smith (ed.), *Norwich Papers: Essays in Memory of Janine Deakins and Michael Parkinson*, 4, 313–19
——, 2003, 'The Politics of the Wound: Jean Genet's Ethical Commitment', *Journal of European Studies*, 33:2, 161–76
——, 2005, 'The State of Genet studies', *Contemporary Theatre Review*, 15:4, 470–5
——, 2006a, 'Between Negativity and Resistance: Genet and Committed Theatre', *Contemporary Theatre Review*, 16:2, 220–34
——, 2006b, 'Theatre in a Graveyard: Site-Based Performance and the Revolution of Everyday Life', in C. Finburgh, C. Lavery and M. Shevtsova (eds), *Jean Genet, Performance and Politics* (Basingstoke: Palgrave Macmillan), pp. 95–105
——, 2006c, 'Interview with Terry Hands' in C. Finburgh, C. Lavery and M. Shevtsova (eds), *Jean Genet, Performance and Politics* (Basingstoke: Palgrave Macmillan), pp. 199–207.
——, 2006d, 'The Theatre of Genet in Sociological Perspective', in C. Finburgh, C. Lavery and M. Shevtsova (eds), in *Jean Genet, Performance and Politics* (Basingstoke: Palgrave Macmillan), pp. 44–53
Lavery C. and P. Woodward, 2006, 'Jean, Ron, Franko and Me: Genet, Body Art and Abjection', in C. Finburgh, C. Lavery and M. Shevtsova (eds), *Jean Genet, Performance and Politics* (Basingstoke: Palgrave Macmillan), pp. 117–27
Lecuyer, M., 1972, '*Les nègres* et au-delà', *Obliques*, 2, 44–7
Little, J. P., 1990, *Les nègres* (London: Grant & Cutler)
Lloyd, D., 1987, 'Genet's Genealogy: European Minorities and the Ends of the Canon', *Cultural Critique*, 6, 161–85
Lucey, M., 1997, 'Genet's *Notre-Dame-des-Fleurs*: Fantasy and Sexual Identity', S. Durham (ed.), *Genet: in the Language of the Enemy*, *Yale French Studies*, 91:1, 80–102
Magedera, I., 1998, *Les bonnes* (Glasgow: University of Glasgow French and German Publications)
Magnan, J. M., 1966, *Essai sur Jean Genet* (Paris: Editions Seghers)
Mailer, N., 1961, '*The Blacks*', *Village Voice* (18 May: 11, 14)
Marcel, G., 1991, 'Le procès de Jean Genet', in B. Bellity Peskine and A. Dichy (eds), *La bataille des Paravents* (Paris: IMEC), pp. 61–2
Marowitz, C., 1966, 'Notes on a Theatre of Cruelty', *Tulane Drama Review*, 11:2, 152–72
Martin, G. D., 1975, 'Racism in Genet's *Les nègres*', *Modern Language Review*, 70:3, 517–25
Marty, E., 2003, *Bref séjour à Jérusalem* (Paris: Gallimard)
Mayer, H., 1982, *Outsiders: A Study in Life and Letters*, trans. D. M. Sweet (Cambridge, MA: MIT Press)
McMahon, J. H., 1963, *The Imagination of Jean Genet* (New Haven, MA: Yale University Press)
Melcher, E., 1962, 'The Pirandellism of Jean Genet', *French Review*, 36:1, 32–6
Melia. M., 2007, 'Architecture and Cruelty in the Writings of Antonin Artaud, Jean Genet and Samuel Becket' (Ph.D. dissertation, Kingston University)
Millet, K., 1991, *Sexual Politics* (London: Virago)
Moraly, J.-B., 1988a, *Jean Genet: la vie écrite* (Bordeaux: Editions de la Différence)
——, (ed.), 1988b, *Les nègres au Port de la Lune: Genet et les différences* (Bordeaux: Editions de la Différence)

Nelson, B., 1963, 'The Balcony and Parisian Existentialism', Tulane Drama Review, 7: 3, 60–79
Neutre, J., 2002, Genet: sur les routes du sud (Paris: Fayard)
Nugent, R., 1964, 'Sculpture into Drama: Giacometti's Influence on Genet', Drama Survey, 3:3, 378–85
John Orr 'Terrorism as Social Drama and Dramatic form' in J. Orr and D. Klaić (eds), 1990, Terrorism and Modern Drama (Edinburgh: Edinburgh University Press), pp. 48–64
Oswald, L., 1989, Jean Genet and the Semiotics of Performance (Indiana: Indiana University Press)
Pickering, K., 2005, Keys Concepts in Drama and Performance (London: Palgrave Macmillan)
Piemme, M., 1979, 'Scenic Space and Dramatic Illusion in The Balcony', in P. Brooks and J. Halpern (eds), trans. K. Kinczewski, Genet: A Collection of Critical Essays (New York: Prentice Hall), pp. 156–71
Plunka, G., 1992, The Rites of Passage of Jean Genet (New Jersey: Fairleigh Dickinson Press)
Pronko, L., 1962, Avant-Garde: The Experimental Theatre in France (Cambridge: Cambridge University Press)
Pucciani, O. F., 1963, 'Tragedy, Genet and The Maids', Tulane Drama Review, 7:3, 42–59
Read, B. and I. Birchall (eds), 1997, Flowers and Revolution: A Collection of Writings on Jean Genet (London: Middlesex University Press)
Redonnet, M., 2000, Jean Genet: le poète travesti (Portrait d'une oeuvre Paris: Grasset & Fasquelle)
Reed, J., 2005, Jean Genet: Born to Lose: An Illustrated Critical History (London: Creation)
Ross, K., 1997, 'Schoolteachers, Maids and other Paranoid Histories', S. Durham (ed.), Genet: in the Language of the Enemy, Yale French Studies, 91:1, 7–27
Running-Johnson, C., 1995, 'Reading Life Signs in Jean Genet's L'Atelier d'Alberto Giacometti and ce qui est resté d'un Rembrandt', P. Bougon (ed.) L'Esprit Créateur, 35: 1, 20–9
Said, E., 1995, 'On Genet's Late Work', in J. Ellen Gainor (ed.), Imperialism and Theatre (London: Routledge), pp. 230–42
——, 2006, On Late Style (London: Bloomsbury)
Sandarg, R., 1986, 'Jean Genet and the Black Panther Party', Journal of Black Studies, 16:3, 269–82
Sartre, J.-P., 1988, Saint Genet: Actor and Martyr, trans. B. Frechtman (London: Heinemann)
Savona, J., 1981, 'Jean Genet Fifteen Years Later: An Interview with Roger Blin', Modern Drama, 24:2, 127–34
——, 1983, Jean Genet (London: Macmillan)
——, 1985, 'Théâtre et univers carcéral: Jean Genet et Michel Foucault', French Forum, 10:2, 201–13
Scarborough, M., 1973, 'The Radical Idealism of Genet's The Screens', Modern Drama, 15:4, 355–68
Schechner, R., 1982, 'Genet's The Balcony: A 1981 Perspective on a 1979/80 Production', Modern Drama, 25:1, 82–104
——, 2006, 'Interview with Carl Lavery', in C. Finburgh, C. Lavery and M. Shevtsova (eds), Jean Genet, Performance and Politics (Basingstoke: Palgrave Macmillan), pp. 213–22
Shevtsova, M., 1983, 'Social Actors/Stage Actors: Jean Genet and the Sociology of the Theatre', in S. Knight and S. N. Mukherjee (eds), Words and Worlds: Studies in the Social Role of Verbal Culture (Sydney: Sydney Studies in Society and Culture), pp. 163–87

——, 1987, 'The Consumption of Empty Signs: Jean Genet's *The Balcony*', *Modern Drama*, 30:1, 35–45
——, 2006, 'The Theatre of Genet in Sociological Perspective' in C. Finburgh, C. Lavery and M. Shevtsova (eds), *Jean Genet: Performance and Politics* (Basingstoke: Palgrave Macmillan) pp. 44–53
Sigal, M., 1998, 'Genet's *The Screens* Directed by Peter Sellars', *Theatre Forum*, 13, 76–83
Simon, A., 1976, *Les signes et les songes. Essai sur le théâtre et la fête* (Seuil: Paris)
Sinfield, A., 1998, 'How transgressive do we want to be? What about Genet', in *Gay and After* (London: Serpent's Tail), pp. 129–45
Stephens, E., 2004, 'Disseminating Phallic Masculinity: Seminal Fluidity in Genet's Fiction', M. Hanrahan (ed.), *Genet*, special issue of *Paragraph*, 27:2, 85–97
——, 2006, 'Corporeographies: The Dancing Body in '*adame Miroir et Un chant d'amour*', in C. Finburgh, C. Lavery and M. Shevtsova (eds), *Jean Genet, Performance and Politics* (Basingstoke: Palgrave Macmillan), pp. 159–68
Stewart, H. and R. McGregor, 1993, *Jean Genet: From Fascism to Nihilism* (New York: Peter Lang)
Strehler, G., 1980, *Un théâtre pour la vie* (Paris: Fayard)
Taubes, S., 1963, 'The White Mask Falls', *Tulane Drama Review*, 7:3, 85–92
Taylor-Batty, M., 2007, *Roger Blin: Collaborations and Methodologies* (Bern: Peter Lang)
Thody, P., 1968, *Jean Genet: A Study of His Novels and His Plays* (London: Hamish Hamilton)
Twitchin, M., 'What Do We See in Theatre?', www.people.brunel.ac.uk/bst/documents/mischatwitchin.doc (accessed January 2008)
Valogne, C., 1966, 'Les lettres de Genet à Blin', *Tribune de Lausanne* (18 September)
Walker, D., 1984, 'Revolution and Revisions in Genet's *Le balcon*', *Modern Language Review*, 79:4, 817–30
Warner, K., 1983, '*Les nègres*: A Look at Genet's Excursion into Black Consciousness', *CLA Journal*, 26:4, 397–414
Warrick, J., 2006, '*The Blacks* and its Impact on African-American Theatre in the United States', in C. Finburgh, C. Lavery and M. Shevtsova (eds), *Jean Genet, Performance and Politics* (Basingstoke: Palgrave Macmillan), pp. 131–42
Webb, R. C., 1979, 'Ritual, Theatre and Jean Genet's *The Blacks*', *Theatre Journal*, 31:4, pp. 443–59
——, 1992, *File on Genet* (London: Methuen)
Wellwarth, G., 1965, *The Theatre of Paradox and Protest: Developments in the Avant-Garde Drama* (London: MacGibbon and Kee)
White, E., 1993, *Genet* (London: Chatto & Windus)
——, 1995, 'Genet and Europe', P. Bougon (ed.), *L'Esprit Créateur*, 35:1, 5–10
Zanotto, I., 1973, 'An Audience-Structure for *The Balcony*', *The Drama Review*, 17:2, 58–65
Zimbardo, R., 1965, 'Genet's Black Mass', *Modern Drama*, 8:3, 247–58

General articles and books

Adereth, M., 1967, *Commitment in Modern French Literature: A Brief Study of Littérature Engagé in the works of Péguy, Aragon and Sartre* (New York: Gollancz)
Adorno, T., 2004, *Aesthetic Theory*, G. Adorno and R. Tiedeman (eds), trans. R. Hullot-Kentor (London: Continuum)
——, 2007, 'Commitment', trans. F. McDonagh, in *Aesthetics and Politics: Debates Between Ernst Bloch, Georg Lukács, Bertolt Brecht, Walter Benjamin and Theodor Adorno* (London: Verso), pp. 177–95

Allen, T., 1994, *The Invention of the White Race*, 2 vols (London: Verso)
Appadurai, A., 1996, *Modernity at Large: The Cultural Dimension of Globalization* (Minneapolis: University of Minneapolis Press)
Archer-Shaw, P., 2000, *Negrophila: Avant-garde Paris and Black Culture in the 1920s* (New York: Thames & Hudson)
Aristotle, 1967, 'The Poetics', trans. T. S. Dorsch, in *Aristotle, Horace, Longinus: Classical Literary Criticism* (London: Penguin)
——, 1969, *The Politics*, trans. T. A. Sinclair (London: Penguin)
Badiou, A., 1990, *Rhapsodie pour le théâtre* (Paris: Imprimerie Nationale)
——, 2000, 'Théâtre et philosophie', *Frictions: Théâtre/écritures* 2, 133–41.
——, 2003, *On Beckett*, trans. A. Toscano (Manchester: Clinamen)
——, 2005, *Metapolitics*, trans. J. Barker (London: Verso)
——, 2007, *Being and Event*, trans. O. Feltham (London: Continuum)
——, 2008, *De quoi Sarkozy est-il le nom?* (Lignes: Clamécy)
Baker, J. and J. Bouillon, 1977, *Josephine*, trans. M. Fitzpatrick (New York: Harper & Row)
Barthes, R., 1986, *Mythologies*, trans. A. Lavers (London: Paladin)
Bataille, G., 1997, 'Architecture', in N. Leach (ed.), trans. P. Hegarty, *Rethinking Architecture: A Reader in Cultural Theory* (London: Routledge), pp. 21–3
Benjamin, W., 1969, *Illuminations: Essays and Reflections*, H. Arendt (ed.), trans. H. Zohn (New York: Schocken)
——, 1988, *Understanding Brecht*, trans. A. Bostock (London: Verso)
——, 2003, *The Origin of German Tragic Drama*, trans. J. Osborne (London: Verso)
Berliner, B., 2002, *Ambivalent Desire: The Exotic Black Other in Jazz Age France* (Amherst: University of Massachusetts Press)
Bhabha, H., 1985, 'Signs Taken for Wonders: Questions on Ambivalence and Authority under a Tree outside Delhi', *Critical Enquiry*, 12:1, 144–65
Blanchard, P., E. Deroo and G. Manceron, 2001, *Le Paris Noir* (Paris: Hazan)
Bloch, E., 1986, *The Principle of Hope*, vol. 1, trans. N. Plaice, S. Plaice and P. Knight (Oxford: Blackwell)
Brecht, B., 1976, 'The Caucasian Chalk Circle', in J. Willett and R. Mannheim (eds), trans. J. Stern, T. Stern with W. H. Auden, *Bertolt Brecht Collected Plays*, vol. 7 (London: Eyre and Methuen)
Buchloh, B., 1982, 'Allegorical Procedures: Appropriation and Montage in Contemporary Art', *Artforum*, 21:1, 43–56
Butler, J., 1993, *Bodies that Matter: On the Discursive Limits of 'Sex'* (London: Routledge)
Case, S. E., 1991, 'Tracking the Vampire', *Differences: A Journal of Feminist Cultural Studies*, 3:2, 1–20
Certeau, M. de, 1984, *The Practice of Everyday Life*, vol. 1, trans. S. Rendall (Berkeley: University of California Press)
Dalton, K. and H. L. Gates, Jr., 1998, 'Josephine Baker and Paul Colin: African American Dance Seen through Parisian Eyes', *Critical Enquiry*, 24:4, 903–34
Day, G., 1999, 'Between Deconstruction and Dialectics', *Oxford Art Journal*, 22:1, 105–16
Debord, G., 1983, *Society of the Spectacle* (Detroit: Black & Red)
Derrida, J., 1981, *Writing and Difference*, trans. A. Bass (London: Routledge)
——, 1994, *Spectres of Marx: The State of the Debt, the Work of Mourning and the New International*, trans. P. Kamuf (London: Routledge)
Dewitte, P., 2004, 'L'immigration: l'émergence en métropole d'une élite africaine' in P. Blanchard and S. Lemaire (eds), *Culture impériale: les colonies au cœur de la République, 1931-1961* (Autrement: Paris), pp. 201–11
Dine, P., 1994, *Images of the Algerian War: French Fiction and Film 1945-1992* (Oxford: Clarendon Press)
Dolan, J., 2005, *Utopia in Performance: Finding Hope at the Theater* (Ann Arbor: University of Michigan Press)

Drake, D., 2002, *Intellectuals and Politics in Post-War France* (Basingstoke: Palgrave Macmillan)
Dyer, R., 1997, *White* (London: Routledge)
Eagleton, T., 1990, *The Ideology of the Aesthetic* (Oxford: Blackwell)
Edwards, R. and K. Reader, 2001, *The Papin Sisters* (Oxford: Oxford University Press)
Fabre, M., 1991, *Black American Writers in France 1840-1980: From Harlem to Paris* (Urbana: University of Illinois Press)
Fanon. F., 1970, *Black Skins, White Masks*, trans. C. L. Markmann (London: Paladin)
——, 1980, 'Algeria Unveiled', trans. H. Chevalier, in a *Dying Colonialism* (London: Readers and Writers), pp. 13-42
Fischer-Lichte, E., 1997, *The Show and the Gaze of Theatre: A European Perspective*, trans. Jo Riley (Iowa City: University of Iowa Press)
Foucault, M., 1991, *Discipline and Punish: The Birth of the Prison*, trans. A. Sheridan (London: Penguin)
——, 1997, 'Of Other Spaces: Utopias and Heterotopias', in N. Leach (ed.), *Rethinking Architecture: A Reader in Cultural Theory* (London: Routledge), pp. 350-6
Frankenberg, R. (ed.), 1997, *Displacing Whiteness: Essays in Social and Cultural Criticism* (Durham, NC: Duke University Press)
Freedman, J., 2004, *Immigration and Insecurity in France* (Aldershot: Ashgate)
Fried, M., 1980, 'Art and Objecthood', in M. Philipson and P. J. Gudel (eds), *Aesthetics Today*, revised edn (New York: New American Library), pp. 214-39
Freud, S., 1990a, 'Psychopathic Characters on the Stage', in A. Dickinson (ed.), trans. J. Strachey *et al.*, *Art and Literature*, vol. 14 (London: Penguin), pp. 119-27
——, 1990b, 'The Uncanny', in A. Dickinson (ed.), trans. J. Strachey *et al.*, *Art and Literature*, vol. 14 (London: Penguin), pp. 335-76
Garner, S. B., 1994, *Bodied Spaces: Phenomenology and Performance in Contemporary Drama* (Ithaca: Cornell University Press)
Garner, S., 2007, *Whiteness: An Introduction* (London: Routledge)
Gibson, A., 2005, 'The Unfinished Song: Intermittency and Melancholy in Rancière', in M. Robson (ed.), *Jacques Rancière: Aesthetics, Politics and Philosophy* (Edinburgh: Edinburgh University Press), pp. 61-76
——, 2006, *Beckett and Badiou: The Pathos of Intermittency* (Oxford: Oxford University Press)
Gregory, D., 1994, *Geographical Imaginations* (Cambridge, MA: Blackwell)
Grotowksi, J., 1995, *Towards a Poor Theatre*, E. Barba (ed.), trans. J. Andersen and J. Barba (London: Methuen)
Hallward, P., 2003, *Badiou: A Subject to Truth* (Minneapolis: University of Minnesota Press)
——, 2006, 'Staging Equality: On Rancière's Theatocracy', *New Left Review*, 37, 109-29
Hardt, M. and A. Negri, 2001, *Empire* (Cambridge, MA: Harvard University Press)
Hargreaves, A., 1995, *Immigration, 'Race' and Ethnicity in Contemporary France* (London: Routledge)
Harris, G., 1999, *Staging Femininities: Performance and Performativity* (Manchester: Manchester University Press)
Harvey, D., 1995, *The Condition of Postmodernity* (Oxford: Blackwell)
Harvie, J., 2005, *Staging the UK* (Manchester: Manchester University Press)
Hetherington, K., 1998, *Expressions of Identity: Space, Performance, Politics* (London: Sage)
Hewlett, N., 2007, *Badiou, Balibar, Rancière: Re-thinking Emancipation* (London: Continuum)
hooks, b., 1997, 'Representing Whiteness in the Black Imagination' in R. Frankenberg (ed.), *Displacing Whiteness: Essays in Social and Cultural Criticism* (Durham, NC: Duke University Press), pp. 165-79
House, J. and N. MacMaster, 2006, *Paris 1961: Algerians, State Terror and Memory* (Oxford: Oxford University Press)

Howells, C., 1989, 'Derrida and Sartre: Hegel's Death Knell', in H. J. Silverman (ed.), *Derrida and Deconstruction* (London: Routledge), pp. 168–91
Jameson, F., 1998, *Brecht and Method* (London: Verso)
Johnson, D., 2008, 'Perverse Martyrologies: An Interview with Ron Athey', *Contemporary Theatre Review*, 18:4, 503–13
Kant, I., 1978, *The Critique of Judgement*, trans. J. Meredith (Oxford: Oxford University Press)
Kear, A., 2001, 'Speak Whiteness: Staging "Race", Performing Responsibility', in P. Campbell and A. Kear (eds), *Psychoanalysis and Performance* (London: Routledge), pp. 192–202
——, 2004, 'Thinking out of Time: Theatre and the Ethic of Interruption', *Performance Research*, 9:4, 99–110
——, 2005, 'Troublesome Amateurs: Theatre, Ethics and the Labour of Mimesis', *Performance Research*, 10:1, 26–44
Kelly, T., 1997, *Reinventing Allegory* (Cambridge: Cambridge University Press)
Kobialka, M., 2003, 'Theatre and Space: A Historiographic Preamble', *Modern Drama*, 46:4, 558–79
Lacoue-Labarthe, P., 1998, *Typography: Mimesis, Politics, Philosophy* (Stanford: Stanford University Press)
Lefebvre, H., 2004, *The Production of Space*, D. Nicholson-Smith (Oxford: Blackwell)
——, 2005, *The Critique of Everyday Life*, vol. 3, trans. G. Elliot (London: Verso)
Lehmann, H.-T., 2006, *Postdramatic Theatre*, trans. K. Jürs Munby (London: Routledge)
Lionnet, F., 2001, 'Des clichés et des villes, entre Paris et Los Angeles', *L'Esprit Créateur*, 41:3, 1–9
Lott, E., 1993, *Love and Theft: Black Face Minstrelsy and the American Working Class* (Oxford: Oxford University Press)
MacMaster, N., 1997, *Colonial Migrants and Racism: Algerians in Paris 1900–62* (New York: Macmillan)
Man, P. de, 1979, *Allegories of Reading: Figural Language in Rousseau, Nietzsche and Proust* (New Haven, MA: Yale University Press)
McAuley, G., 2000, *Space in Performance: Making Meaning in the Theatre* (Ann Arbor: University of Michigan Press)
—— (ed.), 2006, *Unstable Ground: Performance and the Politics of Place* (Brussels: Peter Lang)
Mignon, P.-L., 1999, *Jean-Louis Barrault: le théâtre total* (Monaco: Rocher)
Muñoz, J., 1999, *Disidentifications: Queers of Colour and the Performance of Politics* (Minneapolis: University of Minneapolis Press)
Nancy, J.-L., 1991, *The Inoperative Community*, trans. P. Connor et al. (Minneapolis: University of Minnesota Press)
Newton, H., 1996, *War against the Panthers: A Study of Repression in America* (New York: Harlem River Press)
Nield, S., 2006, 'There is Another World: Space, Theatre and Global Anti-Capitalism', *Contemporary Theatre Review*, 16:1, 51–61
Osborne, P., 2006, 'The Dreambird of Experience: Utopia, Possibility, Boredom', *Radical Philosophy*, 137, 36–44
Owens, C., 1980, 'The Allegorical Impulse: Towards a Theory of Postmodernism', published in two parts, *October*, 12, 67–86 and *October*, 13, 59–80
Quick, A., 1997, 'Performing Displacement: Desperate Optimists and the Arts of Impropriety', *Performance Research*, 2:3, 25–9
Rancière, J., 1998, 'The Cause of the Other', *Parallax*, 4:2, 25–33
——, 1999, *Disagreement: Politics and Philosophy*, trans. J. Rose (Minneapolis: University of Minnesota Press)
——, 2000, 'Literature, Politics, Aesthetics: Approaches to Democratic Disagreement. Jacques Rancière interviewed by Solange Guénon and James H. Kavanagh', *Substance: A Review of Theory and Literary Criticism*, 92, 3–24

——, 2002, 'The Aesthetic Revolution and Its Outcomes', *New Left Review*, 14, 133–51
——, 2003, *Les scènes du peuple: les révoltes logiques 1975-1985* (Lyon: Horlieu)
——, 2004, *Malaise dans l'esthéthique* (Paris: Galilée)
——, 2005, 'From Politics to Aesthetics?', in M. Robson (ed.), *Jacques Rancière: Aesthetics, Politics and Philosophy* (Edinburgh: Edinburgh University Press), pp. 13–25
——, 2006, *The Politics of Aesthetics: The Distribution of the Sensible*, trans. G. Rockhill (London: Continuum)
——, 2007, 'The Emancipated Spectator', *Artforum*, 65:7, 270–81
——, 'Misadventures of universality', www.Rancière.Blogspot.com/20008/12/Rancière-Talk-at-Moscow-Biennale.html (accessed 31 December 2008)
Read, A., 2008, *Theatre, Intimacy and Engagement: The Last Human Venue* (Basingstoke: Palgrave Macmillan)
Reader, K., 1987, *Intellectuals and the Left in France since 1968* (Basingstoke: Palgrave Macmillan)
Reinelt, J., 2004, 'Theatre and Politics: Encountering Badiou', *Performance Research*, 9: 4, 87–94
Retort (Iain Boal, T. J. Clark, Joseph Matthews, Michael Watts), 2006, *Afflicted Powers: Capital and Spectacle in a New Age of War* (London: Verso)
Roediger, D., 1991, *The Wages of Whiteness: Race and the Makings of the American Working Class* (London: Verso)
Rokem, F., 2000, *Performing History: Theatrical Representations of the Past in Contemporary Theatre* (Iowa City: University of Iowa Press)
Rose, P., 1990, *Jazz Cleopatra: Josephine Baker in Her Time* (London: Chatto & Windus)
Ross, K., 1995, *Fast Cars, Clean Bodies: Decolonization and the Reordering of French Culture* (Cambridge, MA: MIT Press)
——, 2002, *May '68 and Its Afterlives* (Chicago: University of Chicago Press)
——, 2008, 'Managing the Present', *Radical Philosophy*, 149, 2–5
Rousso, H., 1991, *The Vichy Syndrome: History and Memory in France Since 1944*, trans. H. Goldhammer (Cambridge, MA: Harvard University Press)
Sartre, J.-P., 1967, *What is Literature?*, trans. B. Frechtman (London: Methuen)
——, 1976, *Sartre on Theater*, M. Contat and M. Rybalka (eds), trans. F. Jellinek (London: Quartet)
Schiller, F., 1977, *On the Aesthetic Education of Man: In a Series of Letters*, trans. R. Snell (New York: Fred Ungar Publishing)
Sedgwick, Kosofsky, E., 1991, *Epistemology of the Closet* (Hemel Hempstead: Harvester Wheatsheaf)
——, 2004, *Touching Feeling: Affect, Pedagogy, Performativity* (Durham, NC: Duke University Press)
Seidman, M., 2004, *The Imaginary Revolution: Parisian Students and Workers in 1968* (Oxford: Berghahn)
Shepard, T., 2006a, *The Invention of Decolonization: The Algerian War and the Remaking of France* (Ithaca, NY: Cornell University Press)
——, 2006b, '*Pieds noirs, bêtes noires*: Anti-"European of Algeria", Racism and the Close of the French Empire', in P. Lorcin (ed.), *Algeria and France 1800-2000: Identity, Memory, Nostalgia* (Syracuse, NY: Syracuse University Press)
Silverman, M., 1992, *Deconstructing the Nation: Immigration, Racism and Citizenship in Modern France* (London: Routledge)
Soja, E., 1996, *Thirdspace: Journeys to Los Angeles and Other Real-and-Imagined Spaces* (Oxford: Blackwell)
States, B. O., 1985, *Great Reckonings in Little Rooms: On the Phenomenology of Theatre* (Berkeley: University of California Press)
Stora, B., 2001, *Algeria 1830-2000: A Short History*, trans. J. M. Todd (Ithaca: Cornell University Press)

Stovall, T., 1996, *Paris Noir: African Americans in the City of Light* (Boston, MA: Houghton Mifflin)
Stovall, T and G. van den Abbeele (eds), 2003, *French Civilization: Nationalism, Colonialism Race* (Lanham: Lexington Books)
Strehler, G., 1980, *Un théâtre pour la vie* (Paris: Fayard)
Sweeney, C., 2001, 'La revue nègre: Négrophilie, Modernity and Colonialism in Inter-war France', *Journal of Romance Studies*, 1:2, 1–14
Taleb-Khyar, M., 1991, 'An Interview with Maryse Condé and Rita Dove', *Callaloo*, 14:2, 347–66
Todd, J.-M., 1986, 'Autobiography and the Case of the Signature: Reading Derrida's *Glas*', *Comparative Literature*, 38:1, 1–19
Tompkins, J., 2003, 'Space and the Geographies of Theatre: Introduction', *Modern Drama*, 46:4, 537–41
——, 2006, *Unsettling Space: Contestations in Contemporary Australian Theatre* (Basingstoke: Palgrave Macmillan)
Twitchin, M., 'What Do We See in Theatre?', www.people.brunel.ac.uk/bst/documents/mischatwitchin.doc (accessed January 2008)
Warner, M., 1993, 'Introduction' in M. Warner (ed.), *Fear of a Queer Planet: Queer Politics and Social Theory* (Minneapolis: University of Minnesota Press)
Weber, S., 2004, *Theatricality as Medium* (New York: Fordham University Press)
Wegner, P., 1998, 'Horizons, Figures and Machines: The Dialectic of Hope in the Work of Fredric Jameson', *Utopian Studies* 9:2, 58–74
Wiles, D., 2003, *A Short History of Western Performance Space* (Cambridge: Cambridge University Press)
Wright, E., 1988, *Postmodern Brecht: A Re-presentation* (London: Routledge)

INDEX

Note: 'n' after a page reference number indicates the number of a note on that page. Numbers in italics refer to illustrations.

121 Manifesto 24, 24n.5, 83
17 October 1961 173–4

abjection 19, 27, 52, 54, 55, 56, 57n.7, 67, 68, 72, 136–67, 178, 185, 230
  See also Blacks, *The*
Adamov, Arthur 110
Adorno, Theodor 41, 97–100, 124–5
  See also aesthetic politics
aesthetic politics 19, 39–45, 48, 50, 65, 75, 78–101, 123, 146, 167, 184, 187, 198
  See also political aesthetics
Akalaitis, JoAnne 18, 19, 198, 208–12, *213–14*, 219
Algerian Liberation Front (FLN) 23, 39, 172–4, 178
Algerian War 5, 24, 40, 64, 66, 85, 168–94
  See also Screens, *The*
Alleg, Henri 175

allegory 17, 60, 105–35, 157
anarchism (anarchist) 2, 34–9, 180, 182
Andre, Carl 130
Arafat, Yasser 30
Archer-Shaw, Petrine 148
Arendt, Hannah 25
Aristotle (Aristotelian and Aristotelianism) 82, 112–13, 119, 123, 125, 156, 163, 186
Arrabal, Fernando 206
Athey, Ron 197, 197n.2
Auriol, Vincent 70n.20
axiom of equality 28, 118

Baader, Andreas 37
Badiou, Alain 5, 13, 15–16, 26, 27, 28, 34, 38, 76, 98, 165, 183–4, 184n.24, 186, 197
  See also axiom of equality; event; state of the situation

Baker, Josephine 147, 147n.15, 148n.17, 149, 149n.18
Barthes, Roland 80n.6, 110, 130, 163, 163n.33
Bataille, Georges 55, 92
Baudrillard, Jean 110
Beckett, Samuel 98, 117, 203, 211, 212
Benjamin, Walter 17, 19, 28, 43, 43n.26, 81n.7–9, 105, 108n.5, 115–16, 126
See also allegory; *Trauerspiel*
Bersani, Leo 3, 4, 53, 55–61, 61n.11, 70, 72
Bharucha, Rustom 2, 3, 5, 196
Black Panther Party 21n.1, 23, 26, 29–31, 32, 33, 34, 38, 43, 45, 46, 53, 73n.22, 80, 207
Blin, Roger 16, 19, 22, 25n.6, 83, 136n.1, 142, 143n.14, 146, 148–67, 168–94, 210
See also Blacks, The; Screens, The
Bloch, Ernst 80n.5
Bonnet, Christian 170
Bougon, Patrice 3, 27
Bourseiller, Antoine 188
Bradby, David 17n.27, 64, 67n.18, 179n.18, 182n.22, 194n.27
Brecht, Bertolt (Brechtian) 9, 40n.24, 80–2, 80n.7, 86, 86n.14, 128, 164, 178, 212
See also aesthetic politics
Brook, Peter 106, 106n.2, 130, 189, 217
Butler, Judith 50

Casares, María 169, 194n.27
Case, Sue Ellen 55
Castoriadis, Cornelius 110
Césaire, Aimé 67, 146
Chalaye, Sylvie 3, 143n.13, 146
Chaudhuri, Una 7, 7n.10, 93, 127n.21, 155, 155n.24, 156
Cixous, Hélène 3, 54n.3
Claudel, Paul 88, 204
Cleaver, Eldridge 29
Cohn-Bendit, Daniel 24, 182
Colin, Paul 147

colonialism 31–9, 45–8, 136–67, 168–94, 195–8, 217–18
colonisation of everyday life 35–7, 108–11, 118–19
Committee Djali 24
Compagnies Républicaines de Sécurité (CRS) 173, 183
Condé, Maryse 136, 136n.1, 138, 159, 165n.34
Confédération Générale du Travail (CGT) 173
Corvin, Michel 8n.11, 17n.27, 79n.4, 128n.22, 155n.25, 186n.26, 227n.2
Craig, Edward Gordon 92
Creech, James 51, 58
Critchley, Simon 3, 7n.9, 50n.1, 73n.22

Debord, Guy 17, 26, 37, 37n.22, 106, 118–35
See also Balcony, The; *détournement*; society of the spectacle
decolonisation 6, 18–20, 31–9, 47, 64–9, 101, 136–67, 168–94, 195–8, 206, 218
See also Blacks, The; Screens, The
De Gaulle, Charles (General) 109, 140, 140n.8, 160, 169n.2, 170–5, 181
Delanoë, Bertrand 174
Deleuze, Gilles (Deleuzian) 4, 27, 46
Delgado, Maria 17n.27, 128n.22, 129n.23, 177n.15, 179n.18, 194n.27, 201n.1
De Man, Paul 125, 125n.16
Derrida, Jacques (Derridean) 3, 26, 27, 47n.31, 50, 50n.1, 120, 120n.14
détournement 17, 19, 136–67, 168–9
Dichy, Albert 8n.11, 22n.3, 79n.4, 169
Diderot, Denis 61
Dien Bien Phu 66, 172
disidentification (disidentify) 13, 13n.19, 14–15, 68, 77, 83n.10, 96, 101, 126, 136–67, 171, 181, 182

Index

distribution of the sensible 13–14, 44, 82, 99, 123, 125n.18, 152–61, 164
Dollimore, Jonathan 3, 67, 73n.22
Dort, Bernard 8n.9, 80n.6, 108n.5, 115n.10, 142n.11
Dunham, Katherine 144, 228
Duras, Marguerite 154
Durham, Scott 3, 4, 27–8, 43n.27, 44, 105n.1

Eagleton, Terry 40
Eribon, Didier 3, 8n.12, 52–7, 57n.4, 69, 106n.1
Espert, Nuria 205
event 15–16, 19, 23, 28, 49, 50n.1, 69–77, 183–4, 184n.24, 186, 193
Excalibah 18, 19, 147, 167, 198, 206, 215, 216, 217, 221–4, *225–6*

Fanon, Frantz 34, 137, 138n.3, 139n.7, 145, 175
Fassbinder, Rainer Werner 206
Fichte, Hubert 80, 81, 87
Finburgh, Clare 3, 8, 19, 34n.18, 93n.19, 120n.14, 227–34
Foucault, Michel (Foucauldian) 10, 11n.16, 24, 59, 127n.21, 152, 159
See also heterotopia
Franco, General 116, 201, 202, 205, 207
Frankel, Gene 142, 142n.12, 156n.26, 166n.36
Freud, Sigmund 112, 134, 134n.30
Fried, Michael 130, 130n.28
Front de Libération Nationale (FLN) 23, 39, 172, 173, 174, 178
Fuchs, Elinor 155n.24, 157

Gaitet, Pascale 3, 8n.12, 51, 54
García, Víctor 12n.18, 15n.24, 22, 61n.12, 128, 129, 129n.23, 132n.29, 202, 205
Garner, Stanton B. 17
Garner, Steve 162
Gaullist consensus 19, 47, 166, 169, 171, 175, 183, 194, 206

Gautier, Jean-Jacques 185, 192
Genet, Jean
   'Avertissement' to *The Balcony* 15n.24, 65, 83–4, 93–6, 111–18, 124, 126, 132, 134
   Balcony, The 1, 6, 6n.8, 7, 9, 12n.18, 15n.24, 18–19, 29, 47, 49, 50, 51, 60, 60n.8, 61n.12, 62, 64, 65, 66, 67, 68, 69–73, 79n.4, 84, 86, 93, 96, 99, 105–35, 136, 153–4, 168, 180, 186, 188, 190, 192, 201–7, 208, 210
   Blacks, The 1, 6, 6n.8, 9, 18, 19, 33, 36, 38, 47, 51, 57, 60, 61, 64–9, 73, 84, 93, 96, 99, 117, 136 –67, 168, 176, 178, 180, 186, 188, 190, 192, 195, 196, 204, 215–24, *225–6*
   commitment 21–48
   early theatre, cinema and dance 57–64
   Genet criticism 2–5, 21–3, 50–66
   immigrant workers 31–3
   novels 50–7
   'Preface to *Soledad Brother*' 29, 39
   'Preface to *The Blacks*' 15n.24, 19, 65, 93, 96, 136–67, 195, 227–34
   Prisoner of Love 8n.11, 22, 22n.3, 27, 31n.13, 38, 41, 45, 57, 73n.22, 95n.21, 179n.17, 196, 198
   queer readings 50–7, 69–70
   'Rembrandt's Secret' 73–4, 93, 193
   resistance 50–64
   revolution 21–48
   Screens, The 6, 6n.8, 8n.11, 9, 12n.18, 16, 17n.27, 18, 19, 22, 23n.4, 24n.5, 27, 31, 33, 38, 39n.23, 51, 60, 64–9, 73, 82, 83, 85, 96, 164, 168–94, 193, 206, 208–12, *212–13*, 217–20
   'That Strange Word' 65n.17, 82, 135, 180n.19, 186
   'The Studio of Alberto Giacometti' 50, 73–5, 91–3, 193
   'The Tightrope Walker' 76, 89–91, 94

Genet, Jean (*cont.*)
  theory of theatre 78–101, 188–94
    enchantment 188–90
    obliqueness 85–8, 101, 124, 184,
      188, 190, 191, 192, 193
    wound, the (*'la blessure'*) 78–101
  'Violence and Brutality', 37
  'What Remains of a Rembrandt'
    50, 70–4, 76, 91–3, 193
  wound, the (*'la blessure'*) 4–7, 14,
    16, 19, 26, 28, 49–50, 69–77,
    78–101, 126–35, 136, 137, 142,
    160, 165, 166, 169, 180, 184, 186,
    193, 197–8, 211, 220, 230, 237
Gibson, Andrew 4, 100n.26
Giscard d'Estaing, Valéry (President)
  32
Godard, Jean-Luc 175
Goldmann, Lucien 106–8, 111, 114,
  126n.20
Griots, Les 146, 218
Grotowski, Jerzy 95n.22, 206
Group d'Information sur les Prisons
  24
Guattari, Félix 3, 46

Hallward, Peter 14, 183
Hanrahan, Mairéad 3, 54n.3
Hansberry, Lorraine 143
Hardt, Michael 3, 4, 27–8, 32, 44, 46,
  46n.29
Hargreaves, Martin 3, 58, 197n.2
heterotopia (heterotopic) 10, 11,
  11n.16, 14, 47, 69, 100, 130, 134,
  136, 152, 159, 167, 194
Ho Chi Minh 66
Hocquenghem, Guy 25, 26n.8
Hubert, Marie-Claude 7n.9, 73n.22,
  86

immigration 19, 31–3, 136–67,
  168–94, 195–8, 218
Ionesco, Eugène 107, 110, 155, 186

Jackson, George 29, 30
Jameson, Fredric 47n.31, 86

Jeunesse Communiste
  Révolutionnaire (UJC) 182
Kani, John 217
Kant, Immanuel 40–1, 80, 97
Kantor, Tadeusz 90
Kear, Adrian 96, 112n.8, 184n.24
Kelly, Theresa M. 115
Kemp, Lindsay 197
Knapp, Bettina 79n.2, 127n.21,
  143n.14, 154
Kobialka, Michal 11n.15, 100
Koltès, Bernard-Marie 33, 179n.18,
  182n.22, 197, 204, 206, 207
Kosofsky Sedgwick, Eve 51, 63,
  63n.14
Kristeva, Julia 159–61
  See also abjection; *Blacks, The*

La Carnicería Teatro 197
Lafargue, Paul 34
Lane, Christopher 61, 61n.11
Lavaudant, Georges 128
Lavery, Carl 4, 7n.9, 23n.4, 55n.4,
  61n.12, 64n.15, 86n.14, 180n.19,
  196n.1, 197n.2, 210
Lefebvre, Henri 10–11, 13, 13n.19, 26,
  36–7, 69, 108–11, 134, 159
  See also Balcony, The; colonisation
  of everyday life; modernisation;
  representational space; spatial
  representation(s)
Lehmann, Hans-Thies 17, 100, 131–3,
  191–2
Le Pen, Jean-Marie 169
Liaison des Etudiants Anarchistes
  (LEA) 180
Liebknecht, Karl 116
Lietzau, Hans 129, 170n.5
Living Theatre, the 61n.12, 206
Lorca, Federico García 69, 205
Lukács, Georg 118
Luxemburg, Rosa 116

Mailer, Norman 166, 166n.36
Maldoror, Sarah 154
Malraux, André 170

Mao Zedong (Maoist) 24, 26, 34, 66
Marcel, Gabriel 161, 178, 179, 185, 192
Marcuse, Herbert 26
Marowitz, Charles 151n.20, 189
Marston, Joanna 215, 224
Marty, Eric 3, 34n.17, 78n.1
Marx, Karl (Marxist) 19, 88, 26n.9,
    66, 116, 118–19, 122–3, 126, 187,
    204
May (1968) 10, 16, 22, 23–9, 32, 34,
    37, 47, 51, 168–94, 196
    See also Screens, The; student
    politics
Mayer, Hans 56
Meinhof, Ulrike 37
Meyerhold, Vsevolod 186
Mill, John Stuart 5
Mitterrand, François 37, 173n.9, 174
modernisation 18, 20, 33, 64, 67–9,
    101, 105, 108–11, 133–41, 171–5
Mollet, Guy 172
Monnet, Jean 108
Morin, Edgar 110, 140n.9
Mouvement National Algérien
    (MNA) 172, 173
Müller, Heiner 81n.7, 90, 133
Muñoz, José Esteban 83

Nancy, Jean-Luc 133
Negri, Antonio 3, 32, 46, 46n.29
negrophilia 137, 144, 148
negrophobia 137–42
neo-imperialism (neo-imperialist) 3,
    33–9, 47, 196
Neutre, Jérôme 3, 3n.5, 34n.19,
    35n.21, 68, 86n.16
Newton, Huey P. 29

Occident Group 169, 169n.2
Odéon-Théâtre (de France et de
    l'Europe) 16, 34, 128n.22,
    168–84, 193, 194, 203, 204, 209,
    209n.1, 219
Ohno, Kazuo 197
Organisation de l'Armée Secrète
    (OAS) 173

Paine, Thomas 5
Palestinian Liberation Organisation
    (PLO) 23, 30
Palestinians, the 21n.1, 27, 28, 29–31,
    32, 34, 35, 38, 41, 46, 53, 57, 69,
    73 n.22, 86, 207
Papin sisters 60, 60n.9
Papon, Maurice 173, 174
Paris 137–42, 169–84
Paris Commune 10, 88, 116
Parti Communiste Français (PCF)
    24, 173
Parti Socialiste (PS) 24
Pasqual, Lluís 18, 19, 128, 128n.22,
    198, 201–7
Piemme, Michèle 117
Plato 14, 89, 112, 157–8
political aesthetics 19, 39–45, 48, 87,
    99, 184, 198
Pontecorvo, Gillo 175, 177, 187
Poujade, Pierre (Poujadist) 109,
    109n.6
Prado, Patrick 88
privatisation 69, 110–11, 121, 134–5
Proudhon, Pierre-Joseph 34
Pucciani, Oreste 61n.11

Quick, Andrew 152, 160
Quintero, José 129, 130n.26

Rabaté, Jean-Michel 3, 27
Rancière, Jacques 13–15, 26, 26n.9,
    27–9, 34, 34n.18, 40n.25, 42,
    43n.26, 44, 44n.28, 46, 78, 82, 85,
    99, 100n.26, 118, 137, 137n.2,
    152, 158, 159, 164–6, 182, 198
    See also Adorno, Theodor; aesthetic
    politics; disidentification;
    distribution of the sensible;
    political aesthetics; wrong, the
Reader, Keith 24, 60n.9
Red Army Faction 24, 37
Redonnet, Marie 2, 3, 5, 127n.21
representational space
    'representations of space' 10–11,
    69, 134

Resnais, Alain 24n.5
Retort collective 2, 2n.3
Rimbaud, Arthur 88, 187
Rokem, Freddie 20
Ross, Kristin 18, 25n.7, 26n.8, 60,
    60n.10, 66, 67, 110, 111n.7,
    138–42, 181–2
    See also Blacks, The; decolonisation;
    May (1968); modernisation

Said, Edward 3, 6n.8, 39, 66, 97n.23
Sandarg, Robert 23, 29n.12
Sarkozy, Nicolas (President) 196
Sartre, Jean-Paul (Sartrean) 1, 7,
    9, 23, 23n.4, 24, 24n.5, 34, 39,
    40n.24, 49, 50n.1, 55, 58, 60,
    65, 70–1n.20, 94, 95n.22, 107,
    135n.31, 174, 178
    See also aesthetic politics
Schechner, Richard 9n.13, 12n.18,
    18n.18, 61n.12, 117
Schiller, Friedrich 42–4, 87, 99
    See also Spieltrieb
Seale, Bobby 29
Sellars, Peter 197
Senghor, Léopold 146
Shepard, Todd 140n.8, 172, 173n.9,
    175, 181n.20
Shevtsova, Maria 3n.4, 78, 108,
    108n.4, 125, 125n.18
Silverman, Maxim 31n.14, 139n.5,
    180
Sinfield, Alan 51
Situationist International 26, 147, 182
Socialisme ou Barbarie 26
Socialist Party, the (French) (SFIO)
    174
society of the spectacle 19, 37,
    105–35, 197
    See also Balcony, The
Soja, Edward 10n.14
spatial representation(s) 10–11, 134
Spieltrieb 42, 45, 87
state of the situation 15, 16, 16n.26,
    76, 183
States, Bert O. 92–3, 142

Stephens, Elizabeth 3, 54n.3, 58, 59
Stoléru, Lionel 32
Stora, Benjamin 172n.7, 175
Strindberg, August 81, 210
student politics 19, 23, 24, 25, 25n.6,
    26, 34, 138, 168–94

Tati, Jacques 110
Tel Quel 26, 82
Thévenin, Paule 170
Third Worldism 24, 33–7, 66–9, 171,
    174
Tompkins, Joanne 11n.15, 12
Trauerspiel 115–16, 126
Truffaut, François 24 n.5

Ultz 18, 19, 147, 167, 198, 206,
    215–20, 221, 225–6
Union des Jeunesses Communistes
    Marxistes-Léniniste (UJCml)
    180, 182
Union Nationale des Etudiants de
    France (UNEF) 169, 171, 173
utopia (utopian) 3–6, 8, 11n.16, 17,
    22, 25, 27–9, 34–48, 47n.31, 52,
    56, 75–7, 80n.5, 87, 98, 100, 111,
    125n.18, 137, 164, 166, 167, 187,
    195–7
utopic 3, 11, 11n.16, 14, 47, 100, 194

Vawter, Ron 117
Vérité-Liberté Collective 175
Vilar, Jean 64, 194n.27
Vitez, Antoine 80n.6

Warner, Michael 50, 64, 64n.16
White, Edmund 7n.9, 23, 25n.6,
    29n.11, 34n.19, 70, 73n.22, 84,
    106n.2, 156n.26
Wooster Group, The 197
Wright, Elizabeth 86
wrong, the 28, 33, 137, 164–5

Yacine, Kateb 67

Zadek, Peter 106, 106n.2, 129

EU authorised representative for GPSR:
Easy Access System Europe, Mustamäe tee 50,
10621 Tallinn, Estonia
gpsr.requests@easproject.com

www.ingramcontent.com/pod-product-compliance
Lightning Source LLC
Chambersburg PA
CBHW070939230426
43666CB00011B/2494